Roots and Resilience

Volume One

Immigrant Dreams and The Open Road

Dedicated to my great- and great-great-grandparents, whose heroic journeys from Europe to the U.S. in the latter part of the 19th century saved our family from extinction.

Copies of the second volume of this memoir, *Roots and Resilience, Volume Two: Remember the Greenstone,* may be ordered directly from the author or through major online retailers.

View the photo album that accompanies the two volumes of this memoir with the following Internet Archive URL: https://archive.org/details/full-photo-album-31jan-2026

Table of Contents

Prologue
Volumes One and Two

I began writing this memoir to create a living legacy for my children and grandchildren. With them in mind, I use the pronoun "our" rather than "my" when referring to family and ancestors. Our story stretches across six generations, from tight-knit, precarious 19th-century shtetls to full participation in the promise of 21st-century America. It reveals aspirations, traits, and trauma passed through generations. The story begins with the lives of my great-grandparents, seven of whom died before I was born and one who died when I was still a toddler. Since I never knew them, I refer to my great-grandparents and their forebears as our ancestors.

What began as a personal story evolved into a two-volume exploration of the cultural, political, and economic forces that shaped our family's search for identity and belonging. Universal themes like repression, resilience, assimilation, and responsible citizenship come alive through our family's migration from fragile beginnings in cloistered Jewish communities to lives of integration and opportunity in modern America. Our family's journey—infused with love and purpose—reflects a passion for finding fulfillment in the context of engaged community life and communion with nature.

Volume One tells the story of our ancestors' journey from oppression in Central and Eastern Europe—the "old country"—to the Jewish neighborhoods of New York City and, ultimately, Chicago. Volume One then takes us to the suburbs of Chicago and the Jewish enclave of Skokie before proceeding into my adult life and a world beyond the confines of Jewish neighborhoods. Volume Two carries the story into the lives of my grandchildren, tracing the choices that shaped our journey, at times liberating and at times turbulent. Volume Two celebrates the people and places that brought meaning and purpose to our lives.

Both volumes describe elements of the political landscape that moved me to action. Volume One describes activism galvanized by the civil rights, antiwar, and environmental movements that shaped my college years. Volume Two highlights activism spurred by government policies promoting Jewish settlement of large portions of the West Bank, to the detriment of the Palestinian population, and expanded U.S. interests in Mexico and Latin America at the expense of indigenous and working-class communities. This political engagement flows naturally from deeper themes of repression, resilience, and identity.

While viewed through a Jewish lens, the struggles and triumphs described here apply equally to any people made to feel like the "other" in a society that promises prosperity for all who "fit in." Since at least the 4th century BCE when the spread of Greek culture under Alexander the Great reached Jerusalem, Jews have wrestled with the tension between Jewish community and engagement with the host culture. This tension has most powerfully challenged Jewish identity during three eras: the Greek era, culminating in its absorption into the Roman Empire of the first century CE; the Jewish Enlightenment (Haskalah), beginning in mid-19th century Europe and ending with Hitler's rise in 1933; and the American era, beginning in the late 19th century and continuing today.

Assimilation in America is alive and well. Whereas my parents' generation experienced a dramatic rise in religious affiliation, mine has seen a sharp decline—among Christians and Jews alike. In many ways, you might say that Jews climbed into the melting pot during my lifetime. From early childhood, I found myself navigating the waters between Jewish identity and integrated American life. At about age four in Chicago, my parents took me to sit on Santa Claus' lap. Later, as a teenager in Skokie, I turned a large living room plant into a decorated Christmas tree, complete with presents underneath. Throughout my life, I have navigated feelings of intense loyalty to my country—"sweet land of liberty"—and my people—"Klal Yisrael."

Above all, this memoir is about the vitality that flows from family—the cornerstone of society—sustaining our sense of self, inspiring our highest ideals, and anchoring our search for belonging across generations.

Introduction to Volume One

The first volume of this memoir tells the story of our family's migration from Central and Eastern Europe to Chicago at the turn of the twentieth century, as well as my own migration within the United States. Through the eyes of a loving Dad and Papa, I hope to illuminate our shared family history so future generations will know whose shoulders they stand on. I want my grandchildren—and their grandchildren—to appreciate the heroic journeys of our Jewish ancestors who escaped oppressive conditions in Central and Eastern Europe. They fled to a strange land, our land, where they struggled to learn a new language and build new lives from almost nothing.

While Chapter 1 picks up with the lives of my great grandparents, the story of our Jewish heritage begins long before our ancestors lived in Europe. The roots of Jewish identity first emerged in the ancient lands of the Levant. Like their Palestinian cousins, Jews descended from the indigenous Canaanites [1][2]. As shown in Figure 1, the ancient Levant consisted of modern day Israel, Palestinian Territory, Jordan, Lebanon, Syria, the Sinai Peninsula in Egypt, and parts of Turkey. Jerusalem emerged as the center of Jewish life, located at the junction of modern day Israel and the Palestinian Territory.

Two watershed events exiled Jews from Israel-Palestine: the destruction of Solomon's Temple by Babylonians in 586 BCE and the destruction of the Second Temple by Romans in 70 CE. In their aftermath, diasporic Jewish communities took root in Africa, the Middle East, and Europe. During the Middle Ages, Jews who settled in Central and Eastern Europe became known as Ashkenazi Jews—our ancestors. Even as

Jewish identity and community endured, the plague of antisemitism—"hostility toward and discrimination against Jewish people [103]"—persisted.

Had it not been for the long, bitter legacy of antisemitism, our family might never have left Europe, and I wouldn't have grown up in the United States of America. Despite the criticism I will level at our country's imperialist ways, it's a country I love—one I could not leave when I had a golden opportunity to emigrate to a more peaceful part of the world. This memoir often refers to the United States simply as "America." I recognize that this term can be ambiguous, since it technically includes all of North, Central, and South America. Yet, in both common U.S. usage and in much of Latin America, "American" has come to mean someone from the United States. I use it here in that colloquial sense, with no slight intended toward our neighbors across the hemisphere.

This volume's story stretches from shtetls to skyscrapers, and finally to wide-open American landscapes. I responded to a calling of the mountains and rivers, and the environmentally conscious laid-back culture of the West. I also resonated with the sixties ideals that defined my college years and shaped my adult life.

This first volume traces the journeys of eight families whose paths converged on the streets of Chicago. It chronicles family life through emigration, two world wars, the Great Depression, and the Cold War. Finally, it reveals the importance of family in shaping my character—as a devoted father, active participant in university and community life, and lover of adventures infused with a deep appreciation for the natural world.

Part I: Family Origins
Chapter 1
From Shtetls to Chicago

A century of silence shrouded our family's origins in mystery. I knew my four grandparents well, but I never met—nor heard much about—my eight great-grandparents. When asked about my heritage, I used to say, "My ancestors were Jewish." Pressed for more, I'd offer tentatively, "I think they came from Slavic countries around the turn of the twentieth century." That nebulous reply was as unsatisfying to me as it must have been to anyone who asked. This chapter reflects the deep satisfaction I now feel in finally uncovering the lives of our ancestors—and the context for their remarkable journeys.

In my forties, with a wife and children of my own, I began asking questions about our family's past. Using grandparent memory book prompts, I encouraged my mother, Lois, and paternal grandfather, Mort, to share their experiences and the stories they heard growing up in Chicago. I also had rich conversations about family dynamics with my sister Linda, and my Uncle Joe. Further insight came from perusing a database compiled by the organizers of one of my paternal grandmother's family reunions. This process produced notes that I later cross-referenced against source documents—birth certificates, census reports, and other historical records—retrieved from Ancestry.com. Finally, to deepen my understanding, I studied the broader historical forces that shaped our ancestors' lives.

Many of the parents and siblings of these ancestors chose to remain in places I knew only as the "old country." Many died in those places—later targeted for annihilation. It saddens me to think that many of the children and grandchildren of those who stayed behind—our cousins—perished during the Nazi genocide.

I attribute the paucity of information about our ancestors to their efforts to hide their former identities from the "long arm of the Kaiser," as Grandpa Mort put it. It's interesting that, while his father emigrated to avoid conscription into the Russian army, Mort worried more about the German Kaiser than the Russian Tsar. Courland, now part of independent Latvia and once controlled by German overlords, retained its German character when it became part of the Russian Empire in 1795. In addition to avoiding conscription, these ancestors wanted to be accepted in America, thus securing the promise of freedom and prosperity for their descendants. They changed surnames to make them distinctly less Yiddish-sounding and dressed their children to blend in with their gentile peers. They emerged from restrictive European lives into a new homeland, albeit with a dose of assimilation that diluted the rich Jewish culture they had once known.

This chapter recounts how two family lines, emerging from disparate regions of Europe, ultimately converged in a strange new world. The chapter is organized around the lives of my eight great-grandparents: three with German roots, one with Hungarian roots, two with Polish roots, and two with—most likely Ukrainian and Lithuanian—roots in the Russian Pale of the Settlement.

Our German Jewish Roots

Three of my great-grandparents—Aaron Schoen, Fannie Meltz, and Lillie Gaertner—grew up speaking

German in Jewish communities blending Jewish and German culture. Here are their stories.

Great-grandparents Aaron Schoen, 1857-1918, and Fanny Meltz, 1860-1943

Grandpa Mort told me his parents, Aaron Schoen and Fannie Meltz, met and married in Kurland—a region in western Latvia where German Jews first settled in the 16th century. Though later ruled by the Polish-Lithuanian Commonwealth and the Russian Empire, Kurland's Jewish community retained much of its German character. In fact, Mort used the German spelling, Kurland, rather than the more common spelling, Courland, when referring to his parents' birthplace. German influence brought ideas from the Haskalah, encouraging integration and reform. In contrast, Russian rule—building on Lithuanian and Polish traditions—reinforced Orthodox rituals and customs.

Aaron and Fannie married in 1885 and their first child, Ida, was born the following year. According to Grandpa Mort, Aaron faced conscription into the Russian army. Fannie's brother, Avram Meltz—a rabbi and the family patriarch—advised his brother-in-law to change his family name and emigrate with Fannie and baby Ida to America.

At the time, some Jewish men avoided conscription by paying a 500-ruble bribe [20]—about $300 then, or roughly $12,000 today. That sum would easily cover passage for a young family to the United States. For Kurland Jews, avoiding conscription into the Russian army was crucial—not only because of rampant discrimination, but also due to their cultural affinity with Germany, Russia's rival. In 1887, Aaron changed the family name to Goldstein and—with Fannie and their one-year-old daughter Ida—set sail for America.

Mort told me that Uncle Avram also emigrated—adopting the last name Zelig. In an act that set an assimilation tone for the rest of the family, Uncle Avram gave up his role as a rabbi and became co-owner of the Altbach and Rosensen Jewelry Store in downtown Chicago.

A comparison of the 1900 and 1910 U.S. Census Reports reveals conflicted allegiances of Kurland's Jews—controlled by Russia but steeped in German-Jewish culture. The 1900 U.S. Census reports that Aaron, Fannie, and Ida emigrated to the U.S. *from Russia*; whereas, the 1910 Census says they came *from Germany*. The reports agree that Aaron and Fannie's parents were born in Kurland, suggesting we have deep roots in that region.

•••••

The 1910 Census reports that Aaron and Fannie had eight children living at home ranging from Morton (age 7) to Ida (24)–with all but Ida born in Chicago. Ida worked as a telephone salesperson, and three of the younger siblings held jobs that helped support the family. The family lived at 528 Liberty Street on Chicago's West Side near Maxwell Street. Grandpa Mort told me he never knew his father, as he became severely disabled—confined to a wheelchair and unable to speak. I don't know what afflicted him—perhaps a stroke.

Mort recalled that the family connected with the Jewish religious community during their early years in Chicago. However, sometime after Aaron became totally disabled, a delegation from the synagogue showed up at the house. They asked for money before showing any concern for the well-being of an unemployed woman with a disabled husband and at least six children living at home. Incensed, Fannie—the family matriarch—never again graced the pews of the synagogue. I am honored to be named after Fannie (aka Fagey), a woman who held her family together with strength and integrity.

Great-grandmother Lillie Gaertner, 1869-1926

Our German roots on my mother's side come through Lillie Gaertner—Lois' maternal grandmother, whom she never knew. Lillie was born in Germany in 1869. When Lillie was three, her father, Isidor Gaertner, married Julia Winter in Frankfurt. Aside from her first name—Leah—and the reasonable deduction that she died in childbirth, little else is known about Lillie's biological mother.

I envision the Gaertners and Winters having many discussions—within their families and their Jewish community—about whether to remain in Germany or seek new lives abroad. This was not an easy decision. As an aside, the political construct of Germany as a separate nation did not arise until the creation of the German Empire from a loose collection of German-speaking states in 1871. Before 1871, the largest of these states, Prussia, most prominently represented German culture and military power. Another large German-speaking state, Austria, emerged as a powerful empire in its own right, controlled for centuries by the Habsburg dynasty. With the Austrian city of Vienna as its seat of power and cultural center, the Habsburgs grew to control much of Central and Southeastern Europe. Relations between Austria and Prussia generally teetered between uneasy alliance and all-out war.

In the late 18th century, Moses Mendelssohn helped launch the Haskalah (Jewish Enlightenment), a movement advocating Jewish integration into European civil life while preserving Jewish identity. This movement precipitated Reform Judaism, which encouraged German Jews to embrace German culture while maintaining their Jewish identity and sense of belonging within the Jewish community.

Our family must have embraced the Haskalah because I saw no evidence of my grandparents clinging to religious Jewish lives. In fact, I don't remember them belonging to a synagogue. I do remember many Passover celebrations in their homes. Our family was culturally—not religiously—Jewish.

Gradually, Germany opened its doors to Jewish emancipation—with assimilation strings attached. Jews like Isidor and Julia experienced pressure to abandon Yiddish for German, and were told even by their most enlightened supporters that full civil rights would follow only after their "intellectual and moral improvement [6]." Emancipation was finally fulfilled by Otto von Bismarck, whose statesmanship and iron fist unified twenty-five German-speaking member states into one German Empire in 1871—two years before the Gaertners emigrated. Bismarck invoked constitutional support for Jewish emancipation and declared his opposition to antisemitism by saying, "I decidedly disapprove of this agitation against the Jews, be it on religious or on racial grounds [5]."

With a firm grip on emancipation and the protection of a German ruler who stood against antisemitism, it would not have been unreasonable for the rest of Isidor and Julia's families to choose to stay in Germany. Once the dust cleared from the Long Depression (1873-1879), Jews enjoyed a great deal of acceptance. "Three generations after Moses Mendelssohn, Jews were Germans in language, dress, and national sentiment [4]." Albert Einstein exemplified Jewish integration in Germany—achieving global fame while retaining his Jewish identity.

Given the momentum toward Jewish emancipation in 19th-century Germany, why did Julia, Isidor, and so many other Jews choose to leave? From another perspective, one might ask: *Why didn't **more** Jews leave Germany* before U.S. immigration quotas dramatically tightened in the 1920s [9], and before Germany closed the exit doors in the 1930s? By 1942, Nazi Germany had begun building gas chambers for systematic extermination of European Jewry. By 1945, they had murdered two-thirds of Europe's nine million Jews. But hindsight is 20/20. What danger signs influenced Isidor and Julia to emigrate fifty years before it became impossible to do so?

Julia and Isidor were born shortly before the revolution of 1848-49. Jews—the usual scapegoats—were blamed for the failure of the revolution to overthrow the monarchical government [10]. Nonetheless, government policy still favored emancipation with assimilation. This created a double-edged sword. On one hand, it provided Jews with much the same freedoms enjoyed by their gentile neighbors. On the other hand, it allowed Jews into occupations previously reserved for gentiles, breeding jealousy and antisemitism.

Antisemitism—an extreme form of discrimination—blames Jews for the ills of society. The original canard was that the Jews killed Jesus. While religious antisemitism persists to this day, the Middle Ages saw the rise of economic antisemitism, which blamed Jews for the hardships of the masses. Many Jews found niches facilitating the flow of capital and were stereotyped as "moneylenders." Their success as middlemen reinforced the disparaging perception that they fed parasitically off others' productivity.

Karl Marx and Wilhelm Marr stirred the waters of antisemitism. Using the Jewish experience to support his diatribe against religion and capitalism as tools of the State for exploiting the working class, his 1844 essay, *On the Jewish Question,* pejoratively calls Judaism a "worldly cult" with money as its jealous God—"besides which no other god may exist."

In his 1862 treatise, "A Mirror to the Jews," Marr insisted, "Judaism must cease to exist, if humanity is to commence." Shortly before the Gaertners emigrated, Marr coined the term "antisemitism" and framed it as a noble movement aimed at expelling all Jews from Germany, in order to get their "foot off the necks" of the German People.

In this atmosphere of growing antisemitism, it was reasonable for Julia and Isidor to seek greater acceptance, freedom, and economic opportunities in America. There, they would seek a fresh start for a young family. Moreover, since most German Jewish immigrants had arrived in the U.S. before 1870, the Gaertners likely knew people already establishes there.

·····

With Lillie in tow, I envision Julia looking forward to having children of her own in America, and Isidor looking forward to new business opportunities. In October 1873—in the midst of a worldwide depression—Isidor and Julia Gaertner, ages twenty-nine and twenty-seven, left their parents and siblings behind and began their momentous journey to America. They were not alone. The 19th-century saw an increase in the Jewish population of the U.S. from 3 thousand to 1.5

million. Germans fueled much of this dramatic influx, which tended to occur earlier than emigration from Eastern Europe. One-fifth of Germany's Jewish population—including the Grant family—emigrated to America between 1820 and 1880.

When Lillie arrived with her parents in 1873, the family probably moved into a tenement house in "Little Germany," a Lower East Side Manhattan neighborhood with about 50,000 German immigrants, including a large percentage of Jews. Lillie grew up in New York City, where three half-brothers were born. She was nine when her first half-brother was born, and fifteen by the time of her third half-brother's birth.

Depending on when between her 15th and 20th birthdays the family moved to Queens—where Isidor worked as "an importer of ribbons" (commonly adorning women's garments and hats)—Lillie may not have moved with them. In 1889—at the age of twenty—she married Great-grandfather Julius Grant, and they chose to live in East Harlem, a magnet for German Jews. Over the next six years, Lillie bore three children—Hugo, Albert, and Elsie—and Julius developed a business manufacturing women's skirts. I imagine that Lillie and Julius led middle-class lives and associated with a Reform Jewish synagogue near their apartment on East 110th street.

•••••

Family dynamics might have played a role in Julia with her husband, Isidor, and her four-year-old stepdaughter, Lillie, leaving Germany for America. Twenty-eight years later, with Lillie nine years older than her nearest half-sibling, family dynamics might have again played a role as she left New York City with her husband and three children. In 1901 the family left New York and briefly lived in Philadelphia, where Lillie gave

18

birth to her second daughter, Beatrice. Four years later in Chicago, Lillie gave birth to her last child, my Grandma Roselyn, on January 7, 1905.

Our Hungarian Jewish Roots

Great-grandfather Julius Grant, 1857-1923

Julius Grant was born and raised in Hungary, as were his parents and grandparents before him. Thus, our roots run deep in Hungary through Lois' maternal grandfather. Let's explore currents at play in Hungary that might have motivated Ignatz and Josephine to emigrate to America in the early 1870s with their six children. Julius, their oldest, would have been a teenager at the time.

Through many centuries leading up to the revolution of 1848, the Kingdom of Hungary had a sometimes symbiotic and sometimes subservient relationship with Austria's Habsburg Empire. The revolution failed to gain Hungary's independence. In its aftermath, Habsburg Emperor Franz Joseph I, placed Hungary under martial law and a brutal military dictatorship.

Jewish emancipation became a much-debated issue. The Jewish community resisted assimilation and the Habsburgs required it as a prerequisite for full citizenship. Harsh constraints required Jews to keep their heavily taxed shops open on the Sabbath and replace Yiddish with the Magyar language (Hungarian). Jewish emancipation was finally achieved with the 1867 Ausgleich (Compromise) which joined the Kingdom of Hungary with the Austrian Empire to create the Austro-Hungarian Empire. Thus, attitudes toward Jews softened and restrictions were abolished by the time Julius reached his teen years.

Aside from antisemitism, it's likely that economic crisis in Hungary and opportunity in America played a significant role in the Grants' decision to emigrate in the early 1870s [96]. Hungary's Jewish population was fluid at the time, with high birthrates and migration in both directions. Josephine herself gave birth to seven children between 1857 and 1870.

Upon arriving in the U.S., the Grant family moved to Manhattan's Lower East Side. According to naturalization papers and New York City directories, Ignatz worked as an importer of flower extracts, which he might have marketed to pharmacies, candy-makers, beverage producers, and cosmetics companies. It seems he was a successful businessman and the Grants became relatively well-to-do members of the Jewish community.

In 1880, they lived with six of their children at 39 Norfolk Street on Manhattan's Lower East Side. By that time, Julius had moved out and—like his father—worked as "a merchant" in his own business. I have no record of the Hungarian family name before it was changed to Grant, an event that likely occurred shortly before embarking on the voyage to America. If Ignatz and Josephine left siblings behind in Hungary, then their descendants—our cousins—might have been among the two-thirds of all Hungarian Jews who died in the Holocaust.

At thirty-two years of age, Julius Grant—already established in the clothing industry—married Lillie Gaertner, then just twenty years old. It's unclear what brought together the young German belle with the older Hungarian. They did have things in common, as both families arrived in New York around 1873, initially settling on Manhattan's Lower East Side. By the time they met, both would have been fluent in English, and both were shaped by the Haskalah, which embraced

Reform Judaism and cultural integration. In any case, the evidence is clear that they married in Manhattan in 1889.

By the 1900 U.S. Census, Julius was working as a "manufacturer of skirts," with Lillie managing a household including three children, a 53-year-old female "lodger," and a 19-year-old female "servant." The lodger worked as a seamstress, perhaps in Julius' clothing company. The servant worked in a foundry and was probably paid a small wage to help out with the children and the household. The children included Hugo, Alfred, and Elsie, aged ten, eight, and four years old, respectively.

At the time of my grandma Roselyn's birth in Chicago in 1905, Lillie would have been thirty-six and Julius would have been forty-eight. Despite their apparent affluence, I saw little evidence of trickle-down prosperity. When my mother was young, my grandparents Roselyn and Leo lived with Leo's parents. The only lasting reflection of a once affluent family was a baby grand piano in the apartment my grandparents eventually rented. My grandmother was an accomplished pianist, a skill I'm sure she developed while growing up in the culturally rich Jewish neighborhood in Chicago where Julius and Lillie raised her.

Our Eastern European Jewish Roots
Our Eastern European Jewish heritage comes through Lois' paternal grandfather Joseph Herr and paternal great-grandmother Etta Rosenberg; and through Orville's maternal grandparents, Hyman Levin and Sara Mata Silverstein. All four came from regions controlled by the Russian Empire.

*** The Pale of the Settlement***

By way of successful military campaigns and high-stakes diplomacy, three Russian monarchs played major roles in creating one of the most dominant empires the world has known. These monarchs disdained the Jewish community. In 1682, Peter the Great—Russia's first emperor—said, "I prefer to see in our midst nations professing Mohammedism and paganism rather than Jews. They are rogues and cheats. It is my endeavor to eradicate evil, not to multiply it [12]."

Peter's second daughter Elizabeth Petrovna reigned from 1741 until 1761. She implemented a policy of expelling Jews from Russia to neighboring countries in Eastern Europe and the Ottoman Empire. Then came the thirty-five year reign of Catherine the Great who greatly expanded the boundaries of the empire through the partitions of the Polish-Lithuanian Commonwealth and the annexation of Ukraine and the Crimean Peninsula. Her empire reached as far as Alaska and an outpost on the coast of California.

Expansion into Eastern Europe brought more than a million Jews back into Russia and created a "Jewish problem" for the tsarist regime. Catherine attempted to solve the problem by dictating that, with few exceptions, Jews would live in a region called the Pale of the Settlement. The Pale included the modern countries of Lithuania, Belarus, Moldova as well as much of Ukraine, Poland, and Latvia (Figure 3).

During the late 19th-century, over sixty percent of the world's eight million Jews—and an even larger share of Ashkenazi Jews—lived in the Pale. Jews in the Pale led religious lives, with ninety-five percent of them identifying as either Orthodox or Hasidic. Ninety-eight percent spoke Yiddish as a common language and Jewish culture flourished.

The Pale was imprinted with the thought-leadership of the disciples of Israel ben Eliezer (aka the Baal Shem Tov), the famous Ukrainian-Polish rabbi who founded Hasidic Judaism. Hasidism had an 1800s center of gravity in the Belarus town of Lyubavichi. Now it's called Chabad-Lubavitch Judaism, and its center shifted to the Crown Heights neighborhood of Brooklyn, New York. The disciples of the Rabbi Elijah ben Solomon Zalman (aka the Vilna Gaon) also contributed to theological debate in the Pale. The Vilna Gaon founded a rational Lithuanian Judaism opposed to the Baal Shem Tov's ecstatic Judaism, and the debates continue to this day.

An article appearing in a 1923 issue of *The Nation* describes life in the Pale during the 19th century as follows (think *Fiddler on the Roof*): "Beyond all the squalor was a thriving culture, a world defined by rituals, religious or otherwise. Quiet Sabbaths with shops closed and candles glowing in windows. Seasonal cycles of holiday fasts and feasts. Lively market days, close-knit communal life, village squabbles [14]."

The Pale became one of the largest and most intense incubators of Jewish culture and spirituality the world has known. At the same time, isolating Jews in the Pale hampered Jewish contributions to wider Russia, and it made Jews easy targets for the winds of antisemitism.

Great-grandfather Joseph Herr (1871-1936)

Joseph Herr was born around 1871 in Russia when its empire was peaking militarily under the rulership of Tsar Alexander II. Census records report "Russia Yiddish"—code for the Pale of the Settlement—as the place of birth for Joseph and both of Joseph's parents. Joseph emigrated to America as a teenager, between 1884 and 1887—an anxious time for the Jewish community. These were the early years of the great migration of two million Jews, escaping the Russian Empire's religious persecution, poverty, pogroms, and conscription.

Under Alexander II's rule, only the upper classes lived well. The lower classes (especially peasants and the urban working class) led miserable lives characterized by poverty, repression, lack of political representation, high taxes, and unrest. For Jews, the conditions were even worse, as their position in society was even more precarious.

As a ten-year-old child, Joseph would have witnessed a brutal, antisemitic crackdown. Tsar Alexander II was assassinated on March 13, 1881, an act for which Jews were unfairly blamed. As a result, "more than 250 anti-Jewish riots erupted in the Russian Empire [15]." These pogroms destroyed thousands of Jewish homes, impoverished many Jewish families, and killed or injured large numbers of Jews. To make matters worse, by the mid 1880s Joseph would have been looking toward compulsory military service.

Though we know little about Joseph's early life, a single picture captures the dramatic contrast between the old and new worlds. In it, we see Joseph as a large middle-aged man looking fully American with a three-piece modern suit and top hat. He's standing next to his much smaller father, who's sporting a long white beard, Eastern European kaftan-style black overcoat, and Russian Kippah (Jewish skullcap). Thus, we know Joseph emigrated as a teenager with his parents, and we have a dramatic picture of assimilation.

If Joseph's parents left relatives behind, then their descendants (our cousins) would have been at risk for eventual extermination when the Nazis invaded Poland and the Soviet Union during World War II. By the end of World War II, Nazis murdered 90 percent of Poland's 3.5 million Jews. The Nazi invasion of the Soviet Union led to the annihilation of another 2 million Jews, mostly in Ukraine, but also in Lithuania, Latvia and other parts of the Soviet Union. As a tentative teen boarding a ship headed for America, Joseph could not have foreseen the important role he would play in the survival—and flourishing—of his family line.

•••••

The 1910 U.S. Census shows Joseph renting a house on Waller Street on the West Side of Chicago with his wife, Rose, and his three sons Sam (short for Samuel), Jack (short for Jacob), and Leo, who were 18, 16, and 7 years old, respectively. The family reported that Joseph immigrated in 1887 and married Rose in 1891, when he was about 21 and she was about 18 years old. The Census indicates that Joseph was a self-employed "horse dealer"—a trade he likely learned from his father in the old country.

The Columbia University Club's History of Chicago Series describes the "city of horses" as follows. "To understand life in Chicago in the late 19th and early 20th century you must imagine a city filled with horses. Horses were essential to the growth of Chicago and served as a primary means of commercial and public transportation ... Horses transformed the city in a number of ways. They were essential to everyday life, helped industry expand, stimulated the rise of Chicago's downtown consumer economy, and had a profound influence on how urban space was shaped [16]."

Joseph must have been a successful horse-trader, because the 1920 Census shows the family owning their own home—without a mortgage—on Washburn Avenue, still on Chicago's West Side. Joseph operated his horse-trading business in the heyday of the industry.

Beginning at three years of age, Lois—with her parents—lived with Rose and Joseph, who died when Lois was eight. Lois claimed to be the apple of her grandfather's eye. She described him to me as a burly man who walked the streets of the West Side with his big collie dog Teddy. She said, "They backed down to no one and there were days when they both came home bloody."

Great-grandma Rose Rosenberg, 1873-1952
Rose Rosenberg's mother Etta arrived in America in 1870, the year before the Great Chicago Fire. Rose was born in Chicago three years later at a time when the city itself was young—barely four decades after incorporation. Census records report Russia-Yiddish as Etta's birthplace, meaning that, like Joseph, she grew up in the Pale of the Settlement during the reign of Tsar Alexander II. However, she emigrated more than a decade before Joseph, possibly without her parents, at the age of thirteen.

In 1873, when she was just 16, Etta gave birth to Rose. I don't know the identity of Rose's father, and I have no information about the lives Etta and Rose led in Chicago before Rose met Great-grandfather Joseph Herr, the burly horse-trader. Joseph and Rose married in 1891 when she was eighteen and he was twenty-one. A year later, Rose gave birth to her first child, Leo's older brother Sam, and Etta became a 35-year-old grandmother. Jack followed in 1894 and Leo in 1903. The 1910 Census Report shows Joseph as the head of household at 40 years old and Rose at 37, with Etta a 53-year-old widow living with the family. Etta likely died before the 1920 census, as she no longer appears in the household.

Why Etta emigrated as a teenager during a period of reform and relative calm in the Russian Pale remains a mystery. Etta and her daughter Rose were the first of our ancestors known to settle in Chicago. Much about this family line remains shrouded in mystery—extending through my mother Lois, grandfather Leo, great-grandmother Rose, and great-great-grandmother Etta. I know from the 1910 U.S. Census that the line goes at least as far back as Etta and her parents in the Russian Pale, but I have no record of Rose's father or siblings, nor do I have any record of Etta's parents, or siblings. We will probe this mystery in a subsequent chapter, as my mother's trials later in life offer additional insight.

Given Leo's roots in the Pale, his DNA likely carried a rich blend of Eastern European Jewish cultures. My mother mentioned Lithuania to Neala, and wrote "Russia/Latvia" in her *Grandmother Book*, suggesting a heritage grounded in intensely religious traditions. Unaware of each other, teenagers Joseph Herr and Etta Rosenberg left behind cloistered Jewish communities in the Russian Pale. Their paths ultimately crossed in Chicago, where Joseph met Etta's daughter Rose—and together, they planted the seeds for our family to flourish in America.

Great-grandparents Hyman Levin, 1861-1948, and Sara Mata Silverstein, 1865-1921

Shifre's Family

The Silverstein-Hofman Family Reunion took place in 1997 in Chicago. It produced a rich database and directory documenting the family's living members and ancestors. The oldest known relatives are Shimon Silverstein and Shifre Yellin, both born in the Russian Empire after the

Third Partition of Poland divided much of Eastern Europe between Russia, Prussia, and Austria in 1795. Russia divided its share of Poland into two parts: an eastern region merged into the Pale of the Settlement, and a western region called the Province of Poland.

Thus, our Polish Jewish roots come through Shifre and Shimon and a small town named Tykocin. Nine of their ten children were born in Tykocin between 1862 and 1884. Furthermore, Shifre herself was born in Tykocin in about 1837. Shifre lived to see the birth of more than fifty grandchildren and countless great-grandchildren. That branch of the family tree produced hundreds of cousins, and I've only known a few. Mort used to say, "If you drop something from the top of a building, it's bound to hit one of Selma's relatives."

The family appears to have split up during the emigration process. Nine of Shifre and Shimon's children emigrated to the U.S. at various times between 1887 and 1898, and they all settled in Chicago. Five of the children, including Sara Mata, were married at the time that they emigrated and some had children of their own. Ranging in age between 14 and 20, the other four emigrant children found spouses after arriving in Chicago.

The union of Hyman and Sara Mata produced ten children. The last of them was my Grandma Selma, born in 1905 in Chicago. Fannie, the oldest, and three siblings were born in the old country. After emigrating in 1894, Hyman and Sara Mata had six more children, all in Chicago, with Selma the youngest. Sara Mata died six years before Selma gave birth to one of Sara Mata's many grandchildren—my father Orville. My Aunt Sermata, the second child born to Selma and Morton, was named after her grandmother, Sara Mata.

Tykocin and Bialystok

In 1932, Shifre died at age 98 in Chicago. Shimon died at age 66 in 1900 in Bialystok, a Polish town in the western part of the Pale. Tykocin and Bialystok—only about 20 miles apart—were on opposite sides of the border between the Pale and the Province of Poland.

The Silverstein-Hofman database indicates that Leah Silverstein, Sara Mata's sister, married Itzhak Weinstein in the old country and they tried living in America for a year, but decided the Jewish community was "not Jewish enough" for their taste. Leah died in Bialystok while giving birth to the last of her and Itzhak's eight children.

I visited Tykocin in May of 2014. In spite of finding no Jews living there, I discovered a beautifully restored synagogue, originally built in 1643. In 1941, during the Nazi occupation of Poland, the synagogue was desecrated. After the war, the postwar all-gentile Tykocin population repurposed the synagogue as a fertilizer warehouse.

In the 1970s the people of Tykocin restored the synagogue to its original glory and made it into a museum which now attracts 40,000 visitors a year, many—or more likely, most—of them Jews whose ancestors were murdered by the Nazis. All but 150 of the Jews living in Tykocin were transported—by the Nazis with the help of the Polish police—out of town and into the forest, where they were massacred on August 25-26, 1941. The 150 who escaped the massacre were forced into the nearby Bialystok Ghetto.

Inherited Trauma

In June 1941, the German armed forces overran Bialystok and on June 27, a day that became known as "Red Friday," the Nazis murdered 2,200 Jews, including

1,000 men who were locked inside and burned alive when the Nazis set fire to the synagogue. Then, the Nazis rounded up as many as 50,000 Jews and confined them in the Bialystok Ghetto before systematically "liquidating" them—by firing squads or by deportation to one of the extermination camps in German-occupied Poland: Chelmo, Sobibor, Belzec, Majdanek, Treblinka, or Auschwitz.

Another Nazi attack came in February of 1943. Ten thousand Jews were deported from Bialystok to the Treblinka concentration camp, where they were murdered. Meanwhile, two thousand Jews—too old, weak, or sick to travel—were shot on the spot in Bialystok. These two thousand probably included the late Leah's 70-year-old husband, Itzhak Weinstein, who was killed in the Bialystok Ghetto in 1943. Two of Leah and Itzhak's children died in Poland—probably murdered by Nazis—and it's likely that they had children of their own—our cousins—who also perished.

Until embarking on this writing project, I didn't think about having not-so-distant relatives who were murdered in the Holocaust. I grew up often thinking about the Holocaust, but not in personal terms. Regrettably, I gave little thought to the generations before my grandparents. My parents and grandparents didn't talk about the old country. Perhaps they avoided such talk, because of the pain it would bring to the surface. Perhaps they thought talking about it would hold me back from embracing the opportunities available in the U.S.

I have always taken atrocities committed against the Jewish People personally. Subsequent chapters explain those feelings in more detail. For now, I'll say that in addition to anger, I feel a deep indignation when I see today's all-gentile Tykocin population profit from Jews returning to mourn at sites of atrocity. There they find a once-sacred synagogue functioning as a museum that offers little acknowledgement—much less reverence— for the annihilation of the Jewish community that once filled the sanctuary with prayer, song, and celebration of life.

•••••

The next chapter explores the challenges and triumphs of my grandparents—all but one a first generation American—as they establish a foothold in Chicago, while embracing the American dream.

Chapter 2
Embracing the American Dream

All of my grandparents were born in Chicago—three on the West Side and one on the South Side—between 1903 and 1905. Three were born to immigrant parents and one had an immigrant grandparent living with her. All four would have heard Yiddish spoken at home. They were old enough to know what was going on, but not old enough to serve in World War I. They met, courted, married, and had their first child during the Roaring Twenties. Very exciting. Let's take a closer look.

Grandma Roselyn Grant (1905-1972)
Rosa May begets Rose begets Roselyn

Julius and Lillie Grant named my maternal grandmother "Rosa May" when she was born on January 7, 1905. During her childhood, she was known as Rose. I only knew her as Roselyn. She likely chose the name Roselyn because after a few years on their own, they moved in with Leo's parents. She likely adopted her new name to avoid confusion with Leo's mother, Rose. I expect that the name Roselyn felt like a fresh start with a new family. She chose well and knowing her loving personality, I believe that when the rest of the family called her Roselyn, it was a term of endearment.

A Refined Early Life

With a decade of married life in New York City under their belts, the Grants must have arrived in Chicago with savings and earnings potential. They obtained a mortgage and bought their first home on Chicago's South Side—at 438 West 42nd Place. Census reports indicate that they had a "houseman" named George

Mason. Perhaps George helped out around the house in exchange for a rent-free room. Having a houseman suggests a level of affluence.

At the time of her birth in 1905, Roselyn had two older sisters and two older brothers. The 1920 Census shows Julius still working in the clothing industry, Lillie managing the household, and Roselyn at 15 with all her siblings except Elsie still living at home. Roselyn grew up surrounded by a close-knit family in a culturally rich Jewish community. Raised with refined tastes, she grew up playing the piano and became good enough to aspire to become a concert pianist.

South Side Neighborhoods

Roselyn grew up in a neighborhood at the north end of Canaryville, known at that time for having a mix of Jewish and Irish residents—with the Irish ruling the roost. It was one of the roughest and toughest neighborhoods in Chicago [22]. The neighborhood was only about a mile west of the Bronzeville and Grand Boulevard neighborhoods that attracted many German Jewish immigrants to Chicago's South Side in the late 19th and early 20th centuries.

The house was just a few blocks east of the Chicago Stockyards. The stockyard stench reportedly reached downtown Chicago—four miles away—so the Grants surely smelled it. Between slaughtering at the Union Stockyards and muck spewed into the dying Chicago River, the smells of Chicago could be brutal. Meatpacking was a lucrative industry and at that time Chicago supplied more than eighty percent of domestic meat consumed in the country. It was the center of the meat-packing industry.

Maybe the smell drove them away, because by the time Roselyn was fifteen, the family had moved to a house they rented on Prairie Avenue just west of Washington Park. In the 1920s, Washington Park became a center of racial tension, gang violence, and the criminal activities of the Jewish and Italian mafias. Organized crime had a major impact on Chicago's economy, most notably in promoting illegal gambling and drinking during the prohibition years—from 1920 to 1933.

World War I and the Spanish Flu

In June 1914, news arrived that a Serbian revolutionary operating in Bosnia assassinated the Archduke Franz Ferdinand—heir apparent to the throne of the Austo-Hungarian Empire. This must have piqued the interest of the Grant family, given Julius' Hungarian roots and Lillie's German roots. At the age of nine, Roselyn would have been old enough to participate in the conversation.

One month after the assassination, Austria-Hungary declared war on Serbia, a Russian ally. A few days later, the dominos representing all of Europe's intricate alliances set off a chain reaction and propelled most of Europe into World War I. A generation earlier, Bismarck's diplomacy established a defensive alliance system as a way of securing the German Empire against aggression from its European neighbors—especially Russia—and not as a prelude to war. Kaiser Wilhelm II fired Bismarck in 1890 and destabilized the alliances by withdrawing from Bismarck's treaty with Russia. He inflamed the region with aggressive posturing and in 1914 promised unlimited support to Austria in its prosecution of war against Serbia. Many historians blame the magnitude of World War I on Wilhelm II's belligerence. Initially, the German, Austro-Hungarian and Ottoman empires formed the Central Powers and lined up against the Allies, which included the Russian, French, and British empires. A terrible conflict was shaping up and Roselyn's oldest brother Hugo joined the ROTC (Reserve Officers' Training Corps) after it was founded under the National Defense Act of 1916.

Roselyn was twelve and Hugo was twenty-seven in 1917 when President Woodrow Wilson—for the first time since the Civil War—signed a bill reintroducing a national draft. Coming from the ROTC, Hugo enlisted and served as an army captain. He was in good company as 225,000 Jews fought for the U.S. in World War I. Like Hugo, most came from families who had emigrated from enemy territory. Furthermore, 100,000 Jews still lived there and fought—willingly or not— on the side of the Central Powers [23].

When the German military finally had enough, Kaiser Wilhelm II abdicated the throne of the German Empire. The war ended with an agreement signed by Germany on Armistice Day—November 11, 1918. By that time, more than 53,000 U.S. soldiers had died in combat, and another 63,000 had died from the Spanish Flu. More than six-hundred thousand people in the U.S. and 50 million people worldwide died of the disease during one of the deadliest pandemics in history.

Sibling Stories

As indicated by the 1920 Census, Hugo lived with his parents and siblings for a short time after returning from the war. In 1920, Julius and Albert worked in the clothing industry, and Hugo worked as a draftsman creating designs for electrical machinery in the automobile industry. By the time of the 1930 census, Hugo lived with his wife and three young children in Chicago's South Shore neighborhood. A vibrant center of 1920s Chicago Jewish community and affluence, the neighborhood was home to a large and influential contingent of German Jewish immigrants. Perhaps Hugo's affinity for the German Jewish community stemmed from his mother Lillie's German origins.

Hugo's two oldest children reflect his success in life. Born two years before my mother, her close cousins—the twins Alan and Jeanne Grant—lived lives in the limelight. Alan became an aircraft propulsion engineer, and Jeanne became a professional singer. Alan had appointments at major universities, and Jeanne performed in Broadway theatrical productions, including *Sound of Music* and *Fiddler on the Roof*.

Roselyn's sister, my Grandaunt Beatrice, married Henry Polachek in 1921 when she was just 20 years old. The secretive story portrays Henry and Beatrice becoming Christians, because Henry couldn't get the job he wanted as a Jew. At first, he worked as a production superintendent in Chicago's railway supplies industry. In the 1940s, the family moved to Winona, Minnesota, and Henry continued his work as a production superintendent, but this time in the mill waste industry. Henry and Bea's children, Wilbur, Ralph, and Herbert grew up unaware of their Jewish heritage.

Meeting Leo, Letting Go

It must have been traumatic for Roselyn, at 18 years old, to lose her dad, and at 21 years old to lose her mom. Losing her dad might have intensified her relationship with Grandpa Leo, whom she met around the same time.

At 19 years old (almost 20), Roselyn eloped with Leo on New Years Eve in 1924. For several years, they lived in their own apartment in the Cicero neighborhood about eight miles west of Prairie Avenue. In 1927, at 22 years of age, Roselyn gave birth to my mother Lois—whom neither of Roselyn's parents lived to meet. Sidetracked by the death of her parents, her marriage to Leo, her pregnancy with my mother, and the financial stress of the oncoming depression, my Grandma Roselyn's ambition to perform as a concert pianist slowly slipped away. Failing to pursue it was a major disappointment in her life. Knowing this made me feel sad for her.

Grandpa Leo Herr (1903-1972)

Early Life

My Grandpa Leo was born on August 21, 1903 to Rose Rosenberg Herr (age 29) and Joseph Herr (age 31). Leo's brothers Sam and Jack were 11 and 9. In 1910, Joseph was running his horse-trading business, the two older boys worked as clerks, and Leo was in school. Rose's mother Etta, then 52, also lived with the family. Like Roselyn, Leo grew up in a stable Jewish home. He had older siblings to guide him, and a tight-knit family for support. However, educational attainment didn't seem a priority. Census Reports suggest that all three boys left school around age 16.

West Side Roots

The 1910 Census indicates that the Herr family rented a house in the 1200 block of Waller Avenue on Chicago's West Side. At that time, the epicenter of West Side Chicago Jewish commercial activity was at the intersection of Maxwell and Halsted Streets. The famous Maxwell Street Market covered a nine-block area extending from that location and constituting the largest open-air market in the country.

The market was "established in the late 19th century by newly arrived Jewish residents from Eastern

Europe [25]." The Herrs started out living about 6 miles due west of that intersection. They were in good company, because Jews had begun spreading into neighborhoods west of crowded Maxwell and Halsted Streets. They lived in West Garfield Park, next to Lawndale—a vibrant center of Eastern European Jewish culture in early 20th century Chicago [26].

The West Side Herrs would have enjoyed some great years for Chicago Cubs baseball during Leo's childhood. The Cubs won the National League championship four times during the 12 years between 1906 and 1918, and in two of those years (1907 and 1908) they won the World Series. Memorable players include the dynamic double play combination of Joe Tinker, Johnny Evers, and Frank Chance. I can still hear the phrase "Tinker to Evers to Chance" running through my mind and I never saw them play!

In 1906, the Cubs and White Sox faced off in a cross-town rivalry and one of the most exciting World Series of all time. The White Sox played home games in a South Side park and the Cubs played home games in a West Side park. Thus, the Grants rooted for the Sox, and the Herrs rooted for the Cubs. In this third edition of the World Series, the Sox upset the heavily favored Cubs, winning the series four games to two. When Leo met Roselyn for the first time, there would have been friendly banter endorsing their respective teams. That's not all that separated them.

An Unlikely Union

Leo and Roselyn—both wonderful grandparents—were in many ways an unlikely couple. The West Side where Grandpa Leo grew up probably felt a world apart from the South Side where Grandma Roselyn grew up. In actual distance, they grew up only seven miles apart. Culturally, they lived across a great divide.

The more liberal Reform Movement dominated South Side Jewish neighborhoods with their earlier Central European (mostly German) Jewish immigrants. Tradition and Orthodoxy dominated West Side Jewish neighborhoods with their Eastern European Jewish immigrants. South Side Jews had generally fared better in the old country during the mid-19th century, and they generally had more money to bring with them than West Side Jews. Roselyn's father was a merchant and Leo's father was a horse-trader. While both families fared well in Chicago, Roselyn's family brought a degree of cultural refinement, while Leo's family reflected a more working class tradition.

So how did Leo and Roselyn come together? Notes from my mother say Leo traveled to Roselyn's South Side neighborhood for a blind date. After an apparently brief courtship, they eloped a week before Roselyn's 20th birthday. Perhaps they eloped to avoid the cost and formality of a wedding—maybe they had reason to fear the two families would not see eye-to-eye on planning the affair. Lillie had lost her husband, Julius, just a year before, and she may have been in poor health herself, as she died only two years later. Whatever the circumstances, their decision speaks to youthful passion, independence, and perhaps a bit of defiance.

Given the obstacles she overcame, Roselyn must have been head over heels for Leo, who likely knew how to have a good time. Meeting in the middle of the "Roaring Twenties," Leo and Roselyn must have had fun courting in what was an exuberant time to be Jewish in Chicago. When they met, the U.S. had recently been instrumental in the Allied victory in World War I. They must have been flying high—at least until the Great

Depression began with the stock market crash of October 1929, but more on that later.

From the 1880s to the 1920s, the Jewish population of Chicago grew from 10,000 to 225,000 people, 8% of the general population. I imagine the 1920s were a fun time to be Jewish and courting in Chicago. Maybe Leo's Eastern European roots and Roselyn's German-Hungarian background made their courtship more interesting. Beyond baseball games, what did they do for fun?

The Roaring Twenties

The 1920s saw Chicago transitioning from horses to automobiles for transportation, but Leo's father, Joseph, was still in the horse-trading business. I'm sure he had a horse-drawn carriage which Leo could use to impress Roselyn. However, my guess is that they mostly got around town riding the trolley, a streetcar attached to an elevated electric wire.

While dating, Roselyn and Leo would have put their cross-town rivalry aside and joined forces to root for Chicago Bears football. The team excelled in the 1920s, with two national championships, all-time great players—including Red Grange (the "Galloping Ghost") and Bronislau ("Bronco") Nagurski—and one of the best managers the game has ever known, George Halas. I'm sure Roselyn and Leo had lots of fun listening to Bears, Cubs, and Sox games on the radio, a favorite pastime in those days. When my grandparents were young, Chicago had its heyday as a sports town. Chicago teams competed at the highest levels in baseball, football, boxing, sailing, golf, track and field, horseracing, and tennis. Chicago has always been a powerhouse sports town, but never with as much success across the board as during my grandparents' youth.

I bet Roselyn wanted to take Leo to the symphony to listen to piano concertos. Built in 1904 by renowned architect, Daniel Burnham, Orchestra Hall has thrilled Chicago audiences with world-class performances for more than 120 years. Under Frederick Stock's direction (1905-1942), the Chicago Symphony attracted some of the world's finest musicians—a tradition that continues to this day. In 2008, the Chicago Symphony Orchestra was voted the best in the U.S. and the sixth best in the world by the British classical music magazine, *Gramophone*.

I'm sure Leo wanted to take Roselyn to racetracks, speakeasies, and boxing matches. Betting on horses has always been a favorite Chicago pastime, and the city had six racetracks—more than any other city in the U.S. at that time. Speaking of boxing, they could not attend the big heavyweight championship match between Jack Dempsey and Gene Tunney at Soldier Field on September 22, 1927, because my mother was born just eight days later. The event drew more than 100,000 people, the all-time record for attendance at a boxing match. It was the famous "long count" fight, where Dempsey knocked Tunney down. A delay in the start of the count—due to Dempsey's failure to immediately go to a neutral corner—helped Tunney survive and go on to win. At the end of the fight, Dempsey purportedly said to Tunney, "you're the best," and then retired from boxing. I bet my grandfather listened to the fight on the radio. He loved boxing!

Siblings and Other Relatives

Fortunately for Leo, he was too young for World War I and too old for World War II. His brothers, however, would have been of draft age when Wilson signed the Selective Service Act. I don't know if they were "selected to serve." Less than 12% of the 24 million men who registered were actually drafted. Sam enlisted as a volunteer in the Navy in June of 1918 and served until a month after Armistice Day. I'm sure there was shouting in the streets by the Grants and the Herrs, along with other Americans when the news came on November 11, 1918 that the war had ended [27].

Prohibition came to Chicago in 1920, ushering in illegal drinking and gambling at speakeasies run by gangsters like Al Capone and our cousin Sam Hare. According to my Uncle Joe, Sam Hare partnered with Al Capone and associated with his Chicago Outfit. Sam owned several speakeasies, including the Schiller Café, Hare's Club, and The Dells. With their patently illegal drinking and gambling—made possible by bribing poorly paid police officers—speakeasies became centers of music, dancing, and illicit fun. Prohibition and the Roaring Twenties connoted a time when the mafia ruled Chicago's underworld, making illicit pleasures widely available [28].

Sam Hare's Morton Grove location of the Dells became famous for the kidnapping of Jake Factor from his car as he was returning home from a party at the establishment. Like Sam Hare, Jake "the Barber" Factor was affiliated with the Chicago Outfit, and whether the kidnapping was real remains a mystery, but the story—like the times—was steeped in danger, spectacle, and intrigue. Many believed the kidnapping was staged to create sympathy during Factor's extradition case.

Grandpa Morton Goldstein/Shane, 1903-1992

Morton ("Mort") and Selma both came from large families, typical of Eastern European Jewish households shaped by traditional values and religious observance. This section focuses on Grandpa Mort, and the next section focuses on Grandma Selma, as well as the courtship of Mort and Selma.

Mort's Early Life

On January 11, 1903, Fannie Goldstein, nee Meltz gave birth to my grandfather, Mort. At the time, Fannie and her husband, Aaron Goldstein, lived on Liberty Street on Chicago's West Side with seven of Mort's siblings, ranging from an age of three to seventeen. The home stood a short distance from the bustling, overcrowded Maxwell Street Market. Grandpa Mort told me that when he was about six, the family moved to 1350 S. Avers Street, and when he was in third grade the family moved just a half-mile down the road to a three-flat at 1428 S. Central Park Avenue. Mort lived there and functioned as the house caretaker until he got married.

Both the Avers Street and Central Park Avenue homes were within a couple of blocks of Independence Boulevard, the main drag between North Lawndale and East Garfield Park. Living downstairs in the two-flat on Avers Street was an electrician named Mr. Goding. Grandpa Mort told me that he thought this electrician was "a God," because of his tool collection and how good he was at fixing just about anything. Though not religiously observant, Mort was a God-fearing man. One of his favorite sayings stayed with me, "I can only give you the facts. God has to give you the understanding." His interactions with Mr. Goding inspired Mort to become an electrician later in life.

Mort was a good athlete, too. He told me about his success as a wrestler, speed skater, golfer, and sprinter. He was mighty proud of his best golf score, 79 for 18 holes!

Odd Jobs

As a teenager, Mort held several interesting jobs. He worked the candy counter in the famous Auditorium Theater. Designed and built in 1889 by the famous architectural firm Adler and Sullivan, the Auditorium Theater was already known for its perfect acoustics and impeccable stage productions—mainly opera—in Mort's time. When Mort was nine years old, Teddy Roosevelt gave his famous Armageddon speech—"we stand at Armageddon and we battle for the Lord"—at the Auditorium Theater, as he launched the National Progressive Party, more affectionately known as the "Bull Moose Party." Making the strongest showing of any third party in U.S. history, Roosevelt garnered twenty-seven percent of the vote, coming in ahead of incumbent Howard Taft in the 1912 election, only to lose to Woodrow Wilson. Later generations would feast on performances by Aretha Franklin, Jimi Hendrix, and Itzhak Perlman, among many others. The theater has also thrilled audiences with productions like *Les Misérables* and *Phantom of the Opera*.

Mort also made some money selling score cards and peanuts at Sox and Cubs baseball games. At seventeen years old he had a temporary job as a short-order cook and dishwasher on the Santa Fe Railway. He traveled as far as Los Angeles, spending six days at a time on the train.

A New Last Name

Although the youngest in the family, Mort was not one to "be seen and not heard." Illustrative of his chutzpah (gumption), during his teenage years, Mort changed his family name from Goldstein to Shane. As you may recall, back in Kurland, Aaron's family name was Schoen, a German surname pronounced the way Grandpa Mort spelled it. Mort must have had considerable sway within the family, because he changed the name, not just for himself, but also for his mother and all but one of his sisters.

Mort had some ambivalence when talking about his father. On one hand, he pictured his father as disabled, unable to interact. On the other hand, he took his father's first name as his own middle name: Aaron. When I probed, he said, "There was another Morton Shane in the phonebook, so I needed a middle name."

My grandaunt Ann, along with Mort's two brothers, changed the family name to sound like Shane, but with a "y" in the middle. Both spellings evoke Irish origins. We have no Irish blood of which I'm aware. I surmise that all of the siblings were on board with a phonetic spelling of the original Schoen name, but they disagreed on how that should look. The family also agreed that they wanted a less Jewish-sounding name. This makes sense, given our earlier story about Fannie's indignance over a contingent of the local synagogue's leaders coming to the house to ask a woman with a disabled husband and a brood of children for a donation to the temple.

I am grateful to Grandpa Mort because I prefer Phil Shane to Phil Goldstein. I think my life would have been quite different with Goldstein as a last name. With the name, Goldstein, I might have worn my Jewish heritage on my sleeve. I might not have spread my gene pool with a non-Jewish spouse, a decision I've never regretted. I also prefer the Shane spelling, because I'd be forever explaining that I'm not Irish if the name was spelled Shayne.

Man about Town

Mort was too young to serve in World War I, but during the summers of 1917 and 1918 he had a job working on a farm in Independence, Iowa, filling in for men away at war. After two years of high school, he quit so he could "make some money to buy a car." At the age of 18, Mort became an apprentice electrician, and at the age of 22 he became fully licensed.

He told me that in 1923, he managed a down payment, got a loan for the rest of the $1,023 price, and bought his first car, a Model T Ford Sedan. At a time when fewer than half of Chicago men drove, and even fewer 20-year-olds, Mort must have cut quite a figure behind the wheel of his new Model T.

Sibling Stories

Of Mort's many siblings, I personally remember Aunt Ann who was tough like Mort, Aunt Rose, kind and gentle, and Aunt Esther who always seemed somewhat frail. Grandpa Mort spoke fondly—and sometimes admiringly—about his siblings.

Jeannette dated Hyman G. Rickover, who gave her his pin when she was a student at the University of Wisconsin. Rickover became an admiral and war hero known as "the father of the U.S. nuclear navy." Jeannette and Hyman were the same age and must have grown up together—both graduated from Marshall High School.

Tragically, Jeannette fell ill and died shortly before graduating from the University of Wisconsin in 1923. Grandpa Mort remembered, "Her grades were so exceptional that she was awarded a Phi Beta Kappa key on her deathbed." Mort would have been 20 years old at the time. The loss must have been traumatic for the whole family.

Grandpa Mort's sister Ida worked for a large department store, and his brother Joe was an auditor and accomplished billiards player who "could have played with the best in the country." His sister Esther was a piano teacher, Ann was a kindergarten teacher, and Rose was a saint who took care of anyone who was sick, including, at various times, Aaron, Fannie, Ida, and Jeannette. Rose also worked as an internal auditor for a large Chicago department store.

Famous Friends and Acquaintances

Mort had famous friends. Abe Marovitz was a federal judge and the first ever Jewish State Senator. Buck Halperin was a standout football player and war hero. He also was known as one of the best yachtsmen in the world with an Olympic bronze medal, a Pan American Games gold medal, and even had a sailing trophy named in his honor: The Buck Halperin World Championship Trophy.

Halperin became a successful businessman and owned Commercial Light, where Mort worked for twelve years as an electrician. Grandpa Mort told me that he eventually became a foreman and also worked in the front office. He said he became "part of the family."

I wouldn't call them friends, but Mort knew Al Capone and, according to family lore, interacted with him from time to time. My cousin Mickey told the following story. Mort was walking along the street minding his own business when a car pulled up with thugs inside. One of them opened the door and told Mort to get in, which he did. They told Mort that Capone's hideout needed rewiring, they were taking him there, and he would have to wear a blindfold. As far as I know, everything went as planned at the

Wisconsin hideout and the thugs drove Mort back to Chicago. The hideout is now a tourist attraction. This story has always held equal parts pride and amusement in my family—having evidence that it actually occurred would kill the humor and make the pride dubious. In any case, it reflects the colorful, dangerous world of Chicago.

Grandma Selma Levin, 1905-1985

A Big Family!

My Grandma Selma's family makes Grandpa Mort's family look small. Selma was the last of 10 children born to Hyman and Sara Mata Levin. I know nothing about Hyman's family of origin but, thanks to the July 1997 Silverstein-Hoffman Reunion, I know a lot about Sara Mata's family. Her parents, Shifre Yellin and Shimon Silverstein, lived in Tykocin, Poland before the family emigrated to America.

Aside from those belonging to Sara Mata and Hyman, I counted 69 of Shifre and Shimon's children and grandchildren already living in the U.S. when Selma was born on December 16, 1905. At least, that's the birthdate inscribed on her headstone. According to family lore, this was a made-up date, as her birth certificate was irretrievably lost or never created. With so many children arriving in rapid succession, it was easy to get lost in the shuffle. Our Eastern European family believed the world needed more Jews and, by golly, they did their part!

By the time of Selma's birth, most of her expansive family had settled in either Los Angeles or Chicago. Shifre was buried in Chicago's Waldheim Cemetery in 1932, so Chicago was a center of gravity for the family when Selma was growing up. Grandpa Mort didn't want to be buried with Grandma Selma's relatives at Waldheim, so he bought a family plot in Shalom Park Cemetery in Arlington Heights, a northwest suburb of Chicago. Mort, Selma, and my parents are buried there.

Early Life

In 1921, when Selma was just fourteen, her mother, Sara Mata, died. She left behind a bustling household, including young grandchildren and her mother Shifre, who never spoke English. I hope Hyman, who was 57 years old at the time of Sara Mata's death, was getting all the help he needed. Hyman provided for the family with his earnings as a tailor, a trade he probably learned in the old country, perhaps in Bialystok.

Bialystok had a thriving textile industry, the third biggest center for textile production in Europe after Moscow and Lodz. Hyman had his own shop, specializing in ladies' clothes. He must have been a particularly good tailor to support such a large family. Other working members of the household held jobs as an auto mechanic, a bank teller, a notions salesperson, and a fruit salesperson. These jobs were typical of other branches of Shimon and Shifre Silverstein's exceptionally large family in California and Chicago.

Grandma Selma was a loving, nurturing, warm-hearted person and a great cook, characteristics I presume were passed down from her mother. After her mom died, Selma at 15 years old likely took on a heavy share of nurturing and cooking in a bustling household of 12 that included young children.

Selma was also the most culturally Jewish of my four grandparents. I remember her "pushke," a container used in Jewish homes to collect money to support the temple and give to the poor. She religiously fed the pushke whenever anyone in the family was traveling or otherwise needed protection.

By the time she was four years old, Selma's family had moved to 736 S. Hermitage Avenue and by the time she was 14 they lived at 1331 S. Troy Street. Like Mort's family, Selma's family lived solidly on the West Side. Though they lived only eight short blocks and a little over a half-mile apart, they didn't meet in the neighborhood.

Meeting Mort

When I interviewed him in 1985, Grandpa Mort told me that he met Selma in the summer of 1922 at a resort in South Haven, Michigan. At that time, she would have been a pretty, impressionable, 16-year-old coming through an intense time in her family. It had only been six months since Selma lost her mother, and she was living with her father and five older siblings, two of whom had a husband and infant child.

In the summer of 1922, Selma was ready to emerge from her cocoon—and Grandpa Mort must have been a breath of fresh air. He would have been a handsome, athletic, 19-year-old apprentice electrician saving money to buy his first car. He would have been trying out his new last name, Shane, and he would have talked proudly about his accomplished older siblings.

South Haven, Michigan, a port city where the Black River meets Lake Michigan developed as a resort community in the early 1900s, complete with an amusement park, recreation buildings, cottages, and of course the beach. Getting there—by steamship or a lovely 120-mile drive along the coast of Lake Michigan— was part of the fun. In the early 1900s, South Haven became a magnet for Chicago's Jewish community, and it remained so at least through my childhood.

With reference to its better-known counterpart in New York, South Haven became known as the "Catskills of the Midwest." "At its height, South Haven had sixty-three resorts run by Jewish immigrants for Jewish vacationers [29]." Mort and Selma must have really hit it off in South Haven in the summer of 1922. It led to two and a half years of courting followed by marriage on February 1, 1925, one month after Leo and Roselyn eloped.

Like Grandma Roselyn, Grandma Selma was 19 years old when she married. Unlike Roselyn and Leo, Mort and Selma got married "in a restaurant with a hall for weddings on the West Side." The families approved of their union. Grandpa Mort remembered their honeymoon at the Rogers Park Hotel on Sheridan Road, "in those days a very fine hotel." They moved in together at 3359 Lexington, still in the vicinity of their Independence Boulevard stomping grounds.

•••••

The lives of my four grandparents, Mort, Selma, Leo, and Roselyn, reveal a rich European Jewish heritage, along with an open-armed receptiveness to U.S. culture and "the American dream." I suspect the family's roots go through many generations of ancestors in the Central and Eastern European places where I found them.

Escaping oppressive governments, economic hardship, and antisemitic cultures meant they necessarily left few traces behind. Consequently, my research efforts penetrate two or three generations beyond each of my grandparents' lives before reaching dead ends. Nonetheless, each of their lives carries the flavor of a distinct family journey—landing in Chicago.

Mort's family from Kurland experienced Baltic culture with a strong German influence. Deeply steeped in Polish Jewish culture, Selma's family of origin is more traditional and more religious than the families of my other three grandparents. Selma knew the most Yiddish words and probably could converse in Yiddish. Leo's family came from the Eastern European melting pot known as The Pale of the Settlement, while Roselyn's family came from Germany on her mother's side and Hungary on her father's side.

Overall, our heritage blends the Reform Jewish movement and Jewish Enlightenment with the Jewish orthodoxy that permeated Poland and most of The Pale of the Settlement. The next chapter will reveal that my grandparents raised my parents without much taste for orthodoxy. Instead, we'll see an orientation toward assimilation balanced by a strong sense of Jewish identity.

Chapter 3
The Greatest Generation

Orville Shane and Lois Herr Arrive

In 1927, at the height of the Roaring Twenties—before the winds of The Great Depression and World War II began to blow—stocks soared, spirits ran high, and Orville and Lois burst on the scene. I bet the Shane, Herr, Grant, and Levin families celebrated my parents' births with champagne despite Prohibition—not enforced as long as you played nice with the Machine and the Mafia. All four of my grandparents were the babies of their respective families. I'm sure lots of "oos and ahs" from siblings and parents greeted the birth of each couple's first child. Let's take a look at the receptions.

In March 1927, Mort's mother and seven older siblings looked on, while Selma's father and her nine older siblings looked—figuratively—over her shoulder. My father arrived on the 29th, and they named him Orville. I'm sure he received plenty of adoring attention, at least until—twenty months later—he had to share it with his sister Sermata. By the time of the 1930 Census, Mort, Selma, Orville, and Sermata Shane were living in an apartment at 3309 Warren Blvd., just a few blocks from Garfield Park on Chicago's West Side.

The names Orville and Sermata warrant discussion. Orville was named after Mort's Uncle Avram, the old country rabbi turned new country jeweler, and Sermata was named after Selma's mother, Sara Mata. Normally, my dad would have been named after Mort's father, but Mort already took his deceased father's given name, Aaron, for his own middle name. Mort adored his uncle—and liked doing things his own way.

Selma also had a say in my dad's name. Jewish tradition does not require either the Hebrew or English first name to be the same as the person's namesake, but the phonetic sound at the beginning of all four names should be the same. Grandma Selma gave her first child the Hebrew name Avram, and—taking a bit of liberty with the English name—claimed the sound at the beginning of Orville matched the sound at the beginning of Avram. My dad grew into his name, which came to reflect the humility, integrity, competence, and strength that defined my dad's character.

Shortly after Orville's birth, Selma had her say in another way. Grandpa Mort told me that he had to get rid of his all-time favorite pet, a toy-bulldog, because Grandma Selma "found him in Orville's crib when he was just two months old." You didn't mess with Selma when it came to her kids.

While Orville was still an infant, my mother Lois arrived across town on September 30 at South Shore Hospital. Roselyn's hospital choice reflected her South Side roots rather than Leo's West Side orientation. Leo's brothers, Sam and Jack, looked on from the West Side, while Roselyn's siblings gathered on the South Side. Three of them—Hugo and Beatrice on Roselyn's side, and Jack on Leo's—already had children of their own. All told, Lois had six first cousins close to her age. Since Lois was the first born after their Grandmother Lillie's death, she had the honor of being named after her.

Chicago Politics

In 1930, Sam Herr lived at home with his parents, and the census listed his occupation as providing "public service" for the "county," which meant he was part of the Democratic Machine. The Machine—one of the strongest Democratic political organizations in U.S. history—formed from the Cook County Democratic Party [30]. Uncle Sam supported the household, as neither his 66-year-old father Joseph nor his 57-year-old mother Rose worked.

Sam would have worked hard to help Anton Cermak defeat the Republican incumbent—crooked Big Bill Thompson—in the 1931 mayoral election. Openly allied with Al Capone, Thompson became known as one of the most corrupt mayors in American history. Cermak's monumental victory ushered in a century of Democratic Machine-dominated Chicago politics. Mayor Cermak was the unintended victim of an assassin's bullet aimed at President Franklin D. Roosevelt (FDR), as the two men met briefly at a Miami park in February 1933. Immediately thereafter, Patrick Nash, chairman of the Cook County Democratic Party, hand-picked Edward J. Kelly as the next mayor, launching the "Kelly-Nash Machine" that would dominate Chicago politics for the next 16 years [31].

When Kelly became too progressive—pushing for fairer real estate practices affecting the city's Black population—the very Machine he built withdrew its support leading him not to seek reelection. Then came Democratic Mayor Martin H. Kennelly, who served two four-year terms, followed by Democratic Mayor Richard J. Daley, who was elected six times between 1955 and 1976. You didn't mess with Mayor Daley throughout my formative years in Chicago. Though not a public figure, my Uncle Sam remained an insider in the Chicago Democratic Machine throughout the Daley era and until his death in 1980. He was appropriately named Uncle Sam [32], as he knew how to help when someone in the family needed a political favor—especially his brother Leo, who was eleven years his junior.

The Great Depression
Though my parents were born in the Roaring Twenties, The Great Depression shaped their childhood. The Depression began with the 1929 Stock Market Crash, when Orville and Lois were two years old, and it lingered for twelve years—until the U.S. entered World War II. The 1930 Census reports Leo, Roselyn, and Lois living on the West Side with Leo working as an electric streetcar conductor. That would have been a tough job to get in those days—likely requiring connections. Fortunately, Leo's brother, Sam, could provide them.

The shock of the Stock Market Crash of 1929, followed by The Great Depression, must have hit the young Herr family hard. For support, before Lois turned four, they moved in with Uncle Sam and Leo's parents, Joseph and Rose. Sam moved out sometime in the 1930s, and as already mentioned, Joseph died in 1936. I'm sure Lois grieved the loss of her grandfather—the horse-trader who adored her.

By 1940, Leo, Roselyn, Lois, then twelve years old, and Lois' new brother, Joe, were living with Rose. Roselyn gave birth to Joe on April 1, 1940, and the family lived in a house Rose rented at 823 Independence Boulevard one mile southwest of Marshall High School. Marshall opened its doors around the turn of the 20th century, and it quickly became an icon of the West Side's Jewish community.

When they moved to Independence Boulevard, Prohibition had ended, and Leo began working in the liquor industry. He worked mostly as a liquor salesman and, for a time, co-owned a bar with his brother Sam. Interestingly, Mort owned a bar for a while, too. Mort also ran *"Mort's Service Station"* after struggling to find work as an electrician during the Depression.

The Great Depression took a heavy toll on Mort and Selma's young family. As I was growing up, Grandpa Mort used to tell me that, during the Depression, "I didn't have two nickels I could rub together." Much later he told me about the big gamble he made. Remember, Mort dropped out of high school to work and save money when he turned 18 in 1921. Over the next five years he saw the Dow Jones Industrial Average double in value. Meanwhile, his savings account earned just 3% interest.

Mort decided he'd like to participate in this Roaring Twenties boom, and he learned he could easily do so by opening a margin account with a stockbroker. As a budding electrician with a wife and work history, showing a strong sense of responsibility, he would have looked like a good bet to a stockbroker. In those days, he could borrow on margin, meaning that with just $1,000 in cash—easily borrowed from his bank—he could buy $10,000 worth of stock.

As the prices of stocks kept rising, Mort could borrow and invest even more. Most investors continued borrowing, and they poured money into riskier stocks. This was an exuberant time, to say the least. Overall, stocks increased in value by 400% between 1921 and 1929. Then, the bottom fell out. Over the next three years, blue chip stocks lost 89% of their value. Banks called loans, brokers issued margin calls, and investors couldn't pay. Twenty thousand companies declared bankruptcy, nine thousand banks failed, and nine million savings accounts were wiped out. Mort told me, "I lost everything."

As described in *The Encyclopedia of Chicago*, "The Great Depression was particularly severe in Chicago because of the city's reliance on manufacturing, the hardest hit sector nationally. Only 50 percent of the

Chicagoans who had worked in the manufacturing sector in 1927 were still working there in 1933 [33]." Chicago's unemployment hovered between 40 and 50 percent—well above the national peak of 25%. The city's emergency relief funds were exhausted, and funds from charitable organizations dried up. Frustratingly long bread lines were woefully inefficient in getting food to the poor.

Amid these hardships, Mort and Selma welcomed another child on November 19, 1937 and named her Ila. Mort told me, "The most horrible experience I ever had was trying to raise three children and provide for my wife during the Depression." But he did it, and he told me, "I'm proud that I was able to pull myself up and do what I needed to do to take care of my family."

FDR became President in 1933, ushering in the "New Deal" era, during which the federal government sponsored many programs to put U.S. residents back to work. These programs helped, but the end of The Depression didn't come until December 7, 1941, when the U.S. entered World War II. This created a wartime economy that provided jobs for those who fought and for those who stayed behind to produce the weapons and supplies needed to fight.

In 1933, the Century of Progress World's Fair drew millions to a city staggering under 40% unemployment and the burdens of The Great Depression. But conditions were never too harsh to have a good time in Chicago. My parents had the fondest memories of their West Side neighborhood with its vibrant Jewish community of predominantly U.S.-born kids whose parents and grandparents had emigrated to escape oppression in Eastern Europe.

Orville and Lois' families were, I'm sure, enjoying "Da Bears," led by "Papa Bear" George Halas. The

Chicago Bears won the National Football League Championship in 1932 and 1933 and had an 18-game winning streak across two seasons going into the 1934 championship game against the New York Giants. The heavily favored Bears were ahead 13-3 at the end of the third quarter. The Giants won by scoring 27 points in the fourth quarter, an NFL record that stands to this day. It's known as "the sneaker game," because in the second half, the Giants changed shoes—to sneakers borrowed from a basketball team—to purportedly improve traction on their home field that was iced over in a storm the night before.

I know they enjoyed music—I wonder whether that included the blues, which came to Chicago with The Great Migration. Around 300,000 African Americans moved to Chicago mainly from Mississippi, Alabama, and Louisiana, fleeing persecution in the country that had once enslaved them. Roughly the same number of Jews had arrived in Chicago during the late nineteenth and early twentieth centuries, escaping persecution in Europe. The blues they brought with them—raw, expressive music born of hardship and resilience—helped define Chicago as the "home of the blues."

The 1930s saw blues legends Big Bill Broonzey and Sonny Boy Williamson, among many others, performing on The Stroll, a stretch of South State Street between 26th and 39th Streets. The Stroll was part of the Bronzeville neighborhood and was the center of Chicago's 1930s music scene. Bronzeville was one of the first Chicago neighborhoods settled by German Jewish immigrants in the latter part of the nineteenth century, eventually becoming a hub of Jewish life. With The Great Migration, African Americans moved in and Jews relocated further south to places like the South

Shore neighborhood, where Hugo Grant and his family lived.

Marshall High School

While I never heard about the families knowing each other, Orville and Lois grew up living three blocks apart in the heart of Chicago's Jewish West Side just a mile from Marshall High School. The 1940 Census shows 12-year-old Lois living with her parents and grandparents at 823 Independence Boulevard and 13-year-old Orville living—in the 3700 block of West Arthington Street—with his parents and sister a short walk away. Lois' family had moved to Independence Boulevard early in the 1930s, so she would not have remembered life elsewhere. Sometime during the decade, Orville's family moved to Arthington Street from just a mile away, so he likely had no memory of life outside the neighborhood.

Lois carefully recorded her life story in a *Grandmother's Memories* book during the summer of 1999. In it, she reported that she started dating when she was 15, and she met Orville "at the corner drug store" after she turned 16. At that time, she would have been a sophomore and he would have been a junior at Marshall High School. Lois wrote that they went to a movie and out for ice cream on their first date. Maybe they saw *Heaven Can Wait* with Don Ameche and Gene Tierney, or *For Whom the Bell Tolls* with Gary Cooper and Ingrid Bergman—both popular movies at the time. When Lois and Orville were dating in high school, they warmed up to each other's much younger sibling—Joe, twelve years younger than Lois, and Ila, ten years younger than Orville.

My mom and dad had a great time at Marshall High School, where 90% of the kids were Jewish, where life revolved around basketball, and where my dad was captain of the team. The basketball team was known as the Marshall Commandos, and they competed in two divisions. Orville was just under 5'8" tall, allowing him to compete in the junior division.

Orville had a rare blend of toughness, stamina, team spirit, athletic ability, and a highly developed sense of responsibility—traits that suited him for the style of Marshall's legendary coach, Lou Weintraub. Mort raised Orville to be tough and responsible, Selma raised him to have compassion, and Coach Weintraub helped mold it together into a big-hearted fighting machine.

Mort told me much later, "My proudest moment was when my son played on the Marshall High School basketball team that won 98 straight games, and he was picked co-captain and most valuable player." Orville received honorable mention for the all-city team that year. The remarkable run of the team—with its iconic coach—was chronicled in a 1944 issue of *Time Magazine*, and both Lou and his team were inducted into the basketball hall of fame in 1985. A whole book, titled *Fast Break to Glory: Marshall High School's 98-Game Basketball Winning Streak* [38], has immortalized the achievement. No wonder Lois, as popular and vivacious as she was, fell for Orville. All this fun and excitement existed against a backdrop of an increasingly perilous world, with Nazi Germany exterminating Jews and seizing territory in Europe.

World War II

I wonder what discussions the Grants, Herrs, Shanes/Shaynes, and Levins were having in their own families and with their neighbors—on the South Side for the Grants and on the West Side for the other three families—as they heard about Hitler coming to power in 1933. The warning signs of Nazi determination to eradicate Europe's Jewish population should have been alarming.

The lack of response by Great Britain, France, and the U.S. to these warning signs should have been equally alarming. Great Britain and France adopted an appeasement strategy of throwing Hitler bones in hopes he would eventually become happy enough to leave the rest of Europe alone. FDR's attitude didn't help. "In the 430 press conferences that FDR held from January 1933 until September 1938, he never criticized Hitler's persecution of German Jews [34]." The League of Nations was equally ineffective.

Some Jewish people in the U.S. openly protested the lack of resistance to oppressive Nazi posturing toward Jews. One such protest took place on May 11, 1933 in the immediate vicinity of Chicago's West Side Jewish neighborhoods. Jews organized the march [35], which began at Ashland and Roosevelt Road just a half-mile west of the Maxwell Street Market. The route proceeded east along the market's southern border and on to Grant Park, the site of the 1933 Century of Progress World's Fair. Perhaps some members of the Shane-Herr expansive families participated.

Like the majority of Jews living in the U.S., they probably focused more on surviving The Great Depression and avoiding antisemitism at home and less on growing antisemitism and military posturing in Germany. The most egregious example of U.S. indifference to the plight of Europe's Jews came "in June 1939 (when) the German ocean liner, *St. Louis*, and its 937 passengers, almost all Jewish, were turned away from the port of Miami, forcing the ship to return to Europe; more than a quarter died in the Holocaust [36]."

Antisemitism was not restricted to Europe. It was alive and well in the U.S. Two of its strongest agitators were Henry Ford, inventor of the Model T, and the Reverend Charles Coughlin. Ford's widely circulated newspaper, *The Dearborn Independent*, and subsequent four-volume book set, *The International Jew*, spread antisemitic tropes throughout the world. Hitler was so enamored that he hung a picture of Henry Ford in his office. Father Coughlin's popular radio show promoted antisemitism in the U.S. between 1926 and 1942. Finally, the Ku Klux Klan had 50,000 members in Chicago, more than any other U.S. metropolitan area.

I expect that many Jews in Chicago had ambivalent feelings about confronting antisemitism, wanting to protest Nazi practices in Europe while at the same time worrying it would trigger a backlash at home. In fact, a 1939 New York rally in Madison Square Garden drew a crowd of more than 20,000 people chanting "Heil Hitler" [37].

Throughout the 1930s, the U.S. had an extreme isolationist attitude toward Nazi Germany. This attitude was stubbornly maintained, in spite of news of escalating Nazi atrocities. In 1938, the Kristallnacht attracted worldwide attention, as paramilitary forces destroyed 267 synagogues and 7,000 Jewish businesses, and arrested 30,000 Jewish men, while the Nazi government looked the other way.

The Allied forces did little to dissuade the Nazi offensive until Germany invaded Poland on September 1, 1939. Two days later Great Britain and France declared war on Germany, but didn't seriously engage the enemy. By mid-1940, Germany had overrun most of Western Europe. By late 1942, it controlled much of the continent, including parts of the Soviet Union.

In 1941, the Nazis forbade all Jewish emigration. Then came the "final solution" with its deportation of Jews to concentration camps—mostly in Poland—where they were systematically murdered in gas chambers or by other ghastly means. Torture and murder typified concentration camps between December 1941 and January 1945.

The U.S. maintained its isolationist stance until Germany's ally, Japan, decided to take the war to the U.S. Japan was for many years trying to build an empire with access to much-needed oil and other resources. With ambition to build an empire rivaling the British Empire, Japan tried and failed to win army battles attempting to take control of parts of the oil-rich Russian province of Siberia and the coal-rich Chinese province of Manchuria. So, Japan turned its sights southward, where it could rely on its navy to win battles in Malaysia. The U.S. responded with embargos that crippled Japan's oil supply.

The Japanese sought to neutralize the U.S. navy, so it built a large military presence in the Pacific two or three hundred miles north of Hawaii—where the U.S. maintained its largest fleet of naval resources. On December 7, 1941, Japan attacked the U.S. naval arsenal at Pearl Harbor. According to plan, this surprise attack crippled the U.S. fleet which took months to recover. Meanwhile, Japan fulfilled its objectives of rapidly building an empire and accessing much needed oil and other resources from conquered foreign lands.

Orville to the Rescue

Orville and Lois were 14 years old when Japan attacked Pearl Harbor. Orville would have been a freshman at Marshall High School and Lois would have been in eighth grade. This would have been a stressful time.

They may not have been close with any of their cousins who went to war in 1942, but surely they would have known people responding to the call when the country began mobilizing its resources. I found many examples of Orville and Lois's cousins who were either drafted or who enlisted between 1940 and 1945. The Selective Training and Service Act of 1940 ultimately required all men between the ages of 18 and 45 to register with their local draft board, which would receive a quota and conduct a lottery to fill it.

Bobby socks and basketball were in full swing at Marshall High School while the country was at war in Europe. Orville was only 17 when he graduated from high school, so he went to the University of Illinois for a year before enlisting in the Army on May 17, 1945. Germany had surrendered 10 days earlier; Japan would follow less than four months later.

My dad, who was never stationed overseas, used to say that Germany and Japan must have gotten wind that he was prepared to join the fight, thus hastening their surrender. Of course, in Japan's case, capitulation was hurried along by dropping atomic bombs on the cities of Hiroshima on August 6 and Nagasaki on August 9. Japan surrendered on August 15.

To this day, the U.S. remains the only country that has resorted to the use of atomic weapons. In its immediate aftermath, the decision to obliterate Hiroshima and Nagasaki was wildly popular in the U.S., with a Gallup Poll showing 85% public approval [39]. The decision became controversial much later and remains so to this day [40].

The war officially ended on September 2, 1945, and my dad was eventually discharged as part of the massive demobilization effort that, in 1946 and early 1947, set the stage for the baby boom. Twelve million U.S.

servicemen were discharged, including eight million stationed overseas. My dad didn't get to go to the front of the line, because he had served at a stateside military base. Nonetheless, he had enlisted and had been ready for anything required to serve his country.

A Promising Union

Orville was officially discharged on October 22, 1946, and he and Lois didn't waste time before getting married and starting a family. They became engaged in August of 1947, while my father was taking courses at Northwestern University to prepare for the CPA exam. They married on March 3, 1948 and I arrived—eleven months later—on February 6, 1949. Our first home was a Near North Side apartment at 840 West Montrose Street, just one mile north of Wrigley Field, home of the Chicago Cubs since 1914.

By 1950, Orville was working 50 hours per week for a largely Jewish public accounting firm known as Himmelblau and Company. Abraham Himmelblau founded the firm in 1930 and his son, David Himmelblau, ran it when Dad worked there. I asked my dad how he got into accounting, and he told me that his favorite uncle—his father's 12-years-senior brother and billiards player extraordinaire—was an auditor/bookkeeper and that sparked his interest. Orville emulated his Uncle Joe by becoming a CPA.

I sometimes reflect on uncomfortable parallels between the modern accounting profession and the derided "moneylenders" of the old country. I recoil at hearing antisemitic tropes—like someone saying they were "jewed" out of money by a person with greater financial acumen—that echo the old prejudices. Regardless of the stereotypes, my dad loved his work and took pride—as did I—in how much he helped struggling businesses across Chicago.

My mom was a good writer, and I think her plans for a career in advertising dissolved when she became pregnant with me just two months after marrying my father. She wasn't alone—1949 set a new record with 3.9 million births. It wasn't simply that more women were having children. The fertility rate reached an all-time high of 3.8 children per mother in 1957. My parents' generation birthed the name of my generation: Baby Boomers. I don't think any generation before or since derived its name from the activities of the previous generation. The Greatest Generation really was great!

The Greatest Generation's exuberance associated with victory in World War II and the economic boom that followed made the decade following World War II a wonderful time to be born. The stage is set for the early years of my own life. The next chapter describes the next great migration. Chicago's West Side Jews moved almost *en masse* to Chicago's Near North Side. By the time I reached the age of eight, Jews were moving again, this time from the North Side to the suburbs, and we moved with them to Skokie. Life in Skokie will wait until Chapter 5.

Part II: Upward Mobility

Chapter 4

Growing up During the Cold War

It must have been exhilarating and a little disorienting for Jewish soldiers returning to Chicago from World War II to find a mass migration underway—from the Old West Side neighborhoods to the North Side and the suburbs. Signed by Roosevelt in 1944, the GI Bill expanded the middle class by providing affordable financing to buy homes or rent apartments and sending an unprecedented number of young men (mostly) and women to college.

As much as my mother liked the Montrose studio apartment's proximity to the beach, I'm sure she relished the next move. When I was almost two, we moved to a one-bedroom apartment at 3816 N. Sheffield Avenue, a block or two north of Wrigley Field. My dad supported us on $50 a week (about $2,500/month today) as a newly minted CPA working for David Himmelblau. These were lean but lively years.

Child's Play

Against the backdrop of the Cold War, the Greatest Generation with its indomitable optimism made the years on Sheffield Avenue a great time to be growing up in America. My earliest memories include lots of unsupervised outdoor play with my best friend, Alan Esrig. Alan lived across the courtyard. With other friends, we would run around playing cops and robbers or—I'm ashamed to say—cowboys and Indians.

We also played pinners—a wonderful game with a hard rubber ball—in the alleyway behind the apartment. A short flight of stairs jutted from a landing into the alley, with a wall behind to stop missed throws. If you hit the corner of a stair perfectly, the ball would sail into the alley over everyone's head … a home run! One day the ball went over a neighbor's gate and we all rushed into the yard to get it. I was first in and last out—which meant I was the one bitten by the dog. Fortunately, this event didn't sour my lifelong love of dogs.

On many days, I crossed the street to the schoolyard and played baseball with older kids and a hard ball. I played catcher without protection—a badge of toughness in their eyes. I may have run from butterflies in the courtyard—never have liked insects—but I didn't flinch at foul tips. I developed quick reflexes and attracted positive attention. I don't remember ever getting hurt.

TVs became affordable for families like ours when I was about five. Alan's younger brother Gary often joined us as we huddled around our new 12-inch black-and-white TVs to watch *Captain Kangaroo*, *The Mickey Mouse Club*, and *Superman*—pure magic! I had a younger brother, too, but he was too little to tag along. Rick, known as Ricky in those days, was born on December 12, 1953. At four, I was surely excited to have a little brother, but I don't recall our interactions during the three and a half years that we lived together on Sheffield Avenue. I suppose I was absorbed in my own little world. Unaware of the looming threat of nuclear war, I focused instead on dodging butterflies and chasing friends.

Isn't He Cute?

My mother and her friends loved oohing and aahing over my cuteness. I remember one day when Mom and a friend plopped a new hat on my head—with flaps that covered my ears—and exclaimed, "Oh he'd be such a cute girl!" I was mortified. It felt like a threat to the budding masculine image I wanted to embrace. I must have effectively expressed my displeasure because I never saw the hat again. Around that time, I began to see my nickname—"Flip"—as too cute. But I had to wait several years before insisting on being called "Phil."

Life with Mom's friends around wasn't all bad. One of them had a daughter my age named Carla. They visited on some Saturdays. Carla and I each got ten cents for the ticket and a little extra for a treat. Then, we'd walk a block or two up Sheffield Avenue to the neighborhood movie theater that showed cartoons for kids. At six or seven, it felt like my very first date.

Deep Inside My Head

Instead of public school kindergarten, my parents sent me to the Anshe Emet Jewish Day School. Mom walked me to school, and when she picked me up, Grandma Roselyn sometimes joined her. As we walked several blocks to one of our two apartments, I distinctly remember Mom and Grandma Roselyn wondering, "What is he thinking? It seems he's in a world of his own." Of course, that didn't help. I simply retreated further into my make-believe world. I'm reminded of the words to a John Prine song—apropos to a Cold War upbringing:

> *The lonesome friends of science say,*
> *'the world will end most any day.'*
> *Well, if it does then that's OK.*
> *Cause I don't live here anyway.*
> *I live down deep inside my head.*
> *Where long ago I made my bed.*

This wasn't the only clue that I had my own agenda. Fortunately, enough of it overlapped with my family's expectations to keep them happy. The rest I quietly fought to protect. Withdrawal was my shield—wielded only when necessary. Kiddieland with its famous *Little Dipper* rollercoaster was all the rage, and my parents loved taking me there. They would've liked it better if I smiled, screamed, or even vomited on the ride. Any emotion or physical reaction would have reassured them. But I just wasn't into it. Not my kind of thrill. I needed more active engagement—like playing catcher without a catcher's mask.

Lessons Learned

One day, Mom and I set off for the grocery store a couple of blocks north on Sheffield Avenue—she walked and I rode my bike. She had a stroller or basket to carry groceries. The store sat in an old-fashioned strip mall with a large cement courtyard—perfect for bike riding. Once she finished grocery shopping, Mom went to another store and I stayed outside. I rode around and around, faster and faster, until … *smack!* I ran into an elderly lady exiting the store with bags of groceries that went flying. *Oh no, what have I done!* I was terrified.

Three options flashed through my mind. I could run away and hide until my mom came out. I could approach the woman who was now in the middle of a throng of people trying to help her. Or I could find my mother, confess, and accept the consequences. I chose the last option, and Mom was surprisingly calm about the whole thing. She told me, "go find that woman and apologize!" There was no reward for apologizing, but at least the woman wasn't hurt. I felt forgiven and embarrassed.

I tried to be more careful after that, but it wasn't the last of my accidents requiring an apology. On another occasion I had to confess to Mom that while walking through the school yard with my friends, Alan and Billy, I was casually swinging the bat when one big swing ended with a *smack* to Billy's head. A bump the size of a baseball immediately emerged and, although he was still conscious and able to walk home, I thought I'd inflicted permanent brain damage. You know the ropes. My mom said, "you go apologize to him *and* his mother."

For first grade, I went to Le Moyne Elementary School. I loved running around the schoolyard at recess. Unfortunately, the schoolyard doubled as a parking lot at one end. To reach the open play area, I took a shortcut and ran through the space between two parked cars. As I emerged, *smack!* I ran straight into the belly of an older kid, who was twice my size, and my flight ended with a faceplant to the pavement. When I came to my senses, I saw half of my freshly grown front tooth lying on the pavement. I thought *this is serious*, and decided crying would be appropriate. It didn't take long for my mother to respond to the nurse's call. The dentist installed an ugly black-and-silver cap, which I sheepishly wore throughout adolescence.

Mom, Dad, and Me

Bonding with Dad

My earliest memories include infrequent weekend trips with my dad to his office, where I played with the adding machines while he finished up work that spilled over to the weekend. The adding machines with their keypads, cranks, and narrow rolls of paper fascinated me, but more than that—I was with my dad.

Eventually, Dad left David Himmelblau and Company to start his own firm with two very smart former Himmelblau employees, Jerry Engerman and Herb Goldstein. Herb once told me, "Your dad is the best accountant among us." I was proud—and I knew it was true. He was like a family doctor making house calls and tending to each client with care. His most famous client was Mahalia Jackson, widely considered the greatest gospel singer of all time [104]. Most clients owned small businesses. With efficiency and grace, he helped them solve problems, and they held him in the highest esteem.

Learning to ride a bike was a huge event for me. One weekend, on a day when the Cubs didn't have a game, Dad and I walked my bike down to the stadium, and we used the very wide sidewalks as the perfect training ground. I took to it like a duck to water and I'm sure Dad and I both were proud. Soon, I was riding laps around our giant city block.

Attachment to Mom

I spent a lot of time with my mother when we lived on Sheffield Avenue. In her early twenties and still growing up herself, Mom leaned heavily on her parents for help taking care of me. I grew fond of my Grandma Roselyn and Grandpa Leo, who by that time had moved to Uptown, another North Side neighborhood attracting Jewish families from the West Side. I didn't have older brothers or sisters, so I was pleased to find that Grandma Roselyn and Grandpa Leo had someone else living with them. My Uncle Joe was less than nine years older than me, and we became more like brothers than uncle and nephew. In fact, he was closer to me in age than to his twelve-years older sister—my mother Lois.

My mother required strict loyalty. I remember an incident where Mom was throwing books across the living room at Dad who was standing in the hallway. I thought this looked like fun, so I joined my mother's side. I was probably four years old. While I didn't grasp its meaning until much later, this event reflects an unhealthy connection between Mom and me. She made me the apple of her eye—and expected the same devotion in return.

As I approached adolescence, I began thinking I could meet Mom's emotional needs better than Dad, and she encouraged or perhaps even stimulated this perspective. She was used to a lot of devotion, as she enjoyed her first twelve years as an only child, and until age eight, she and her parents lived with her grandparents, Joseph and Rose. Both Leo and Joseph adored Lois. Then my dad adored her, and much later she even had her father-in-law Mort wrapped around her finger. It was no wonder that people adored her— she was vivacious, beautiful, magnetic, and knew how to light up a room. However, she also struggled with some emotional challenges rooted in her family history. The struggles also afflicted Great-grandma Rose and Grandpa Leo—perhaps a legacy from Great-great-grandma Etta or the unidentified man who impregnated her at fifteen.

Family Triangles

My dad likely had a similarly close and complicated relationship with his parents. Unlike my mother, Selma—last of ten children and born without a birth certificate—wasn't raised to be the center of attention. Furthermore, she bore the brunt of Mort's emotional abuse—which spared few—so intensely that my aunts, Sermata and Ila, often had unkind things to say about him. Everyone in the family idolized my dad—the oldest child and only son. He played a savior role in the family and must have felt the urge to protect his mother, thus complicating his relationship with his father.

Despite Cold War anxiety—communism, nuclear war, Korea, and Vietnam—the 1950s were a good time in the U.S., and our little family rode the wave of upward mobility. In 1953, we traded our one-bedroom apartment for a two-bedroom apartment that rented for more than a smaller family in our building could afford. We swapped and agreed to pay the other family's rent while they paid ours. Dad made a $10 side-payment to the other family, and for reasons I didn't understand, Mom hit the roof. On that dispute, I quietly took my dad's side. Only much later in life did I begin to understand the family dynamics that led to Mom's volatile emotions.

The Cold War

My parents' generation earned the name "The Greatest Generation" largely because of their community spirit and the challenges they overcame. The generation's pride in victory in World War II bred an unshakable confidence in American exceptionalism. I don't think any generation before or since has taken greater pride in being American. The Greatest Generation proudly built the stage for America's emergence as a global superpower. As the U.S. moved to stop the spread of communism, it increasingly used its power to protect its capitalist interests around the world—often with devastating consequences for other nations.

The Soviet Union emerged from World War II as the other global superpower. Stalin pushed the German offensive back through Russia into Germany, ultimately leading to the capture of Berlin and Germany's surrender on May 8, 1945. Meanwhile, Truman's bombing of Hiroshima and Nagasaki brought Japan's surrender on August 15, 1945. Both the U.S. and the Soviet Union emerged from World War II with voracious appetites for expanding their interests and influence throughout the world.

Initially, it appeared that the U.S. and the Soviet Union would work together to create a more peaceful world order. The two countries were founding members of the United Nations—replacing the League of Nations—with the express purpose of promoting cooperation and peace among all the nations of the world. However, the U.S. soon adopted a foreign policy of "containment" to stop the spread of communism.

George Kennan, a career Foreign Service Officer, formulated the containment policy and the president formalized it with the Truman Doctrine, which promised democratic countries protection from the spread of communism. The first major application of the Truman Doctrine occurred in 1950 in Korea, a peninsula extending from China's eastern border just 120 miles from Japan across the Korea Strait.

The Korean War

Korea was a Japanese colony from 1910 until the disintegration of the Japanese Empire at the end of World War II. In August 1945, the Soviet Union and the United States agreed to expel the Japanese from Korea, with the Soviets taking responsibility for the northern half and the U.S. taking responsibility for the southern half of the country.

At the Moscow Conference of Foreign Ministers in December 1945, the United States, the Soviet Union, the United Kingdom, and China agreed that Korea would be ready for reunification and self-rule after five years of trusteeship. Much to the dismay of the Korean people, this never happened as the Soviets moved to establish a communist government in the north, led by Kim Il-Sung, a popular freedom fighter, and the U.S. moved to establish an authoritarian anti-communist government in the south, led by Syngman Rhee, a puppet dictator whose authority rested entirely on U.S. support. Each government claimed to restore Korea to the sovereignty it enjoyed for a millennium before Japanese occupation. Each government also imposed sovereignty-destroying pressure requiring allegiance in the fight against opposing ideology.

In June 1950, with the backing of the Soviet Union and China, the Democratic People's Republic of Korea in the north attacked the Republic of Korea in the south with the goal of unifying the country. Several western countries sent troops to South Korea, but 90% of the troops came from the U.S. After three years of combat, the war ended with two and a half million people dead, including 36,000 U.S. military personnel, and no territory won or lost.

After years of brutal repression under Syngman Rhee, followed by military rule, South Korea evolved into one of the world's strongest capitalist economies, albeit with a corrupt authoritarian government maintaining outward forms of democracy. Meanwhile, Kim Il-Sung created a dynastic communist country, ruled by him for 46 years and now ruled by his grandson Kim Jong-Un. North Korea became the most isolated and controlled communist country in the world, with Kim Il-Sung immortalized as a North Korean demigod, despite his government's brutal oppression of dissent.

While the Truman Doctrine defined U.S. foreign policy aimed at stopping the spread of communism, FBI director J. Edgar Hoover and Senator Joseph McCarthy led the fight against communism on the home front.

Julius and Ethel Rosenberg

At the height of its hunt for suspected communists, the FBI arrested Julius and Ethel Rosenberg—both born to Jewish immigrant parents on New York's Lower East Side—on charges of conspiracy to commit espionage. The charges and especially the sentences—death by electrocution—reflected the dangers of dissent during the early stages of the Cold War. The Rosenbergs are the only ones in U.S. history to be executed for espionage during peace time [41].

The Jewish judge, Jewish prosecutors, and lack of sympathy within the Jewish establishment reflected the intense assimilation pressures of the time. Jews turned on their own rather than risk an antisemitic reaction to a perception that loyalty to Jewish community exceeded loyalty to country. Like most Jewish families, my parents allowed pursuit of the American dream to displace unquestioned loyalty to Jewish community. Jewish families were not about to risk opportunities to prosper in America by *looking a gift horse in the mouth*. From this perspective, it's easy to see why the Jewish community turned its back on the Rosenbergs. A New York jury devoid of Jews—despite Jews constituting 25% of the population—convicted Julius and Ethel, and both were sentenced to be executed. During the sentencing, Judge Kaufman said, "your crime is worse than murder," and J. Edgar Hoover called it "the crime of the century."

Over the years following the execution on June 19, 1953, it became clear that Julius Rosenberg was, indeed, a communist spy who recruited others, but his actions were no worse than those of many spies who received far lighter sentences. Ethel, while a member of the Communist Party and aware of her husband's activities, was not herself a spy. Their executions represented punishment far out of proportion to their offenses. Turning a blind eye to the scapegoating left a lingering shadow of guilt and repressed fear within the Jewish community—an elephant in the room—that mostly escaped my childhood awareness.

•••••

As we migrated from Chicago's North Side to Skokie, the Cold War cast a long shadow. The U.S.—with its capitalist ideology—and the Soviet Union—with its communist ideology—faced off in a high-stakes game of cat and mouse. The U.S. had demonstrated its willingness to use nuclear weapons to crush Japan in 1945, and by 1949, the Soviets had developed their own atomic bomb. The Cold War between these two superpowers blanketed the world in fear of nuclear catastrophe. However, such worries lodged well beyond my field of vision. As we prepared to move to the suburbs, I knew Dwight Eisenhower was president and I knew my parents voted for Adlai Stevenson, but I had greater interest in bikes, sports, and the exciting promise of an expanded world in the suburbs of Chicago.

Chapter 5

Embracing Suburbia

Our move to Skokie in 1957 marked the start of a new chapter—geographically, emotionally, and culturally. Amid quiet suburban streets, I navigated the complexities of growing up—building friendships, confronting signs of antisemitism, and developing a sense of self.

Our New Home

I was eight years old when we arrived in Skokie, a sleepy village located just north of Chicago's city limits. With help from the GI Bill, my parents took out a mortgage and bought their first home for about $16,000—roughly $183,000 in today's purchasing power. I remember Sunday drives to observe its construction—from the earliest excavation to the final coat of paint. Our brand-new 1,000-square-foot townhouse at 8346 N. Kilpatrick Avenue sat in a four-unit building with shared side walls.

Ours was the unit at the south end, with a driveway running along the side. I especially liked the unfinished basement with its incinerator, Dad's makeshift office, and an open play area where I whiled away many hours. The townhouse had a small patio in the back and a postage stamp front lawn that seemed large to me at the time. I remember churning up dirt by jumping up and down on a pitchfork as I helped Dad plant our first lawn.

Neighborhood Fun and Friends

Townhouse Community

My parents became good friends with the Jewish families they encountered in the other three units of our building. Lillian and Boomie Iglitz lived next door. Boomie liked to play the horses at the racetrack. Next to them lived Ruth and Otmar, who had heavy East European accents and had escaped the Holocaust. I never got their stories, but I wondered. Shirley and Seymore Presler occupied the corner unit, which to my eight-year-old mind seemed far away and—with its corner lot lawn—highfalutin.

All four families had children. Ruth and Otmar's daughter Iris was a year or two older than me. She was pretty, and I was too shy to talk to her. Natalie Iglitz was about a year younger than me and she had a younger brother about Rick's age. At some point after high school or maybe after college, Natalie moved to Israel, married an Israeli, and lived on a kibbutz. About 40 years later, I visited Natalie and her family in Jerusalem—a story for a later chapter. Shirley and Seymore's kids were younger.

I have fond memories of summer evenings when the parents and all the kids would be outside. With the other kids, I would play hopscotch, Red Rover, and other games, and we would capture fireflies in glass jars. The kids' joy reflected feelings of security in an age of innocence. The parents played traditional roles. The men worked all day, while the women took care of the house and kids and played Mahjong at each other's houses most afternoons.

Phil's Chutzpah (or Perhaps Hubris)

Chutzpah is a fascinating Yiddish word with nothing quite like it in English. It suggests boldness beyond mere assertiveness, approaching—but not quite reaching—hubris. If someone in the family told me I acted with chutzpah, I took it as a compliment.

It wasn't long before we bolted a basketball hoop to the south wall. I don't know how my mother tolerated the constant banging of the ball against the wall outside the kitchen and living room. She never complained. Maybe she secretly hoped I would join the annals of Shane basketball fame—remember Marshall High School.

I was getting good at shooting baskets in the driveway, so I decided to take my game on the road. I worked my way up from eight- to ten-foot baskets in the schoolyard across Main Street—Kenton Elementary. One day, a couple of teenagers saw me practicing and challenged me to a game of HORSE. I won. Then they raised the stakes—we played for money. Big mistake. They won. To collect, they invited themselves to my house, and my mother paid them. So embarrassing! Surprisingly, the only required penance was to promise never to do it again. I wasn't sure if this meant *never gamble*, or never again play those guys for money. Mom must have told Dad, but he never said anything. I had cool parents.

Rick's Chutzpah

An event highlighting Rick's (aka Ricky's) chutzpah occurred on Kilpatrick Avenue when I was about nine and he was around five. One afternoon the neighborhood kids gathered to play Red Rover in the shared space behind our house. We divided into two teams standing about fifteen yards apart, with each team forming a human chain by linking arms. Then, the teams took turns saying, "Red Rover, Red Rover, let _____ come over," with the blank filled in with the name of someone on the other team. The person so named then broke from their team and ran full blast with the goal of breaking through the other team's chain.

When they shouted, "Red Rover, Red Rover, let Ricky come over," no human chain could hold him. He covered the fifteen-yard space in a flash and tore through the other team's linked arms like a rocket—unfortunately right into a metal brace around a telephone pole. It was a bloody affair that left a scar on the side of his eye. He wears that scar proudly to this day. As the big brother, I felt quite protective, and I would have taken his place if I could. Even then, Rick's chutzpah, fearlessness and competitiveness were unmistakable.

Immediate Vicinity

Soon after moving to Skokie, we acquired our first dog Teddy—a mutt named after Great-grandpa Joseph's beloved companion. I loved taking Teddy for long walks, cutting through lots sprinkled through the blossoming neighborhood thirsty for new homes and residents. Teddy and I got along great, but he and Mom had a volatile relationship. His incorrigibility attracted Mom's ire, which escalated into episodes of chasing Teddy under the furniture with a broom—a disconcerting scene for my eight-year-old eyes. I wanted to protect him, but dared not.

In addition to long walks and shooting baskets in the driveway, I discovered the thrill of running—first taking shortcuts through alleyways, then timing myself running laps around our sprawling suburban block. I also remember collecting grasshoppers in the open field behind our house—until I became disgusted with the ugly brown liquid they spat at me. I decided I wasn't cut out for a future in entomology.

School Days

Laughed so hard...

I started school at Kenton in third grade and made an instant friend: Ronnie Verona. Like our neighbors, Ruth and Otmar, Ronnie's parents had heavy accents and must have somehow escaped the Holocaust. Ronnie lived just two blocks down Kilpatrick Street toward Oakton Park. We quickly became best friends and spent many days playing board games at each other's house. Ronnie had quite the sense of humor and we sat next to each other in school. It seemed that all I had to do was look at him and I would try so hard to suppress laughter that it came through my nose and sent a stream of snot down my face to the bottom of my chin. My punishment was exile to a desk in the hallway until I calmed down.

Hebrew School and Bowling

In fourth grade, Ronnie and I joined a bowling league. I also started Hebrew School at the Niles Township Jewish Congregation (NTJC), founded with a Reconstructionist blueprint by Rabbi Sydney Jacobs in 1952. With the same West Side roots as my parents, Rabbi Jacobs graduated from Marshall High School in the 1930s. Skokie's many Holocaust survivors assured a strong Zionist orientation in the synagogue. As Hebrew School students, we raised money to plant trees in Israel.

I loved bowling and didn't like Hebrew School. Our bowling team, made up of four boys from our grade, steadily improved over the next few years. Ronnie excelled with an average in the 150s, and I wasn't far behind. I wish I could say that I caught on to Hebrew School as well as I caught on to bowling. Over the next four years, I was in trouble enough for the principal to put me to work filing papers in his office.

Brush with a Bully

In fifth grade, I made a new friend, Stevie Rosenbaum. Steve lived in an apartment between my house and Oakton Park. On many summer days, we enjoyed riding our bikes to the park, where we swam in the public pool and played games. I had natural athletic ability, and I especially liked tetherball and baseball/softball. Winter in the park was fun, too, with an ice skating rink and warming house.

At about this time, girls—initially with negative attention focused on my "black tooth"—started noticing me. Then, one member of the girls' gang, Debbie Newberg, decided she liked me, and her friends began calling to let me know. In eighth grade, a bunch of us went to the movies and saw *To Kill a Mockingbird*. It left a lasting impression—the quiet strength and moral integrity of Atticus Finch, the dignity of Tom Robinson, the tragic failure of justice, and the painful clarity with which the film exposed a system marred by systemic racism.

I matriculated to Lincoln Junior High School for sixth grade, and my friendship with Steve Rosenbaum was in full bloom. Steve and his older brother, Howie, lived in an abusive household, where their father had a habit of punching them hard enough to create bruises on their arms. This happened in front of my own eyes.

Howie liked to take his frustration and anger out on me. He was on the high school wrestling team and liked to get me into holds that made me beg for mercy. I feared and hated Howie, who became a high school state wrestling champion. Steve and I mostly stayed clear of the bully and enjoyed our own circle of friends. Howie had a future in college wrestling, but he became addicted to drugs, dropped out of college, and ultimately died of a drug overdose.

Spatially Challenged

After three years on Kilpatrick Street, on August 27, 1960, Rick and I welcomed our sister, Linda, to the family. We were bursting with pride at our growing family, and feeling squeezed in our two-bedroom townhouse. Rick and I shared a small bedroom, and Linda had a crib in Mom and Dad's room. We lived there until Linda was almost three, Rick was nine, and I was fourteen years old.

One day in sixth or seventh grade, I decided to walk home from junior high school for the first time. We lived only a mile away, and I figured I could find my way. So, I pointed myself in what I thought was the right direction. Before long I was hopelessly lost. After an hour or so of wandering, I finally made it home—too late for Hebrew School. My parents had mercy, perhaps because they didn't want to rub in the embarrassment. This was probably the first time I realized I was spatially challenged, and I must admit—it never got any easier.

Bar Mitzvah

When 1962 rolled around and the time came for my bar mitzvah, I adequately played my role in the service and then thoroughly enjoyed the party. Steve Rosenbaum, Ronnie Verona, Debbie Newberg, and other friends were there. I remember my eight-year-old brother, Rick, showing everyone up when he did the

Limbo, a dance that involved leaning back as far as possible and—with hands in the air—scooting under a stick that two people held and lowered a little each time someone made it under without falling. Way to go, Rick!

I don't remember the speeches, the candle-lighting ceremony, or even the gifts, but I do remember Ronnie, clearly alarmed, pulling me aside to explain the meaning of the word "horny." He had overheard me using the word while asking a girl for a dance. "I'm horny. Would you like to dance with me?"—or something along those lines. It would be a long time before I figured out how to talk to the opposite sex.

Holocaust Survivors and Antisemitism

While the sting of antisemitism rarely affected me directly, growing up with children of holocaust survivors in Skokie meant the fear of it never slipped too far into the background. When I was growing up in the 1950s and 60s, Skokie became known as the Chicago suburb with more Holocaust survivors per capita than anywhere outside of Israel. The population was about 65,000, including approximately 38,000 Jews—8,000 of them Holocaust survivors [42]. That meant one out of every eight residents—and one in every five Jews—had survived the Holocaust.

Some came because they had relatives in Skokie. Others arrived simply because they heard Skokie had become a haven for survivors. Many arrived as the only surviving members of their families. They married and did their best to build normal lives, often with deep psychological scars due to the trauma they had endured. Their children absorbed the trauma, particularly when they asked their parents why they didn't have any grandparents, aunts, uncles, or cousins on at least one side and sometimes both sides of the family. Support groups for children of Holocaust survivors later became commonplace [97].

Even in a place offering refuge to Holocaust survivors, antisemitism confronted us in jarring, undeniable ways. Just a few blocks southeast was a neighborhood with covenants restricting owners from selling their homes to Jews. Just a mile north was a private golf course—where I caddied from time to time—that would not take Jews as members.

I felt intense anger and indignation over these affronts to the Jewish community. To illustrate how deeply they got under my skin, one night some high school friends and I carved the words "Jew Haters" in a golf course green. The course management had the green repaired without trying to apprehend the culprits. I'm not proud of this vandalism. It was an immature, impulsive act driven by adolescent frustration and outrage—a stark reminder of how deeply antisemitism shaped my emotional landscape.

I was sensitized to a world where no Jew is safe from the emergence of antisemitism in any place or any walk of life. Shaped by the Jewish community's vigilance against antisemitism, my childhood imagination conjured the notion that Jesus—representing a faith historically hostile to Jews—personified the enemy. Feeding this notion was the Nazi concept of "the Aryan Jesus"—picturing Jesus as a militant leader fighting Jewish domination in Europe [98]. Even now, I avoid saying "Jesus" because I can't muster a sense of reverence to overcome the internalized fear of my childhood.

I was so sensitive to antisemitism that just seeing a church from the outside gave me the creeps. I remember walking with my girlfriend and stepping into the foyer of an ornate Christian church one afternoon. We saw no one inside and stayed only a minute. Despite my curiosity, I could not shake my discomfort. Even in that quiet sacred space, something deep and uneasy stirred—my childhood fear of Christian hostility lingered beneath the surface and made my skin crawl. Later, I realized that it's one thing to be sensitized to antisemitism and another to be paranoid.

Growing up Jewish instilled a fear of antisemitism, while growing up in 1950s America instilled a fear of communism—equally real and equally menacing threats in my young Jewish American mind.

The Cold War and Our Island Neighbor

The Bay of Pigs and the Cuban Missile Crisis caught my attention during my years growing up in Skokie. In 1959, Fidel Castro and his revolutionary army overthrew Fulgencio Batista, the unpopular U.S.-backed Cuban dictator. Batista had ruled for much of the time since the U.S. kicked Spain out of Latin America in 1898. Overthrowing Batista ended 60 years of exploitation by U.S. businesses and the U.S. mafia. Castro nationalized U.S.-owned properties in Cuba, aligned himself with Che Guevara, and established Cuba as a communist country just 90 miles south of Miami. Furthermore, he developed close ties with Nikita Khrushchev and the Soviet Union.

Fearing that Castro would organize attacks on the United States and provoke communist revolutions in other Latin American countries, President Dwight Eisenhower developed a plan to topple Castro's government. The plan involved training and equipping Cuban soldiers opposed to Castro and unleashing them to implement a coup. To avoid provoking an all-out war with the Soviet Union, the U.S. military would stay out of the operation's implementation. John F. Kennedy (JFK) took over as president in 1961 and helplessly watched as Castro's revolutionary forces overwhelmed the U.S.-trained Cuban militia at the Bay of Pigs. Castro ruled for five decades—fueling Cold War fears of communist infiltration—and Cuba remains a communist country to this day.

JFK faced another major Cold War test. Nikita Khrushchev became the Soviet Prime Minister after Stalin's death in 1953. In 1962, Khrushchev decided to send nuclear missiles to Cuba. The Cuban Missile Crisis tested JFK's mettle and diplomacy skills to the limit. Ultimately, JFK negotiated the de-escalation of the crisis by agreeing to remove U.S. nuclear missiles from its base in Turkey in exchange for Khrushchev doing the same in Cuba. The Cuban Missile Crisis is widely regarded as the closest the two countries have come to nuclear war.

In the midst of the Cold War, the Soviets launched the world's first satellite, Sputnik, into the earth's orbit on October 4, 1957. The ensuing Space Race inspired enormous progress in science and technology, along with the proliferation of sophisticated long-range war machines like intercontinental ballistic missiles (ICBMs). Families like ours wondered whether we needed a bomb shelter. We rejected that idea, but it lingered in the back of our minds. We hunkered down in our corner of the world, and I learned that as an American I should fear communists and as a Jew I should fear all non-Jews because antisemitism was everywhere. Nonetheless, I led a sheltered life with the freedom— within reason—to enjoy an unconstrained childhood.

Chapter 6

Mentors and Sports Metaphors

Go Go White Sox

I was only 10 at the time, but I'll never forget the 1959 baseball season. With a 94-60 regular season record, the "Go Go" White Sox were playing in the World Series for the first time since the 1919 Black Sox Scandal. Most of Chicago's North Siders were die-hard Cubs fans and wouldn't dream of rooting for the White Sox. Likewise, most South-Siders wouldn't be caught dead supporting the Cubs. I took exception to this either-or mentality. I'll root for the Cubs no matter how bad a season they're having; whereas I'm a fair-weather fan when it comes to the Sox. After all, I have mixed blood: three of my grandparents grew up on the West Side rooting for the Cubs, while one of my grandparents (Roselyn) grew up on the South Side rooting for the Sox.

In 1959, I fell in love with the Sox players. Early Wynn, Billy Pierce, Luis Aparicio, Nellie Fox, Sherm Lollar, Jim Landis, and the manager, Al Lopez, were my heroes. I spent many evenings glued to the radio, following every pitch. Things were looking up when they beat the Dodgers 11-0 in the opening game at Comiskey Park. The Dodgers won the next three games, but the Sox rallied with a win in Game five. Sadly, the Dodgers won the sixth game at Comiskey Park, and the Sox would have to wait another 46 years before winning the World Series.

Mr. Briggs and Mr. Sortal: Mentors Extraordinaire

Fourth grade was a blast. Throughout all my years of school, I never had a teacher I liked more than Mr.

Briggs. He encouraged me in a way that made me want to learn. Math games saw me confidently running to the blackboard to solve problems faster than my opponents. Along with my parents, I think Mr. Briggs instilled in me the desire for learning that has infused my life with meaning. Mom invited Mr. Briggs to walk home with me for lunch one day. I'm sure I was beaming.

During the summer between my freshman and sophomore years of high school, my Senior League baseball coach, Mr. Sortal, saw my potential, nurtured a confidence within me, and helped me excel. When I wasn't pitching, I played center field. I batted third and stole bases every time I got on with no one ahead of me. I stole home on many occasions with headfirst slides after taking off from third base at the beginning of the pitcher's wind-up. Exciting!

Coach Sortal recommended me to his friend, Nick Odlivak, the head coach of the Niles East varsity baseball team. Playing for Coach Odlivak was nothing like playing for Mr. Sortal. Odlivak was a scary guy. He never attacked me like he did some other players, but his intimidating style stifled my confidence. While I could outrun anyone on the team, I never performed as well as I had during that magical year of Senior League. Nonetheless, the year in Senior League instilled a feeling that nothing was out of reach, and it continues to serve me well. I still feel the thrill of stealing home.

Benched

As my confidence soared during that Senior League summer, our digs improved dramatically as well. We moved four blocks east to a four-bedroom, two-story, stand-alone single-family home with a modest backyard. Our new home, a 2,100 square foot house at 8311 N.

Kilbourn was unlike most Skokie homes, as it had no basement. On the main floor was a nice-sized utility room, where I hung a bar from the rafters to use for pull-ups and chin-ups. The home had four bedrooms, a den, and a screened-in porch—luxuries compared to the outgrown townhouse we left behind. Rick and I shared a bedroom, Linda had a bedroom, and Dad made an office out of the extra bedroom, a big step up from his basement office at the Kilpatrick Street townhouse.

I spent my freshman year of high school on Kilpatrick and my sophomore, junior, and senior years, as well as summer vacations throughout college, on Kilbourn. High school had its ups and downs. The reality of high school sports—and high school coaches—hit me hard, and I quickly learned that football wasn't for me.

I made the mistake of saying I wanted to be an end, not realizing that—on this team—the ends blocked for runners. Nonetheless, I earned a freshman practice uniform, which I proudly took home to show to my parents. They looked on with astonishment as—demonstrating the power of shoulder pads—I inadvertently punched a gaping hole in the wall. I bolted up the stairs of the townhouse, and we never spoke of this incident.

I soon found out that the shoulder pads could not power through a player twice my size. In a tackling drill, the coach paired me with one such player who came at me with the speed of a turtle and the force of a tank. With lightning speed and little power, I threw the full weight of my 150-pound body at his legs. I bounced off his legs onto my back, with the wind knocked out of me and pain shooting through my shoulder. That ended my football career before it began.

Other sports worked better for me. I earned varsity letters in basketball, baseball, and cross-country. Making the basketball team all four years was a big deal, because only four seniors made the team. In my senior year, I started at point guard in the opening game against arch-rival Niles North. But I lasted about three minutes before Mark Solock reclaimed his spot. Unfortunately, I had developed a habit of choking in stressful situations. Much later—in my fifties—I was diagnosed with an anxiety disorder that I'm sure played a role. I was great in practice but, aside from one exceptional season, I struggled in high pressure games.

Dad attended most of my high school games even when I was sitting on the bench for most of the game. He tried (over and over) to encourage me to "be more aggressive" and to "have more confidence." Self-consciously feeling that I lack confidence has plagued me all my life. Dad liked to dig out his scrapbook chronicling his Marshall High School basketball exploits. I'm not sure what he hoped for—maybe it was meant to inspire me. But it had the opposite effect—a reminder of the gap between his glory days and my own struggles.

Dad saw that I had plenty of innate ability, and it pained him to see me not reaching my potential. It pained me more, as I desperately wanted to live up to his expectations. I just didn't know how. The harder I tried to fix it, the worse it seemed to get. Later in life, Dad confided in me that lacking confidence was also an issue in *his* life. I was flabbergasted.

Sports accounted for most of my activity during high school. Outside of team practices and games, I was always playing something—basketball, baseball, tennis, golf, football, or even ping pong. High school years were fun in other ways, too. My friends and I enjoyed learning to play bridge. After learning to drive, I got around town driving my parents' old Chevy Impala convertible with holes in the floor. Passengers could see the road fly by underneath the car, and my friends affectionately dubbed the beat-up car the "Shane-mobile." That car, with its patched seats and hole-ridden floor, wasn't much to look at, but it kept moving—with persistence and perseverance—and so did I.

Chapter 7
The Innocence of Youth

Captivating Tunes

During high school, music began to matter—a lot. The Beatles exploded onto the U.S. scene in 1964, just as I was heading into my sophomore year. I had one friend who recognized their genius, but I didn't understand all the hullabaloo. I liked their top 40 songs, but I certainly wasn't going to scream about them or seek mysterious hidden messages by playing their records backwards. On April 4, 1964, the Beatles held the top five slots in the top 40—a feat unmatched to this day.

My favorite Beatles song was *I Saw Her Standing There*, which was the B-side of the number one hit, *I Wanna Hold Your Hand*, released in 1963. Other favorite songs in these years included Roy Orbison's *Pretty Woman*, Herman's Hermits' *Mrs. Brown You've Got a Lovely Daughter*, *Love Potion Number 9* by the Searchers, Donovan's *Sunshine Superman*, *Light My Fire* by the Doors, and *Eve of Destruction* by Barry McGuire, to name a few. I used to count down the Top 40 when left alone working summer jobs in Dad's office on Peterson Avenue. Working alongside Dad on Peterson Avenue deepened our relationship and stimulated my early aptitude for accounting.

Family Life

Halfway through my junior year in high school, Rick, Linda, and I welcomed our brother David to the family. He was born the day after Christmas in 1965. Once again, we were proud of our growing family—and running out of room. I loved our family, and I think I played a role in livening the party with humorous antics and heartening interactions. I used to think our home life was every bit as wholesome and fun as the lives of the characters in our favorite sitcoms: *Father Knows Best, My Three Sons, Leave It to Beaver, The Donna Reed Show, I Love Lucy, Ozzie and Harriet*, and *Make Room for Daddy*—all produced in the late 1950s and 1960s. Life was good; in our little world, it was a time of innocence. Dad was a successful professional, Mom was—from my perspective—a fully engaged homemaker with a contagiously gregarious personality, and I was a happy camper.

Connections with Grandparents

I continued having close connections with my grandparents throughout the years I lived in Skokie. I sometimes spent the night at Grandma Roselyn and Grandpa Leo's apartment, and occasionally at Grandma Selma and Grandpa Mort's. I impressed Grandma Roselyn with my capacity for eating the waffles fresh from her waffle iron—almost as fast as she could make them—with plenty of syrup of course. I also showed an interest in the newspaper puzzles she played. We both hoped that she'd one day win a fortune. Grandma Roselyn did her best to teach me to play the baby grand piano in her living room, but I was rather hopeless.

With Grandpa Leo, I enjoyed watching boxing matches on the small TV in the living room and working on my coin collection. He used to give me silver dollars whenever I spent the night. Once I reached driving age, he let me drive his Plymouth Fury with a manual transmission—"stick shift." I had fun peeling out from stop lights as they turned green, tires screeching (when Grandpa Leo was not in the car with me). Before Uncle Joe left for college, I occasionally hung out with him and his friends, but they liked to pick on me. Like I said, we were more like brothers than uncle and nephew.

Like Grandma Roselyn, Grandma Selma loved to feed me. I think my closest connection with her was when I asked for second or third helpings at family dinners hosted at her apartment. She often knew what I wanted before I asked.

Upon turning sixteen, I became obsessed with getting a driver's license. The pressure of this obsession choked away my confidence and I failed two driving tests. Failing a third time would mean major embarrassment and waiting at least thirty days before taking the test again. Grandpa Mort found out about this and came to my rescue. He knew a driving test guy in Libertyville, a suburb about twenty-five miles north of Skokie. "Whew," I passed, albeit with the testing guy telling Mort to keep an eye on my "heavy foot." That turned out to be prophetic—I've had more than my share of accidents and tickets. No pride in that.

Throughout high school and college, I remember Grandpa Mort as a frequent visitor to our house. He would come over during the day, take care of Mom's list of things that needed fixing, take our big Collie dog Buttons out for walks in the alley behind our house, and sometimes take me on outings. The outings sometimes involved breakfast with his cronies at their favorite diner or a visit to the schvitz (steam bath). At the schvitz, we kibbitzed with more cronies while sweating away bodily toxins, scrubbed away with broom-like bundles of large, soapy eucalyptus leaves, and washed away with cold water delivered through a fat hose.

When we hung out together, Grandpa Mort thought I was a "lousy conversationalist," so he did most of the talking. He often told me about his loyalties to the Democratic Party and especially to his union, the

International Brotherhood of Electrical Workers (IBEW). Mort was a union man through and through. As described earlier, Mort's favorite job of all time was at Commercial Light. But he cherished his independence and for most of his career he moved from one union job to the next as a journeyman electrician.

Mort's union values placed him squarely in the tradition of Chicago's proud labor history. The IBEW was a major player in the labor movement, which has a long history in Chicago. Most famously, Chicago is home to the Haymarket Affair of 1886, which became an iconic symbol for the worldwide struggle for workers' rights and which prompted an international coalition to establish May 1 as International Workers' Day. In support of labor and commemorating the miscarriage of justice that executed five anarchist labor organizers in Chicago in the wake of the Haymarket riots, most countries celebrate International Workers' Day. Among those that do, only the U.S. and Canada celebrate the holiday in September. At least Canada uses the metric system. The U.S. is one of only three countries that do not. We have a knack for going our own way, not caring about snubbing the international community.

Grandpa Mort enjoyed hanging out with Mom. Especially after he retired in 1972, Mort was a frequent daytime visitor. I didn't notice it much growing up, but later I realized that Mom and Grandpa Mort were drinking buddies. Mort liked to drink and smoke cigars. Mom liked to drink and smoke cigarettes, and she was a *good conversationalist*. They even shared a favorite song: "My Way," composed by Paul Anka and performed by Frank Sinatra.

"And may I say ... not in a shy way ...

I did it my way."

Mort and Lois were "forces of nature," and they seemed to understand one another.

Grandpa Mort told me that while he had friends in both camps, he never worked with Chicago's political machine or mafia. He had the opportunity to be a precinct captain but turned it down. He could have collaborated with the mob when he owned a bar and then a gas station, but he didn't accept their invitations.

Mort let me know that to alleviate financial pressures during the Depression, Selma wanted him to make a deal with the mob. He resisted and resented Selma for pushing. While he remained clean himself, he knew plenty of people who were dirty, and he worried that the mob would come after him because he knew too much. He flinched every time he heard about a mob-related murder.

A Nation in Mourning

The most dramatic and disturbing news during my high school years came on November 22, 1963. I was a freshman, having lunch in the Niles East cafeteria, when we heard the shocking bulletin: President Kennedy had been shot. Thirty minutes later he was pronounced dead.

My grandparents were not yet born when William McKinley was assassinated in 1901, so no one in the family had experienced anything like this. It hit us all pretty hard. In fact, it hit the entire country so hard that nearly everyone who lived through it remembers where they were when they heard the news of JFK's assassination.

Moving On

During the second semester of my senior year of high school, I took a bus ride with some friends downstate to the University of Illinois, located about 150 miles south of Chicago in the twin cities of Champaign-Urbana. This was a rush weekend. The university's 57 fraternities opened their doors and selectively invited newly admitted students to visit. I received invitations to visit several Jewish fraternities.

I was eager to make a good impression, but I may have had a little too much fun testing my ability to hold my liquor, usually served in the form of a spiked punch. After rush weekend—along with several high school friends—I selected Pi Lambda Phi.

I graduated from Niles East High School in June 1967. Early that month, the "Six-Day War" ended with Israel capturing the Gaza Strip and Sinai Peninsula from Egypt, the Golan Heights from Syria, and the West Bank and East Jerusalem from Jordan. The decisive victory intensified my emotional attachment to the State of Israel. In fact, after reading Leon Uris' book, *Exodus*, I fell in love with the Zionist ideal. At that time, my misunderstanding of the conflict was shaped largely by Uris' narrative, which portrayed Palestinians as a pitiful people who—rather than remain and seek peaceful coexistence—had abandoned their homes when promises of support from Arab nations proved empty.

It would take nearly 20 years before I began to understand the deeper complexities of the Israeli-Palestinian conflict and the competing claims to a homeland in the Middle East. That's a story for a later chapter. For now, it's important to point out that I emerged from high school with a deep emotional tie to Israel as a homeland for the Jewish People, and I cheered as its victory in the Six-Day War tripled—from

8,000 to 26,000 square miles—the land under Israel's control.

Beyond politics and history, during high school, many literary works made lasting impressions that helped shape my world view. In addition to *Exodus*, books with lasting impressions included *Walden*, *Catcher in the Rye*, *The Adventures of Huckleberry Finn*, *Brave New World*, and *1984*, among others. Thoreau's *Walden* inspired communion with nature and taught me that three chairs are enough—"one for solitude, two for friendship, and three for society."

J.D. Salinger's *Catcher in the Rye* taught me that having thoughts I couldn't share with my parents didn't make me crazy, and preserving childhood innocence—my own and others—would go a long way toward happiness and wisdom in adulthood. Aldous Huxley's *Brave New World* revealed the importance of promoting individual freedom and critical thinking, and guarding the things that make us human, including creativity and heartfelt emotion. *The Adventures of Huckleberry Finn* taught me about the purity and indomitability of the human spirit.

Finally, George Orwell's *1984* coined the term "Big Brother," while foretelling increased government surveillance and control. Its warning against totalitarianism soon proved prescient, as Senator Joseph McCarthy's anti-communist crusade raged in the early 50s and FBI Director J. Edgar Hoover's COINTELPRO surveillance campaign ramped up in latter part of the 50s and throughout the 60s. Taking Orwell's message to heart, I promised myself I would resist any effort by my government to dictate the direction of my life. I resolved to shape my own destiny.

Part III: Breaking Away
Chapter 8
Pledging

None of my grandparents graduated from high school, and though each of my parents attended college briefly, neither earned a degree. So, technically, I'm a first-generation college graduate—but I was far from underprivileged. My white, middle-class, Jewish upbringing in Skokie, during the heyday of American exceptionalism, all but guaranteed a college education. The University of Illinois—with its affordability and strong reputation—was the obvious choice.

·····

I headed downstate in fall 1967 and moved into the Pi Lambda Phi fraternity house located about six blocks west of the main University of Illinois campus. We had a pledge class of twenty-three freshmen—all about eighteen years old—with at least ten arriving from Niles East or Niles North High School. The vast majority of our class came from the Chicago area. Other residents included members who had already pledged and an ineffective house mother. Like most Jewish fraternities of the time—formed in part because Jewish students had historically been excluded from other houses—the membership lacked racial diversity and included very few non-Jews.

The previous year's class eagerly hazed us pledges. The Marshal led the hazing. His broader role was to educate us on all things Pi Lam and oversee our indoctrination into fraternity life. However, hazing was such a big job—or maybe the brothers enjoyed it so much—that I don't remember much educating. I do remember becoming fast friends with Keith Boxerman who claimed the bunk below mine. We endured frequent hazing raids of the dormitory, and we have remained close friends to this day.

Raids began with a loud whistle jarring us from slumber at about 2 a.m., followed by a stampede from the dorm down two flights of stairs to the basement. The "rack-out" consisted of endless calisthenics, with random pledges called out—just frequently enough to have us all scared—to "assume the position" for paddling. Assuming the position meant the unlucky pledge lowered his trousers, shorts, or pajama bottoms, bent over, grabbed his ankles, and stuck his rear into the air. Then, the Marshal or another brother picked up a wooden paddle and smacked the pledge as many times as the Marshal deemed necessary to make an example. Overall, I valued the camaraderie with my fellow pledges more than I resented the rack-outs or feared the paddling.

Whatever trauma hazing caused us faded quickly, unlike the guilt carried by the Marshal into his post-graduate years. He saw the light and became a strong advocate for the values we embraced during the remaining years of our college experience. Bob Nelson (aka Skull) became one of us. At one of the many campus protests, a campus authority was about to bring a Billy club down on the head of one of my pledge brothers when Skull appeared out of nowhere to grab the club and defuse the situation.

Bob matriculated to the University of Illinois School of Law and became one of the most respected lawyers in the St. Louis region. He married a lovely woman from the area, whose warmth and character matched his own, and they raised a principled family rooted in shared values. Several children became lawyers and joined Bob's practice, which they now run—a remarkable family legacy. I still call Bob "Skull" and proudly count him among my close friends.

Pledging ended with "hell week." In addition to a healthy dose of rack-outs and paddling, hell week included torturous activities such as stuffing as many of us as possible into the house phone booth while blowing in cigar smoke until hacking coughs and labored breathing motivated our release. Hell week ended with a blindfolded trip through a Halloween-like labyrinth, culminating with removal of the blindfolds and a welcome from our new brothers into full-fledged fraternity membership, complete with a secret handshake.

With pledging behind us and friendships fortified by shared adversity, we enjoyed a spring semester filled with fun and exploration. We also began recruiting the next year's pledge class. You might think that during our sophomore year we hazed the new pledges in the same manner that we had been hazed. We didn't. We found ourselves in the midst of a cultural shift—fueled by the Civil Rights, Antiwar, and Environmental Movements— emphasizing peace, love, equality, nonviolence, and earth awareness. Hazing didn't fit in that picture, so we eliminated it.

The pledges coming after us were a more serious bunch, so they didn't take part in much of the reckless fun that some of us modeled. Many of us acquired a taste for alcohol, cigarettes, marijuana, hallucinogens, and free love. Our altered states were conducive to kicking back and listening to music or hiking in Atherton Park, all the while with hearts and minds brimming with enthusiasm for the changes sweeping the country. The early years after college saw the unhealthy habits slip away. Thankfully, our passions for living harmoniously in the natural environment and standing up for the basic human rights of marginalized people endured.

When our parents sent us to college, they could not have foreseen the generation gap it would create. Many did not have college degrees themselves, and even those who had could not relate to our radicalizing experiences—shaped by the era's Civil Rights and Antiwar Movements. The extraordinary patriotism of our parents' generation morphed into a zeitgeist promoting sustainability, world citizenship, and inalienable rights of "life, liberty, and the pursuit of happiness" for all humankind.

Chapter 9
Awakening

Civil Rights and Antiwar Movements
The Civil Rights Movement and the Antiwar Movement ignited the cultural shift we experienced during the 1960s and beyond. In December 1955, the Civil Rights Movement gained national momentum when Rosa Parks refused to give up her seat in the "colored" section of a bus after the white section had filled. A decade later, the Antiwar Movement surged when President Johnson broke a campaign promise and sent the first U.S. combat troops to Vietnam.

In 1968, University of Illinois undergraduates began publishing the *Walrus*, an alternative newspaper advocating radical change. It summed up its orientation with the following prophetic words: "Many students are not realizing that the universities of this country channel young people into institutions and jobs which, instead of correcting the glaring ills of America, simply perpetuate the unjust system to which these students object."

Meanwhile, the generation gap widened between our parents' "greatest generation" that endured the Depression and triumphed during World War II, and the "baby boomer" generation that found no glory in the Vietnam War. It didn't help when we recited the lyrics to Barry McGuire's 1965 protest song [106]:

> The Eastern world, it is explodin',
> violence flarin', bullets loadin',
> you're old enough to kill, but not
> for votin' ... And you tell me over
> and over again my friend how you

don't believe we're on the *Eve of Destruction*.

The voting age was not lowered to 18 until 1971. Songs like *The Eve of Destruction*, *For What It's Worth* by Buffalo Springfield, and *Blowin' in the Wind* by Bob Dylan inspired us to protest against U.S. institutions perpetuating income and wealth inequality, environmental degradation, and our generation's deployment in wars we came to see as ignoble.

After JFK's assassination in 1963, Lyndon Johnson finished Kennedy's term. Then, in November 1964, Johnson won the election on a platform that promised "not ... to send U.S. boys nine or ten thousand miles away from home to do what Asian boys ought to be doing for themselves." Just two months into his full term, Johnson broke his promise and sent the first U.S. combat troops to fight the Viet Cong alongside South Vietnamese troops. This breach of trust outraged supporters like Dr. Benjamin Spock, who encouraged young men to avoid conscription—igniting an epidemic of draft card burning demonstrations on college campuses and fueling a decade of antiwar activism.

MLK and RFK Assassinations

Martin Luther King, Jr. rose to prominence as a leader of the Civil Rights Movement following the Rosa Parks bus incident. His 1963 "I Have a Dream" speech rang through my brain throughout high school. I still hear it, "I have a dream that my four little children will one day live in a nation where they will not be judged by the color of their skin but by the content of their character... With this faith we will be able to transform the jangling discords of our nation into a beautiful symphony of brotherhood..."

King's assassination on April 4, 1968 rocked the world with indignation and grief. As a freshman college student waking up to injustice in America, I was deeply affected. While on the campaign trail, Bobby Kennedy received news of King's death and delivered a speech—immortalized in the PBS film *A Ripple of Hope* and often cited as one of the greatest of all time [47]:

> *What we need in the United States is not division; what we need in the United States is not hatred; what we need in the United States is not violence or lawlessness, but is love and wisdom, and compassion toward one another, and a feeling of justice toward those who still suffer within our country, whether they be White or whether they be Black.*

In his June 1968 victory speech, after the California Democratic Primary, he said, "The people in the United States want a change ... we want to deal with our own problems within our own country and we want peace in Vietnam." Referring to the upcoming Democratic National Convention, he ended the speech with "So my thanks to all of you and on to Chicago and let's win there." Moments later, as he walked through the kitchen toward the exit, he was shot and killed. His death profoundly deepened our disillusionment with what we saw as a racist political economy bent on global domination.

The 1968 Democratic National Convention

Disillusionment with the system set the stage for arguably the bloodiest presidential nominating convention in U.S. history—the Democratic National

Convention held in Chicago between August 26 and August 29, 1968 [105]. I considered attending, but logistical issues and anticipation of violence, arrest, and police brutality kept me away. Nonetheless, my fraternity brothers and I were glued to the television.

Authorities indicted eight alleged instigators in what became known as The Chicago Eight Conspiracy Trial. Along with defense attorneys, William Kunstler and Leonard Weinglass, they became our heroes—Abbie Hoffman, Jerry Rubin, Tom Hayden, David Dellinger, Rennie Davis, John Froines, Lee Weiner, and Bobby Seale—as they stood up to what we all viewed as a repressive system of justice. The fact that three of the defendants (Hoffman, Rubin, and Weiner), both defense attorneys (William Kunstler and Leonard Weinglass), and the judge (Julius Hoffman) were Jewish caught my attention. What can one say about this without being accused of stereotyping? Let's take a closer look at the Jewish people involved and see what they have in common.

Judge Julius Hoffman was born in Chicago to Russian Jewish immigrants—probably from the Pale of the Settlement—and he grew up on Chicago's west side. At just sixteen years of age, he graduated with a philosophy degree from Northwestern University and at nineteen he graduated with a Northwestern law degree. After many years practicing law and a Republican through-and-through, he was appointed by President Eisenhower to serve as a judge for the Northern Illinois District Court. He was an unpopular judge even before the Chicago Seven trial. A survey of Chicago lawyers who had appeared before Hoffman revealed that 78% of them had an unfavorable opinion of the judge.

William Kunstler was born in 1919 to middle class Jewish parents on New York's Upper West Side. He graduated with honors from Yale University in 1941 and subsequently earned a Bronze Star and Purple Heart fighting in World War II, and a law degree from Columbia University. He had an ordinary civil practice until 1960, and during those years, he described himself as an armchair liberal with a membership in the ACLU. In 1960, he represented Paul and Orial Redd, founders of the NAACP, in a housing discrimination case. Then, in 1961, the ACLU asked Kunstler to go to Mississippi to support the Freedom Riders who led boycotts protesting the segregation of bus station restaurants. He watched five young African Americans get arrested for sitting in protest at a lunch counter reserved for whites. This event radicalized the forty-two-year-old lawyer from New York, and he went on to play an important role in Martin Luther King's desegregation campaigns. By the time he accepted the role as lead defense attorney in the trial of the Chicago Seven, he had established a stellar reputation as a defender of civil rights and advocate for the disenfranchised. While both were highly accomplished Jews, it seems Kunstler and Hoffman were polar opposites in their political views and activism. Kunstler made me proud of my Jewish heritage, and Hoffman embarrassed me.

On his way to one of many contempt indictments, Abbie Hoffman spoke Yiddish to Julius Hoffman. Hoffman told Hoffman, "You are a shande far di goyim"—an embarrassment to Jews before Gentiles— implying that the judge's disreputable behavior fueled the flames of antisemitism. Abbie was born in 1936 and raised by middle class Jewish parents in Worcester, Massachusetts. His grandparents immigrated from Russia and Austria. Abbie grew up with a strict father and a rebellious spirit. He may have had Zionist leanings early on, as Israel became a State when he was thirteen;

and at that time of his life, he and his younger brother were fighting to defend themselves against antisemitic neighborhood bullies. Nevertheless, as he matured into an icon of the Civil Rights, Antiwar, and Environmental Movements, he staunchly proclaimed an anti-Zionist perspective in support of the Palestinian cause. Abbie studied psychology as an undergraduate student at Brandeis University and as a graduate student at UC Berkeley. He was heavily influenced by radical and revolutionary-minded professors at both universities. During the run-up to the Democratic Convention, Abbie Hoffman and Jerry Rubin, among others, founded the Youth International Party, more affectionately known as the Yippies.

Jerry Rubin grew up in Cincinnati and was raised by an unlikely couple of Jewish parents. His father quit high school and drove a bread truck before eventually becoming a union organizer. In his book, *Growing Up at 37*, he describes his mother as graduating "from high school and college with honors," He said she "played classical music on the piano…read books constantly…(and) might have been a teacher or writer…(if she wasn't) conditioned to be a housewife." By comparison, he says his father "never read a book." Both of these hyperbolic musings reflect the general feeling on his mother's side of the family that his father was intellectually and morally inferior. His father eventually outshone them all by becoming an effective community and union organizer and, as a parent, a compassionate, encouraging role model. Jerry's parents both died at about age 50—his mother of cancer and his father eleven months later of "a broken heart." In his twenties, Jerry became guardian of his younger brother and decided to move with him to Israel, determined to "convince the Israelis of the rightness of the Arab cause." Failure to do so led to disillusionment and a return to the U.S. with, to paraphrase his words, a Jewish heart and an internationalist mind.

Lee Weiner was the member of the Chicago Seven with whom I resonated most. Ten years my senior, Weiner was born in 1939 and grew up on the South Side of Chicago. Like my Grandma Roselyn's family, Weiner's family lived within smelling distance of the Chicago Stockyards. His mother graduated from the University of Chicago. Like my other grandparents, Weiner's father grew up on the West Side. Most likely, his mother's family emigrated from Central Europe and his father's family emigrated from the Russian Pale. He grew up in an enclave where most of the kids in his school were Jewish.

With his father's connections to the Mob, Weiner grew up tougher and more savvy than typical middle class kids headed from Jewish neighborhoods to post-graduate careers as doctors and lawyers. Upon graduating high school, Weiner attended college downstate at the University of Illinois. Then, he studied sociology at the Hebrew University in Jerusalem on a year-long journey funded by his grandfather. There, he met Jerry Rubin and together they became radicalized by the class-based discrimination they saw within the Jewish community—particularly in the case of Moroccan Jews who were treated, it seemed, even worse than Arabs still living in Israel. Upon returning to Chicago, Weiner earned a graduate degree in social work from Loyola University.

Finally, the team of defense attorneys, led by Kunstler, included another Jewish lawyer, Leonard Weinglass. Weinglass was born in 1933 in Belleville, New Jersey, a suburb of New York City, and he died in 2011. His obituary in the *New York Times* said he was "perhaps the nation's pre-eminent progressive defense lawyer, who represented political renegades, government opponents and notorious criminal defendants in a half-century of controversial cases, including the Chicago Seven, the Pentagon Papers, and the Hearst kidnapping." Raised by Jewish parents, he graduated from Yale Law School and was known as a "modern-day Clarence Darrow."

While I risk overgeneralization, it struck me that half of the ten major players in the Chicago Eight Conspiracy Trial were Jewish. Jews represent only about 2% of the population of the U.S. and only about 0.2% of the population of the world. Nonetheless, 220 of approximately 1,000 Nobel Prizes through history have honored Jews, and approximately 100 of the wealthiest 400 people in America (all billionaires) were Jewish according to a 2010 issue of the *Business Insider*.

Historians and Jewish Studies scholars have long noted the remarkable contributions of Jews to science, arts, and public life, made less surprising by the fact that Jews in America have long graduated from college at twice the rate of non-Jews. But why? These are not coincidences. Scholars often attribute disproportionate Jewish representation on the frontier of possibilities to a historical emphasis on community-preserving education, resilience under adversity, and traditions of questioning and debate. Jews most able to embrace these ingredients, while surviving oppressive antisemitism, ultimately flourished.

Five of the eight defendants in the Chicago Eight Conspiracy Trial received prison sentences for crossing state lines to incite a riot, and they all attracted multiple charges of contempt as the trial turned into a circus. The judge was so prejudiced that all charges were overturned upon appeal. We had come a long way since the execution of Julius and Ethel Rosenberg. As they came of age, our generation's Jews embraced the revolutionary aspirations of the Chicago Eight; whereas, just fifteen years earlier, while still coming of age, the Jews of my parents' generation waved the American flag and turned a blind eye to calls for the execution of the Rosenbergs. Both trials are immortalized in movies and books. Kunstler's role in the trial of the Chicago Seven even inspired me to change my career aspirations. In 1968, I wanted to become a defense attorney.

The Democratic Party imploded after Bobby Kennedy's assassination, and the turmoil at the Democratic convention added fuel to the flames. Vice President Hubert Humphrey looked too much like Lyndon Johnson and would be no match for any candidate the Republicans chose to put forward. With 301 electoral votes, Richard Nixon easily defeated Humphrey in the November election.

Summer Jobs

Summers at home in Skokie felt tame compared to campus life, but they offered interesting work opportunities. Our neighbors the Hollands provided one such opportunity. I became friendly with Nancy and her father Dave offered me a summer job working at his family's clothing store known as Smokey Joe's. The job involved commuting to Halsted Street near Maxwell—the old neighborhood on the West Side, where six of my great grandparents had settled.

Dave's father-in-law, Joseph Bublitz, a Russian immigrant, started Smokey Joe's in the late 1930s. Never mind that Jews soon began migrating to Chicago's North Side. Joseph's son, Morrie, who could sell anyone anything, famously introduced the zoot suit to the African American community. Over time—with celebrities such as Smokey Robinson, James Brown, Sammy Davis Jr., and Michael Jackson—the clientele extended well beyond Chicago. I enthusiastically accepted Dave's invitation to work at Smokey Joe's. My job involved folding clothes, stocking shelves, and serving customers.

Morrie and Dave gave me important instructions. When a customer came in for any single item of clothing, I was to think in terms of a wardrobe. If the customer wanted a shirt, I was to also sell him the tie, pants, socks, sweater, hat, jacket, and underwear to go with it. Furthermore, no customer should leave the store empty-handed. If I couldn't make the sale, I needed to adroitly call over one of the store's super-salesmen to close the deal.

I struggled as a salesman, largely because I found it objectionable to convince customers—virtually all Black and Latino—that they simply must have something they had no idea they lacked until they came into the store. Nonetheless, I cooperated with the rule to transfer my customers to salesmen without my hangups. I remember another college kid named Tommy. He was Black and, as an enlightened 60s college student, I tried to make friends. He wanted no part of it. Looking back, I realize that trust had to be earned, especially across lines of race and privilege.

My most edifying summer jobs involved work for my dad and his partners. One summer, I worked on the audit of Dad's biggest client, Jackson Park Hospital on Chicago's South Side. As I checked bank reconciliations, one account wouldn't reconcile. Dad jumped in and guided me to the reason for the discrepancy. An accounting clerk had siphoned money into her personal account over the course of the past several months. Dad informed the hospital's director, who asked him to dismiss the employee. Normally, this wouldn't be the outside auditor's job. Nonetheless, much to the director's satisfaction and relief, Dad ethically and sensitively handled the dismissal. I was quite impressed and proud of my Dad's character in managing this challenging situation while maintaining his independence from the client.

Chapter 10
Earth, Moon, and Easy

The Environmental Movement

Two environmental events radicalized our view of the earth as a home whose sustainability we should not take for granted. First, on January 28, 1969, a Union Oil facility spilled four million gallons of oil into the ocean. The spill created a slick spoiling 800 square miles of water and 35 miles of beach off the coast of Santa Barbara, killing thousands of large sea creatures and countless birds. Second, on June 22, 1969, the oil-laden Cuyahoga River caught fire near Cleveland. These two events galvanized the Environmental Movement, which combined with the Civil Rights and Antiwar Movements to complete the backdrop to the cultural shift that defined our college years.

The Environmental Movement quickly gained traction with Nixon expediently jumping on the bandwagon as the "environmental president." Nixon's administration enacted several major pieces of environmental legislation, including the Clean Air Act Amendments of 1970, which set clean air standards and equipped the EPA with resources to study environmental problems and to develop and enforce regulations.

William Ruckelshaus, a household name during the EPA's early years, famously said, "We are a long way in this country from taking individual responsibility for the environmental problem." The first Earth Day, on April 22, 1970, reflected our first steps in that direction, as 20 million people participated in demonstrations and teach-ins across the country. Today, one billion people across virtually every country in the world celebrate Earth Day.

One Giant Leap

During the summer of 1969, U.S. citizens came together to proudly celebrate a great achievement that catapulted the U.S. ahead of the Soviet Union in the race for dominance in outer space. On July 20, Neil Armstrong and Buzz Aldrin became the first humans to walk on the moon. This feat fulfilled JFK's goal set in 1961 to land a man on the moon by the end of the decade. I remember Neil Armstrong summing up the achievement with one of history's most famous one-liners: "one small step for man, one giant leap for mankind."

For one brief moment the world was at peace. Even today, those words remind us that all people yearn for peace. Photographs of Earth, taken from the moon, emphasized the fragility of our place in the universe. They reminded us to care for our planet, thus becoming a symbol of the Environmental Movement.

A Beloved Mascot

After all the seriousness of political upheaval and campus protests, let's take a look at a lighter side of campus life. Mike Perlen—a year ahead of me—acquired a dog named Easy. A Dalmatian mix, Easy became our beloved house mascot. Keith became so attached that when Mike moved out and needed to find Easy a home, he gave him to Keith.

My relationship with Easy included taking him with me when I walked the six blocks from the fraternity to my classes. Appropriately named, Easy didn't need a leash, and there were no bags designed for picking up dog poop in those days. The university had a central grassy area called "The Quad," and Easy hung out there while I was in class. He met me when I emerged and we walked home together. Easy convinced me that I should always have a dog in my life.

Woodstock and the Music Scene

The summer of 1969 included a major musical event: Woodstock. This iconic three-day festival happened in mid-August on Max Yasgur's farm in the foothills of New York's Catskill Mountains. I thought about attending, but I was home working that summer, and my parents would not have approved. But I can't blame it all on them. The prospects of spending three days in the mud did not appeal to me, and I couldn't foresee the historical significance of the event. I regretted missing performances of "White Rabbit" by the Jefferson Airplane, "Evil Ways" by Santana, and "Proud Mary" by Creedence Clearwater Revival, among many others.

Music was like a religion to my generation, and it has remained part of my lifeblood to this day. Bob Dylan's music and poetry captivated me, and I immersed myself in lyrics like "He not busy being born is busy dying," and "You'd better start swimmin' or you'll sink like a stone for the times they are a changin'."

We also had some excellent high-energy local bands, including REO Speedwagon and the One-Eyed Jacks, both managed by Bob Nutt and Irving Azoff. REO attracted a substantial following with 40 million records sold worldwide, and Azoff became one of the most powerful players in the recording industry—managing the likes of the Eagles and The Beach Boys. Our parents might have had the Greatest Generation, but we had the greatest music.

The Outhouse

Junior year at the University of Illinois brought a new kind of excitement. I moved from the fraternity into a rental shared with three fraternity brothers—Keith, Ken Batko, and Bob Nelson (whom we all called Skull)—plus Greg Graham, a close friend of Keith's. I lived there during my junior and senior years, and for the first time since I was five, I had my own bedroom. We dubbed our off-campus digs the "Outhouse," because it sat farther from campus than both the fraternity and the raucous house where the rest of my close friends lived—known fittingly as "The Zoo."

Chapter 11
Protest and Purpose

The Moratorium March

At the beginning of fall semester 1969, word spread of a major protest march against the Vietnam War, planned for November 15. I let my parents know that my friend Ken and I decided to go, whereupon my father wrote me the only letter I remember ever receiving from him. In it he implored me not to throw my life away. He was sure I'd be arrested. I let him know that I appreciated his love and concern. However, I stood my ground and gently explained that this was a cause I believed in and something I needed to do. My father's concerns were not unfounded. On November 12, while preparing to embark, news broke that Nixon had ordered 9,000 troops to augment the 1,200 National Guardsmen and 3,700 police officers charged with controlling the throngs of protesters.

Anyone questioning the justification for protesting our government's handling of the war would have received their answer with the next day's news. On November 13, the New York Times published Seymour Hersh's Pulitzer Prize-winning exposé of the My Lai Massacre. The article provided horrific details of Second Lieutenant William Calley and his battalion slaughtering 500 unarmed civilians, including women, children, and the elderly. The American public was outraged to learn that the massacre had been covered up for twenty months.

Sentenced to life in prison, Calley served just three years under house arrest. After all, why should Calley have jail time when the higher-ranking Captain Ernest Medina faced no repercussions for allegedly giving the order to "kill everything that breathes?" At least two dozen soldiers were charged with war crimes, but only Calley was convicted [51]. Unfortunately, this was not the worst of the massacres of Vietnamese civilians by U.S. soldiers [52]. In all, more than two million Vietnamese civilians perished in the Vietnam War, which of course the Vietnamese refer to as the "American War."

Ken and I managed to get a ride on a bus filled with other protesters on their way to D.C. Dozing on the way there, I suddenly awoke to see our bus hurtling toward the car in front of us. I yelled "Watch out!" jolting the driver awake just in time to avoid collision. We arrived in D.C. not knowing where we would sleep, so we went to a church that was offering sanctuary to as many of the arriving protesters as it could accommodate.

Soon, local residents began pouring into the church offering their homes for refuge and a good night's sleep. Awed by this courageous outpouring of generosity, we most appreciatively accepted one family's invitation. The father, a government employee, longed to join the protest but feared for his job. Opening their modest home was a quiet act of resistance—and a gesture of appreciation for protesters like us coming from far and wide.

They fed us and moved their daughters out of their bedroom, so we could have a room to ourselves. Before retiring, we learned much from this family's personal stories and their perspective on the war, the protests, and the inner workings of the Nixon administration. The next morning, we woke to delightful smells of eggs and waffles. After a hearty breakfast, our hosts sent us on our way. We exchanged expressions of gratitude for a heartening encounter and for each other's contribution to a peaceful movement protesting our government's shameful prosecution of a war that was sickening the soul of America.

November 15, 1969 was a glorious day. We joined 500,000 comrades in a peaceful march past the White House, ending with a gathering at the National Mall. There, we heard speeches by Coretta Scott King, Benjamin Spock, and David Dellinger on a stage near the Washington Monument. We also enjoyed performances by Peter, Paul and Mary, Pete Seeger, and Arlo Guthrie. When Pete Seeger led us in *Give Peace a Chance*, our voices rose in a unified cry for peace and our hearts bonded as one.

This experience remains one of the most formative of my life. I still have the march route poster framed and hung in a prominent place in my house. The title in big letters is "We Come in Peace," and that we did. I heard of no violence connected with the demonstrations. We made a powerful statement that peaceful protest can move mountains. Martin Luther King, Jr. and Mahatma Gandhi would have been proud of the reflection of their ideals in the climactic events of that day.

The Draft

I don't remember thinking much about my own draft status. I knew I had a deferment at least until I finished college, and I expected that it would continue through law school. Nonetheless, the first-ever draft lottery on December 1, 1969 attracted my attention. As it turned out, mine was the 347th birthday drawn. This meant that unless they drafted nearly everyone, I was safe.

My friends with low numbers generally avoided the fray in Vietnam by enlisting in the National Guard. I didn't know anyone who went to prison or to Canada, two much less frequently used ways to avoid combat in a war that made no sense to us. American men sent to fight in Vietnam were disproportionately Black and poor, while White men from middle- and upper-class families avoided combat by joining the National Guard. These inequities became a focal point of the Antiwar Movement.

Violence on Campus

By spring 1970, antiwar protests had taken a darker turn. In January 1970, Larry Voss, a student activist confined to a wheelchair, was arrested for throwing a firebomb through the window of Champaign's police department. In February, the ROTC lounge was firebombed, and Dr. Benjamin Spock spoke on our campus. It was music to our ears when Spock said, "the Declaration of Independence states that if people cannot get justice through legal means, they are entitled to cause a revolution."

When University of Illinois administrators rescinded a student-issued invitation for William Kunstler to speak on campus, student protests erupted. In an effort to suppress all-out rioting, administrators reversed their decision and Kunstler spoke [54] [55] [56]. After a short period of relative calm—lasting until the end of April—President Nixon stunned the nation with news that U.S. troops invaded Cambodia. This expansion of the war triggered a new wave of antiwar protests on college campuses.

On the same day as Nixon's announcement, a traffic violation turned into a high-speed chase culminating with a white, Champaign policeman senselessly shooting and killing Edgar Hoults, a 23-year-old Black security guard. "No police officers came to talk (to Hoults' wife) about the shooting; no city official visited to explain the killing to her and her children [56]."

While the shooter never again served on a police force, an all-white jury and a racist criminal justice system cleared the shooter of all charges, including murder. The Hoults affair ignited a new wave of civil rights riots in the Champaign-Urbana community. Community rioters protesting a corrupt criminal justice system merged with rioters on campus protesting the escalation of the Vietnam War.

Then, tragedy struck at Kent State and Jackson State Universities. On May 4, 1970, members of the Ohio National Guard fired into a crowd of Kent State University students, killing four and wounding nine, all of whom were white. The event triggered a nationwide student strike that forced hundreds of colleges and universities to close [57].

On May 6, I joined a protest at the Student Union, where I saw the police and National Guard arrest two professors. I knew one of them: Michael Parenti, a popular political science professor. The police attacked Parenti with Billy clubs and bloodied his face so badly that I thought he might suffer brain damage. The incident sent chills up my spine. Parenti survived the beating and jail time and went on to become a highly regarded political science professor and one of the country's most prolific critics of U.S. foreign policy.

Then, around midnight on May 14, Jackson, Mississippi police fired 400 rounds of bullets at a group of students hanging out outside a girls' dormitory on the Jackson State University campus. The firing started when one of the students threw a bottle in the direction of the police. When it ended, two Black students were dead and twelve were wounded.

White students at Kent State became national martyrs; students at the historically Black Jackson State University received little national attention. The message was unmistakable: the lives of white students drew national outrage; the lives of Black students barely registered. The contrast speaks volumes.

Success of the Antiwar Movement

The May 1970 protests largely succeeded. Nationally, Nixon pulled U.S. troops out of Cambodia. Locally, the University of Illinois Dean of Students pledged that striking students would not face punitive consequences. Instead, a statement released by Chancellor Peltason acceded to the demand for "liberation classes." In classrooms and on the Quad, professors conducted these classes to "carry on discussions of the many problems... in our society [56]." These concessions defused tensions and peace returned to the University of Illinois campus. From the streets of D.C. to the Quad at Illinois, we saw what happened when hundreds of thousands of protesters moved as one in collective peaceful action: change felt possible.

Chapter 12
"California Dreamin'"

California, Here We Come

After a tumultuous junior year at the University of Illinois, my parents surprised me with a brand-new, bright red, $3,000 Plymouth Duster—a belated 21st birthday present. To test drive the car, Ken Batko and I planned a summer trip to California. I had never ventured west of the Mississippi River, so this was a big deal.

We stopped in Colorado, where we experienced the Rocky Mountains for the first time. I was stunned by what my flat Midwestern upbringing kept hidden— trails ascending to jagged mountain peaks, crisp alpine air, rushing rivers, beautiful wildflowers, aspen groves, and abundant wildlife. While we hiked and marveled at our pristine surroundings, I made up my mind that I would eventually live in these mountains.

From Colorado, we made our way to San Francisco, where we needed to find work before running out of money. We saw a boarding house with a help-wanted sign. Upon entering, we realized we were—for the first time in our lives—knowingly entering a world of openly gay people. While we thought our sexual orientation was clear, the proprietor saw something he liked and offered us a job washing dishes in exchange for room, board, and a small stipend. We stayed for two weeks while exploring San Francisco. Then, we headed down the coast to Los Angeles.

We found cheap lodging at a fraternity on the UCLA campus bordering Los Angeles' Westwood neighborhood. Shortly after moving in, I saw a woman about my age trying to get a candy bar from a vending machine. I moseyed over and said, "Here's all you need to do," and I slapped the machine with mock swagger. To our astonishment, the candy bar tumbled out. We laughed and just like that, a friendship began. We discovered that we both needed summer jobs while exploring L.A. I suggested that she—Susie—spend the day sightseeing with Ken and me. The three of us hit it off so well that—later that day—we decided to get our sleeping bags and go to the beach where we could watch the sun set and sleep under the stars.

The next morning, I awoke before Ken and Susie and decided to hunt for a job. I made my way back to UCLA, where I showered and donned my sport coat and tie. I then made my way to Beverly Hills, where I walked around looking for help-wanted signs. I found one at the café in the Beverly Wilshire Hotel, and the manager Gloria offered me a job waiting tables. I told her I had two friends looking for jobs, and she said she could use them, too. I went back to the beach with the good news, and we started work that evening.

Throughout the next two months, Ken and Susie covered the tables and I worked the counter. The café attracted movie stars and other celebrities, one of whom, Frank de Kova, regularly sat at the counter. He had played the role of Chief Wild Eagle in the TV show *F-Troop* between 1965 and 1967. He continued acting until his death in 1981 but seemed to have plenty of time for coffee, refreshments, and chit-chat at my counter in the upscale Beverly Wilshire Hotel.

Invariably, Ken and Susie served more celebrities— like Joey Heatherton and Warren Beatty—and accumulated more tips. I learned that, no matter how hard I tried, waiting on people was not part of my skill set. I regularly mixed up orders and frequently failed to pick them up before the food got cold. The chef had no use for this ineptitude, and regularly read me the riot act.

Challenges at the Beverly Wilshire aside, the summer of 1970 was magical. Ken and I had little money when we started the trip. We earned what we needed to thoroughly enjoy our exploration of the Rocky Mountains of Colorado and the beaches and cities of California. The relationship with Susie was a bonus— and we remained friends for several years. She visited me in Chicago and Champaign, and I visited her in California. *Leaving on a Jet Plane* by John Denver became one of my favorite songs.

Graduation

Back from California for my senior year at Illinois, I had to start thinking seriously about what I would do next. I still dreamt of emulating William Kunstler, so I applied to several law schools, including Boston University, UC Berkeley, Illinois, and Wisconsin. I did reasonably well on the LSAT and had a "B" GPA, but I didn't get in any of these schools. Rejection stung. My credentials would more likely have sufficed in 1970, but 1971 brought more competition, perhaps due to so many students choosing graduate school to avoid the draft. In any case, I didn't give up my dream, and I applied to two Chicago law schools, Loyola and DePaul, both of which accepted me. With my dream of becoming a defense attorney still alive, I chose Loyola.

Chapter 13
Silverton Interlude

Before getting settled in Chicago, I treated myself to a graduation present. I bought a one-way ticket to Los Angeles to visit Ross, who had moved there to try his hand as a performing musician. He was living a Bohemian life in a small apartment, where he learned that "one jar of peanut butter lasts twice as long as a jar of jelly." He played guitar and sang in parks, or wherever people might enjoy a serenade and perhaps contribute cash to the hat in front of his makeshift stage. His rendition of "The Pilgrim" by Kris Kristofferson spoke to me:

> *From the rockin' of the cradle to the rollin'*
> *of the hearse, The goin' up was worth the*
> *comin' down.*

After spending a week with Ross, a few other brothers showed up, including Morry, Keith, and one or two others. One of them had a car and, while Ross stayed behind in his apartment, the rest of us headed east across the Mojave Desert toward the Grand Canyon. I had already seen the Grand Canyon and the others wanted to spend a couple of days there, so we split up. I planned to hitchhike about 300 miles across the Navajo Nation and Ute Mountain Reservations to our rendezvous point in Silverton, Colorado.

After separating from my friends at a convenient spot on the highway, I began my journey. A pickup truck pulled over and offered me a ride on the cargo bed. I threw my backpack over the side and jumped in, only to find myself sharing the bed with a rather large, inebriated, belligerent man. While listening to his threats, I planned my escape. At a highway speed of about 60 miles per hour I planned to throw my backpack overboard, jump after it, and roll to safety.

Before I could execute my plan, the truck stopped at a desolate spot near the middle of the reservation. The two Native American men sitting in the cab jumped out and instructed me to jump in. I didn't argue. I gingerly took my middle seat and finally exhaled when the man sitting to my right said, "We needed to get you out of the cargo bed. That drunk guy in back is unpredictable." Eventually, they dropped me off—still deep within tribal lands—at the intersection of the road toward Silverton and a road toward their homes.

I didn't have to wait long before a car pulled up and the driver, a White man, motioned me to get in. I threw my backpack in the back seat and took the front passenger seat. On this leg of my journey, I learned about the plight of the Navajo as my driver was a social worker dedicated to improving life on the reservation. At the time, most Navajo lived in impoverished homes without access to running water and electricity. I don't remember my driver's name, but I remember his generosity and the positive energy that he poured into his work. We parted at another intersection, still on tribal lands.

The next thing I remember is standing across the road from a diner with my thumb out. When darkness came, the café closed, and cars and trucks whizzed by without a glance in my direction. Eventually, a car stopped about 30 yards beyond me. I ran toward the car and when I was within a few yards, the car sped away. After one more of these annoying episodes, I pulled out my sleeping bag, walked a safe distance from the road and bedded down in the desert until the café opened at the crack of dawn. After an egg, toast, potatoes, and coffee, I ventured back to the road and hitchhiked the rest of the way to Silverton without incident.

Upon arriving in Silverton, I checked into the run-down historic Avon Hotel on the main drag in the center of town. The town was nestled in a valley below the towering San Juan mountains. Like something out of the Old West, the hotel room had an old-fashioned dresser, bed, and a small window that overlooked the street. I imagined crouching by the window, pistol in hand, shooting it out with "bad guys."

I was dead tired with just enough energy to head downstairs with a question for the hotel bartender, "Which of the mountain peaks surrounding this town is highest?" Pointing through the hotel window, the bartender answered, "Kendall Peak at 13,500 feet. You can take a very long walk along the old Kendall Mountain Road most of the way to the top. Or you can bushwhack. But be careful of the scree."

I naively asked, "What's scree?" and learned that it means loose gravel-like rocks. I thanked the bartender and ordered a bottle of whiskey with which to retire. Back in my room, I drank two or three shots—and collapsed on the bed. The next day, I was determined to bushwhack to the top of Kendall Peak. I got an early start and found a hiking trail that seemed to be heading in the right direction.

Bordered by beautiful wildflowers, the trail offered spectacular views of the town and surrounding mountain range, but it ran out of steam at the top of the tree line and the base of a steep, upward-sloping scree field. I could see that I would have to cross this field in order to reach the boulders guarding the peak.

I knew I'd be able to scramble over the boulders, if only I could manage the scree.

I gingerly took my first steps, felt reasonably secure and without looking down, angled upwards across the field. Halfway across, I realized that I had both hands and both boots balancing on loose rocks, one slip from a deadly fall. My whole body shook. Then I became peaceful. As I reviewed my life and contemplated my demise, it saddened me to think of people I'd leave behind, especially my parents. While plastered to the mountain, I carefully looked around and about 100 yards below me and to my right I spotted the old mountain road.

I decided to make a run for it, thinking that if I moved straight to my right across the scree, gravity would take me down toward the old road. I began moving to my right while sliding slightly downward with each step. It worked. After reaching the road, exhausted, I began the long walk to town. At one point, I was so tired that I carelessly collapsed in the middle of the road. Fortunately, no vehicles came to run me over. I wouldn't have cared. After about three hours of walking, I made it back to the hotel.

I went straight to my room, drank another two or three shots of whiskey, and again collapsed on the bed. A few hours later, I woke to a knock on the door. Stumbling to the door, I found that my friends had arrived. They finished the alcohol while I chronicled my adventures to a rapt audience. Over the next few days, we explored the area. We drove on the Million Dollar Highway from Silverton to Ouray and then made our way to Telluride. The colorful scenery took our breath away—red cliffs, multicolored wildflowers, green valleys, and peaks still capped with snow.

In 1971, Telluride was still an enchanting Old West mountain town, and we loved it. Ski lifts didn't come to Telluride until 1972 and the world famous Telluride Bluegrass Festival didn't start until 1974. Many years later we would return to Telluride for a mini-reunion and find that a very hip ski town had replaced the quaint town we found there in 1971. Ouray rests on the third point of the San Juan Triangle, with Silverton and Telluride occupying the other two points.

The San Juan Triangle is one of the most beautiful regions of the U.S., with its colorful 13,000-foot peaks, deep blue lakes, cascading waterfalls, rushing rivers, and glistening streams. While exploring the area, I resolved to one day bushwhack through the Uncompahgre National Forest between Ouray and Silverton (about 15 miles as the crow flies).

Chapter 14
William Kunstler, I'm Not

Upon returning from Silverton to Chicago in the summer of 1971, I began making a new life for myself. My parents graciously agreed to pay my Loyola Law School tuition, and since it was local, they wanted me to live at home in Skokie. I couldn't bring myself to do that, because I worried it would feel like being back in high school. I decided that I would earn the money to support myself in an apartment.

I eagerly looked for a cool place to live with friends in the city. I found a large apartment in a building located just a few blocks southeast of Wrigley Field on Cornelia Street between Broadway and Halsted. Three friends moved in with me. This made it affordable—and fun. I also got myself a dog—a black lab whom I named Huck after my favorite character in literature.

I got a job working in the mailroom at the British Tourist Authority, located in the John Hancock Building—now known as 875 North Michigan Avenue. Completed just a few years earlier, the 100-story building was the tallest building in Chicago and the second tallest in the world—behind the Empire State Building. I enjoyed interacting with the friendly British ladies who staffed the offices, and the job offered flexible part-time hours to accommodate my schedule at Loyola.

During the summer before law school started, I found my happy place listening to blues music with friends at local clubs. I even bought a harmonica and—with little success—tried playing the blues. With Corky Siegel on harmonica and keyboards and Jim Schwall on lead guitar, my favorite band—the *Siegel-Schwall Blues*

Band—performed regularly at *The Quiet Knight*, located just five blocks from our apartment. Other nearby favorite haunts included the *Wise Fools Pub* and *Kingston Mines*. These blues bars attracted some of the greatest musicians of that era, including Muddy Waters, Otis Redding, and Mighty Joe Young. Meanwhile, John Prine was perfecting his unique blend of country, rock, folk, and blues at the *Earl of Old Town*. I discovered John Prine later in life and became a fan.

Even with relatively low rent on the apartment, the British Tourist Authority job didn't provide enough hours or wages to support my lifestyle, so I obtained the required license and signed up to drive a Yellow Taxi. With a poor sense of direction and no such thing as GPS, getting my fares to their destinations was a challenge. When someone flagged my taxi, I would say, "Where to?" Then, I'd follow their answer with, "What's the best way to get there?"

One evening an African American man thanked me profusely for picking him up. Then he revealed that he had a hard time getting any taxi driver to take him to his neighborhood. When we got to his block, he said, "Drop me off at the corner, because it would be too dangerous for you to drive down my street."

Fortunately, while taxi driving came with some excitement and I heard stories of violence, I never got into any real trouble myself, and I did eventually learn my way around the city. I especially liked driving on Lower Wacker Drive underneath the downtown area, requiring quick moves to emerge onto a downtown street.

Law school started in the fall, and I soon became overwhelmed. I juggled two part-time jobs, law school classes, homework, and parties with roommates—who weren't trying to work and go to school at the same time. Unable to care for Huck, Dusty helped me find him a good home on a rural Illinois farm, and we sadly parted ways.

Law school intimidated me. I felt unprepared for professors' cold calls designed to toughen up students for Chicago's courtrooms and law firms. We needed to learn how to make and support arguments for legal positions when there were no "right answers." When called upon to take a position, I invariably froze. I could not recognize my own voice and I couldn't think straight. I experienced the same anxiety that destroyed my concentration during high school basketball games. I made it through my first semester in "good standing," but I had no interest in a second semester. I quit.

I decided I had the wrong personality for high-stakes debate. I didn't like arguing competitively, and I didn't like the fact that a good lawyer could win a case taking either side of the argument. As hard as it was, I had to admit that a future William Kunstler, I was not. My path to self-discovery would have to take me elsewhere.

Chapter 15
The Belly of the Beast

Starting Blocks

Regrouping from my false start in law school, I next decided to explore the possibility of elementary school teaching as a way of making a difference in the world. I discovered an MS Program in Elementary School Education at Northwestern University. Once tentatively accepted into the program, each candidate had to find an internship at a Chicago Public School.

I knew an elementary school principal who lived in our old neighborhood near Kilpatrick Avenue. I had played with him in basketball pick-up games. I approached him and he agreed to establish his school as an internship outlet for education students at Northwestern. On that basis Northwestern accepted me, but I balked when I realized that it would mean two more years of financial hardship. Instead, I decided to rely on my accounting degree to get out of debt and support my modest lifestyle.

I borrowed Barry Greenberg's sport coat and tie, and interviewed for an entry-level professional job at several CPA firms. This was challenging, since 90% of the hiring had already taken place on college campuses during the spring of 1972. I was a walk-on.

Joining a Profession

At an interview with a medium-sized firm, I had to take an accounting aptitude test. I failed miserably, and the proprietor told me to look for another profession. I was shaken, but I persevered and eventually received job offers at three large accounting firms.

I accepted a job at Lybrand, Ross Brothers, and Montgomery, which soon became Coopers & Lybrand and much later became part of PWC. At $11,000, the starting salary was equivalent to $80,000 in 2024 purchasing power. This ample salary would allow me to pay off loans, while greatly enhancing my knowledge of business and accounting. I felt like I was entering the jaws of the complex predatory ways of capitalist enterprise. Rather than leave my ideals at the door, I resolved to be true to them while embracing my chosen profession.

I was in good company with many compatriots who went the way of Jerry Rubin, a folk hero of the almost-revolution. Remember the *Walrus'* warning that we would find our way into "institutions and jobs which, instead of correcting the glaring ills of America, simply perpetuate the unjust system to which (we) object." This warning didn't have the power to stop the vast majority of us from joining the establishment just when the revolution was supposed to prevail. Jerry Rubin wrote, "The movement destroyed its leaders ... (contributing) to (its) disappearance ... as a moral force... By 1972, I was a battered soldier who hated his ego, feared his power, and was contemptuous of his name [109]." Jerry subsequently joined the "human potential movement" and eventually entered the world of Wall Street—as a stockbroker, no less. Hopefully, he did not leave the moral imperatives of sixties ideals at the door.

Navigating Family Trauma

On March 29, 1972—my dad's 45th birthday—my Grandma Roselyn died at age 67 from congestive heart failure. She had complained about her heart condition throughout my college years and it finally caught up with her. I attended three of my grandparents' funerals and maybe even functioned as a pall bearer at one or more. However, I regret to say that I must have been distracted with finding my way in the world, because I don't remember the funerals.

I do remember "sitting shiva" with my family during the week following each funeral. This is a Jewish tradition whereby the family has an open house to receive friends and relatives who want to offer condolences. Each night, the rabbi comes to bless the time set aside to mourn the deceased in the comfort of the family home surrounded by supportive community.

At about the time of Grandma Roselyn's death, Mom was having medical issues that led to a hysterectomy. Her daily calls with her parents were her lifeline. Losing her mother, watching her father's deteriorating health, and undergoing surgery took a heavy toll on Mom's mental and emotional state. Grandpa Leo's death—from prostate cancer that spread to his brain—just eight months after Grandma Roselyn's passing ignited a horror unforeseen by me. My mother became incapacitated by grief and a family predisposition for mental illness—potentially passed down through her great-grandmother Etta, her grandmother, Rose, and her father Leo.

At her low point, Mom attempted suicide and was committed to the psych ward of a hospital where she received electric shock treatments. It's awful to think of this. It must have scared my Uncle Joe who remembered the anguished screams of my Great-grandmother Rose. She must have suffered from schizophrenia or a similarly debilitating affliction. The 1940 Census lists Rose as part of the Herr household, but didn't mention that she was also an inpatient at a mental hospital.

During this difficult phase of my mother's life, I would patiently sit with her and discuss her challenges. I did my best to help work through whatever weighed on her at the moment. The issues seemed eminently surmountable to me, and insurmountable to her. I didn't realize it yet, but the runaway anxiety I experienced in law school had its roots in the same family trauma afflicting Rose, my mother, and potentially my Grandpa Leo. In his book about his famous brother Abbie, Jack Hoffman writes "Every family has its madness." This was ours.

I tried to support my dad in his struggles to care for my mom with her increasingly debilitating mental health challenges. My mom's affliction, along with the profession we now shared, brought my dad and I closer together. We met regularly for lunch and I sometimes joined him for celebratory dinners with his clients at the end of engagements.

Setting the Stage

I didn't dwell on the trauma afflicting my mother. Instead, I focused on preparing to succeed at Coopers & Lybrand. I made an adult decision and didn't renew the lease on my party-friendly apartment on Cornelia Street. I don't remember what my roommates decided, but I know we stayed in touch and continued to frequent blues bars and favorite restaurants. One of my all-time favorite late night haunts was The Villa, near the Howard Street El Station bordering Evanston at the north end of the Chicago city limits. My mouth waters even now as I remember the Italian beef sandwiches, and the ambiance was perfect for late night discussions of our latest adventures.

From Cornelia Street, I moved into a three-bedroom apartment with two high school friends,

Mickey Siegel and Steve Boren. The apartment is just a stone's throw from the newsstand at Chicago and Main Streets and less than a mile to a beach on Lake Michigan. Professional movers with pulleys successfully wrestled Grandma Roselyn's beloved baby grand piano into the living room of my new apartment at 712 Hinman Street in Evanston. We left it there when we moved out about four years later, as the people moving in were happy to have it, and no one else in the family had the space or the wherewithal to have it moved again.

The CPA Exam

During my first year with Coopers & Lybrand, I enrolled in a class to prepare for the CPA exam. The class facilitated absorption of Becker CPA Review materials covering the four sections of the 19½ hour exam taking place over the course of three days. The four sections included Auditing, Business Law, Accounting Theory, and a double dose of Accounting Practice. I worked in the Auditing Division of Coopers & Lybrand, and I had mastered the firm's training manuals, so I didn't think I needed to study for that part of the exam.

Needless to say, when I took this grueling exam for the first time in 1973, I failed Auditing. Fortunately, the rules allowed candidates passing at least two parts to retake only the parts they failed. I studied and easily passed Auditing when I retook that section of the exam in 1974. Then, like my dad, I became a licensed Certified Public Accountant (CPA).

Auditing Economics

During my first summer with Coopers & Lybrand, I spent some time in the "bullpen." This was a place where first year auditors hung out when they weren't assigned to specific clients. It wasn't long before I was assigned to my first real job: the audit of the Hammond Organ Company. I performed well and was next assigned to the DeKalb Agriculture Company, an important "SEC client," meaning the company had publicly-traded stock and, therefore, needed to file heavily regulated financial reports with the Securities and Exchange Commission (SEC).

When Coopers & Lybrand's partners negotiated a price for the DeKalb Ag audit, they had to balance the risk of audit failure against the risk of losing the client to a lower bidder. Ultimately, the partners set a price consistent with an estimate of how many hours it would take a staff of professionals to complete a complex multi-faceted audit, with a tolerably low level of audit failure risk. Audit failure could cripple a firm financially and ruin its reputation. Audit failure occurs when the auditor attests to the credibility of financial statements later found to have—intentionally or inadvertently— misled investors who suffered damages by relying on them.

Pressure Cooker

While working at Coopers & Lybrand, I experienced the tension between making money and guarding against audit failure. For example, in some cases the firm undercut competing firm bids in order to attract new audit clients. This squeezed profit margins and tightened the screws on the audit staff.

I responded to these pressures by underreporting overtime hours spent bringing the quality of my audit work up to my own exacting standards—without breaking the budget. The firm's training programs discouraged underreporting hours, while partners and supervisors turned a blind eye to it. Self-sacrifice within reason was rewarded with salary increases and promotion.

Another source of tension involved pressure on auditors to contribute ideas to the "management letter." While performing the audit, we looked for ways the client might improve its internal controls and operating procedures. The lead partner took responsibility for accumulating our recommendations into a letter to the client—offering our consulting services. This created a conflict of interest for the auditor, whose guard against audit failure might weaken to avoid offending a client more interested in the advocacy of consulting relationship.

The consulting arm of CPA firms earned greater profit margins and eventually grew to provide more revenue than auditing. In the case of the Andersen-Enron debacle, Andersen earned more from its consulting business with Enron than from auditing. The SEC and shareholder lawsuits argued that this conflict of interest played a major role in Andersen's failure to qualify its opinion on Enron's financial statements, subsequently revealed to be scandalously fraudulent. Both Andersen and Enron collapsed, with Andersen partners scrambling for jobs at other firms and members of Enron's senior management team serving prison sentences. This was perhaps the most egregious audit failure of all time.

The Cushion

While working on the DeKalb Ag audit, I became privy to discussions about an account pejoratively known as the "cushion" or "cookie jar." The "cushion"—a flexible tax reserve—could be manipulated to meet earnings targets. While not its main purpose, clients used this account to anticipate outlays for whatever IRS agents might turn up in their audit of the client's complex tax return. This contingent liability later became known as the reserve for uncertain tax positions. Once established, the client could increase income or decrease losses by lowering the reserve account balance to make poor performance look better.

The lead audit and tax partners on the engagement didn't object to the client's misuse of the account, as long as it didn't become too disconnected from reality. At the time, we didn't realize that one penny of fictitious earnings could result in audit failure if that penny brought earnings up to analysts' expectations. Instead of adopting this investor perspective, we assessed materiality by posting all items of disagreement on a schedule and measuring the combined impact of the items as a percentage of the client's reported earnings. If the percentage was less than a "tolerable" amount (usually 5%), then the audit partner felt comfortable accepting the client's reported income number without insisting on adjustments for any one of the scheduled items.

Pro Bono Work

During my years at Coopers & Lybrand, I capitalized on the policy whereby early career stage audit staff logged "bullpen" days when not assigned to an audit. On these unsupervised days, unassigned staff auditors might study the firm's operations manuals, prepare for the CPA exam, or try to look busy while twiddling their thumbs. Once I graduated from the bullpen to actual audits, I performed well enough to have credibility when I made a proposal to the firm's human resource manager. I proposed to supervise new staff members sitting idly in the bullpen in an activity that would give them some practical experience while contributing to the welfare of the community.

With the firm's permission, I identified struggling businesses in low-income neighborhoods and offered free accounting services. The *pro bono* services generally involved developing financial information to help small business owners understand their company's financial condition, obtain financing, and make better operating and financing decisions.

The program's success during its first year attracted the attention of the firm's leaders. The director of human resources invited me and several members of the audit staff—who had participated in the program—to a dinner at a fancy restaurant near the top of one of Chicago's skyscrapers located across the street from our offices. The gourmet dinner was catered by African American servers wearing white gloves. I was encouraged by the firm's interest in institutionalizing the program, and I was disgusted by the opulent ambiance of the venue where we discussed how the firm might take over the program's administration.

"Nail Someone to a Cross"

When I was attending Yom Kippur services in Skokie with my family in 1973, we learned of a shocking surprise attack on Israel by a coalition of surrounding Arab states. Israel retaliated in a war that lasted about three weeks with neither side gaining much in the way of territory. The success of the surprise attack shook Israel's confidence in its own security, inspired U.S. military support, and intensified the fervency of Zionism.

A couple of months after this event, I experienced one of the most jarring moments of antisemitism in my adult life. I was packing up to leave the offices of a client just before the Christmas holiday. A colleague named Mike Higgins and I were the last ones to leave. Mike and I had worked hard together on this audit for several months. He was one year ahead of me, and I thought we had become friends.

As I was leaving the office, I said, "Have a nice Christmas holiday, Mike," and he responded with a callous, "You too … well, I mean, do whatever you people do … nail someone to a cross or something." The sting of that comment made me realize that I had left the comfort of a Jewish enclave. I had moved to a gentile world, and for the first time in my life, I was in the minority.

Later, Mike awkwardly tried to make up for his antisemitic gesture. He invited me to his house for dinner and said he would also invite his cousin—an eligible Irish Catholic bachelorette—whom he wanted me to meet. With heightened Zionist feelings, I politely declined.

Around this time, my friend and fraternity brother Country Bill Shermer and I took a weekend drive to upstate New York in order to attend a meeting designed to provide information for folks considering moving to Israel to work on a kibbutz and ultimately join the Israeli army. Neither of us signed up, but we were certainly sympathetic.

Tax Planning and Compliance

During my second year on the audit staff, I rose to the level of senior, a mentoring role that I found stimulating. I also enjoyed an assignment having me create and present course training manuals. This gave me a taste of teaching, which inspired me to begin thinking about a springboard to an academic career. I began eyeing

Colorado Mountain College, which I had stumbled upon during my travels, just south of Glenwood Springs.

In November 1973, I spoke with Gene Baroni about transferring from the audit staff to the tax department. I had interacted with Gene in his role as the tax partner consulting with the DeKalb Ag audit partner on the tax reserve account discussed earlier. I had been privy to the discussions that took place over a couple of days in a conference room at the DeKalb Ag offices.

Gene impressed me with his deep knowledge, unshakable integrity, and boundless positive energy. He was known for hard work and dedication to his family and his profession. He generally arrived at his office at least two hours before anyone else, and he was always available to discuss difficult issues with colleagues.

I explained to Gene that I wanted to broaden my experience within the firm, and I wanted to work with him on interesting tax planning issues. He said I'd have to also work on tax compliance. I committed to the hard work of becoming a proficient tax specialist. He said that since I was already an audit senior and would have two audit busy seasons under my belt, I could start out as a supervisor.

I began work as a supervising tax specialist in the spring of 1974 and continued until January 1976. In the tax department, I worked on complicated tax compliance issues and creative tax planning engagements. I also regularly consulted with the audit staff on issues related to clients' tax reserve accounts.

I'll never forget one particular client named Jerry. Jerry didn't think much of me when we were first introduced. He thought I was too young and wet behind the ears to be of much help. It perturbed him to think that I would be taking the lead on preparing his family's individual 1974 tax returns, as well as the tax return for his incorporated family business.

The Employee Retirement Income Security Act (ERISA) had just become law, and I structured employee benefit plans for Jerry's family business. My efforts dramatically reduced his family's overall tax bill. Jerry was pleased, but the experience left me with a sour taste, as I knew Jerry would pay a lot less tax that year than many struggling families without access to tax loopholes—like those in the neighborhoods I had targeted for pro bono work. Helping the rich get richer—or worse, becoming one with them—was not consistent with my ideals, and I began thinking in terms of exiting the jaws of predatory capitalism.

Chapter 16
Summer Interludes

I took full advantage of the Coopers & Lybrand policy encouraging staff to use banked overtime to extend vacation time. Each summer, I traveled to the Rocky Mountains for spiritual renewal amid the majesty of the American West. I made the trip alone during the summer following my first busy season.

Traveling solo, I discovered the joys of hiking to the top of a Colorado "14er" and rafting on the Colorado River through Westwater Canyon in Utah. For the rafting experience, I hooked up with a small group and a guide. The guide steered while the rest of us paddled through two days of spectacular scenery and challenging rapids. We stopped for hikes and slept under the stars. I fell in love with these ways of communing with nature, and I resolved to guide my own raft someday.

Whitewater Peril: Big Drop Two and Satan's Gut

Inspired by my solo trip, the next year I invited three friends—Skip and Pat from the audit staff, and Bruce from the tax staff—to join me on a five-day rafting adventure on the Colorado River. This would be a big step up from my previous year's two-day trip with milder rapids. The mere anticipation thrilled me. I looked forward to challenging rapids interspersed with peaceful floats—in tune with the river's powerful current—through a vibrant, living canyon.

I enlisted a guide and two boats for this trip. Our awkward teenager guide morphed into a fearless leader as soon as our boats touched the water. He would control the support boat with a motor, and the four of us would paddle the smaller raft as long as we proved capable. Our guide said, "We'll take it one set of rapids at a time—but don't even think about paddling through Satan's Gut." We'd have ample opportunity to prove ourselves, since the rapids grew increasingly intense over this stretch of the Colorado River—96 miles beginning near Moab, Utah, continuing through Cataract Canyon, and culminating at Lake Powell in Arizona.

The first couple of days were idyllic—developing our paddling skills, stopping for hikes deep into the canyon, and sleeping under millions of stars. This was heaven. On the third day the rapids became more challenging and the canyon more beautiful, as the four of us managed the smaller boat propelled only by the river's current and our paddling strength.

We approached "Big Drop," created by a narrowing of the canyon, with an 80-foot drop and three major rapids. After an exhilarating ride through "Big Drop 1," we came upon "Little Niagara" (aka "Big Drop 2") and our guide instructed us to pull over to shore. Following our guide's instructions, we climbed high enough into the canyon to have a good view and threw sticks into the current. The same thing happened each time. The stick floated toward the left side of a large boulder in the narrowing river. Just before hitting the boulder, the stick disappeared—swallowed by a large hole carved by crushing waves. There was no room to clear the boulder on the right, even if we could fight the current. We had to skirt the left side—edging dangerously close to the hole without plunging in. Our strategy was to just barely hit the boulder and then paddle like hell to pull the boat away from the hole.

Our strategy worked like a charm, *almost*. We headed downstream toward the left side of the big rock with me positioned in the front right. The current was so loud that we couldn't hear each other shout. We approached in good position with my right leg barely grazing the rock, and then we paddled furiously as the current was sucking us into the hole. The waves sent the left side of our raft into the air, and I slipped off the right side and into the river. I grabbed a rope extending from the boat and held on for dear life. Then—I don't know how—but as the raft bobbed wildly from side to side, the river tossed me into the air and into the bottom of the boat.

The thrill didn't end there. An instant after I plopped back in the boat, we realized the current was taking us straight toward "Satan's Gut"—and we had no way to stop. Luckily, the support craft, its motor throttled to hold steady in the current, was close enough to throw us a very heavy rope. We grabbed it and pulled ourselves and our raft toward the bigger boat and—when we came close enough—we jumped aboard. Then, the current caught our raft, pulling it toward Satan's Gut. The rope broke, the raft doubled up so the front and back ends met in the middle. It disappeared under water, and we didn't see it again, until we reached Lake Powell two days later. Risk is its own reward when it produces enough adrenaline to feel the power of rising beyond our limits to meet the challenge at hand.

·····

After the exhilaration of five days of whitewater rafting and the tranquility of sleeping under a sea of stars in the night sky above Cataract Canyon, Bruce headed back to Chicago. Meanwhile, Skip, Pat, and I traded our paddles for hiking boots and headed toward Silverton and the San Juan Mountains. I had convinced Skip and Pat to join me in fulfilling my ambition to bushwhack 15 miles through the Uncompahgre National Forest—from Ouray to Silverton. We camped one night at about 10,000 feet and had a great adventure, without incident—at least until we neared Silverton.

As we descended toward Silverton, we came to a trail leading to the top of Red Mountain No. 3. I asked Skip and Pat if they'd like to do a side trip to the top of Red Mountain. They declined and said they'd meet me at the car. I told them I'd only be an hour behind.

I wasn't tired, and it was great to have some time alone. All was right with the world, as I climbed through an alpine forest and filled my soul with the purity of it all. After a few satisfying, meditative moments at the top, I started my descent. Soon I began to worry, as I realized that I had underestimated the time for the excursion. By the time I saw my companions, Skip was incensed to the point of attacking me. Red-faced, he grabbed me by the shirt, then thought better of it, and let go before I had time to react. Afterwards, my friendship with Skip and Pat cooled. I regretted the fallout, but understood their frustration, and took responsibility for pushing Skip beyond his limits—lesson learned.

Chapter 17
Departure

I disliked the daily suit-and-tie grind—squeezing onto packed trains or crawling through rush-hour traffic—to commute to downtown Chicago. Still, I liked learning about accounting and the inner workings of the corporate world, and I thrived on the camaraderie with colleagues. This tension created internal conflict, as I contemplated following through with my plan to use the experience at Coopers & Lybrand as a springboard. Ultimately, I decided I'd have a better chance at living in line with my values if I left Big 8 accounting behind. After all, its success depended on engagements with some of the wealthiest individuals, highest-paid C-suite officers, and largest corporations in the world—and that didn't appeal to me. In fall 1975, I told Gene Baroni that I planned to leave the firm in January.

At first he tried talking me out of it, explaining that I was one of the very few from my entering class of forty on track to become a partner. I contemplated that compliment for a moment—then did my best to explain my reasons for leaving. In the end, Mr. Baroni supported my decision, albeit without fully understanding it. Years later, I received shocking news that Gene was killed in an automobile accident driving home from the airport after a business trip [61]. He was a giant in the industry and an inspiring mentor—beloved by colleagues, friends, family, and me.

To save a little money, I left my Evanston apartment and moved in with Keith, who had an apartment in Hyde Park on Chicago's South Side. Keith was a resident in the University of Chicago College of Dentistry, kicking off what would become a 45-year career promoting oral health in a warm and friendly atmosphere. Keith's office was more like a home to staff and patients alike. He contributed greatly to the life of the community in and around Santa Rosa, California.

I lived with Keith for three months, while finishing up at Coopers & Lybrand. I thought I might use the post-Coopers interlude to work my way around the world, so I applied for a passport. I also thought I needed a backup plan, so I wrote to Colorado Mountain College to inquire about joining the faculty—never mind that they weren't advertising. With equal parts chutzpah and self-promotion, I touted my education, experience, and professional license—no response. I thought, "Maybe they aren't hiring, or maybe I'm not qualified." I decided that, as part of my backup plan, I'd better earn more credentials. So, I took the Graduate Management Admissions Test (GMAT) and applied to accounting Ph.D. programs.

While living with Keith, I told a woman I was dating about my plans and she gave me contact information for her sister living in Salem, Oregon. Also, I learned that Carla, a friend from college, was planning to leave Chicago for a new life in the west at about the same time as me. I asked if she would like company, as I was selling my car. Carla said she would be glad to give me a ride as far as Colorado, where I planned to stay for a short while with my cousins, Steve and Pettra Pollack. Steve's dad, my Uncle Bob, had been especially encouraging when I drove up to Milwaukee to deliver my car to the dealership where he worked. He gave me a good price, told me to enjoy making my own way in the world, urged me to make my family proud, and sent me on my way.

Of all my friends and family members, I had the hardest time leaving my dad. When he told his partners

I was leaving Coopers & Lybrand, they encouraged him to offer me a job with their firm on a rapid track to partner. I was proud and touched, but I maintained my resolve to strike out on my own. I'll never forget our last lunch date before I left Chicago. I did my best to explain my desire to move west and find my own path in life. Dad said, "I don't understand what you're doing, but I trust you." That meant the world to me.

I thanked Dad for the opportunity to join his firm—the place I had worked part-time throughout high school and college. I felt bad about leaving with my mother leaning so heavily on him, but I didn't think I could help her. He released me by emphasizing that my mother's recovery was not my responsibility. At the time, Mom habitually called Dad multiple times a day and even tried to physically restrain him from leaving the house for work in the mornings. This interfered with his ability to keep up with client demands, and it created tremendous stress. I worried about his health, and said, "I would understand if you left Mom for another woman. You deserve less stress and more happiness." No response.

When my family and friends surprised me with a going away party, I knew there was no turning back. To make sure I stayed warm, my parents gave me a winter coat and down vest as a going away present. The coat is long gone, but I still have the yellow vest hanging in my closet.

Finally, departure day arrived. My possessions consisted of what I could wear on my back and stuff in a backpack. I threw the backpack into the trunk of Carla's car and off we went toward Colorado. As we set forth, we talked about a voice in the wilderness that had appeared on the political scene. He came out of nowhere to win the Iowa Caucuses in January 1976, the same month that Carla and I set out to discover our purpose in shaping a more compassionate, sustainable, and just world.

Carter was a breath of fresh air. He was a Washington outsider and little known governor of Georgia. He promised to "… never tell a lie … never make a misleading statement … never betray the trust of those who have confidence in me … and never avoid a controversial issue." Carter presented a stark contrast to Gerald Ford, the sitting president and a traditional Washington insider who became president in the wake of Nixon's resignation following the Watergate scandal.

The prospects of a Carter candidacy buoyed my spirits. As the westward miles rolled by, I carried with me a short list of big goals. I wanted to get out of my comfort zone, explore the world, find a meaningful career aligned with my ideals, meet a life partner with whom to build a family of our dreams, and deepen my connection to the natural world, not necessarily in that order. The road ahead felt as open and uncharted as the prospects of a Carter presidency. His promise mirrored my hope for a fulfilled life—one in tune with my natural talents and dedicated to building healthy community in a more peaceful world.

Chapter 18
Toward an Academic Life

First Stop: Colorado

On our way to Colorado, we stopped in Iowa City, Iowa, so I could have a meeting with the director of the doctoral program. I don't remember much about this meeting. Both of us were native English speakers, but I'm not sure we were communicating—my first clue that an academic career might come with challenges for which I might not be prepared. My thinking at the time was that—if I decided on an academic career—I wanted to teach at a community college such as the Colorado Mountain College in the Rocky Mountains. I climbed back into the car and we drove to Evergreen, Colorado, home to my cousins, Steve and Pettra. I thanked Carla, and we wished each other Godspeed as we parted ways.

A few years earlier—after graduating from the University of Wisconsin—my cousins had moved from Milwaukee to Evergreen, then a beautiful sleepy village in the foothills about 20 miles west of Denver. I felt close to Steve and Pettra, as we shared family, progressive political views, and love for the environment, while enjoying much the same ways to have a good time. I had visited Steve and Pettra in Madison, and this was not my first visit to the cabin where they lived in Evergreen. Steve drove a bus for the local school district, and Pettra cared for their newborn son, Jeff.

With the birth of his son, Steve started thinking about providing for his family in a style not affordable on a school bus driver's wages. He told me he was thinking about applying to join the MBA Program at the

University of Michigan. Since he had started his undergraduate studies at Michigan before transferring to Wisconsin, this would take some explaining. I offered to help. I suggested that we get a bottle of Scotch, talk it over, and draft an essay. I guess this worked pretty well, since Steve submitted the application and was admitted. I always believed Michigan got the better of the deal, as Steve remains one of the best people I've known.

While visiting Steve and Pettra in January 1976, I met with Professor John Tracy, the director of the University of Colorado doctoral program. Living in proximity to Rocky Mountain National Park and countless mountain and river attractions would fulfill a dream. However, as beautiful as it was, I wasn't ready to move to Boulder with its orientation toward privileged white "trust babies" and ski bums. As it attracted wealth, Boulder was losing its appeal to youthful activists with progressive views. I heard that Oregon—lush fern-covered forests, enticing Cascade Mountains, wild rivers and streams, rugged coastline interspersed with sandy beaches, tranquil Willamette Valley, progressive politics, and stirring counterculture—was the new frontier.

I managed to leave Chicago debt-free, but without any income, not much money in the bank, and no car. I needed to figure out a way to get to Oregon cheaply and then find temporary lodging while I figured things out. I saw an ad in the local newspaper posted by a guy wanting his car transported from Denver to Salem. He would pay all travel expenses, including gas—perfect! I bid my cousins adieu and headed for the new frontier.

Regular phone calls to my parents were not helpful around this time. I didn't get much encouragement from their frequent reminders that I could move back to

Chicago anytime, and I couldn't answer their variously phrased questions about how I was going to support myself or what I was going to do next. So, my calls became less frequent.

Phaedrus and Perpee

Upon arriving in Salem, I found a phone booth—no cell phones in those days—and called the number my ex-girlfriend in Chicago had given me for her sister, whose name I regrettably can't recall. I drove to the house she was renting with her girlfriend, which couldn't have been far from where I made the call. Salem, the capital of Oregon, was a town of only about 100,000 people. The three of us immediately hit it off. The two women, about my age, helped me drop off the drive-away car and invited me to rent the vacant room in the house. I paid one month's rent and said I would need only that much time to figure out my next move.

I had just finished reading the deeply affecting book, *Zen and the Art of Motorcycle Maintenance*. Driven to the brink of madness while defending his dissertation at the University of Chicago, the main character quits the program, buys a run-down classic motorcycle, takes it apart, renovates and shines up each part, puts it back together, and sets out for new frontiers in the western U.S. Though I didn't buy a motorcycle, I did comb the newspaper for an inexpensive car I might take apart and put back together.

The first part was easy. I noticed a drivable 1966 Volkswagen Notchback with a price of $250—perfect! My new friends drove me to pick up the car, and I drove it back to their house. I named the car Phaedrus, the name the Zen book gave to the motorcycle. I resonated with the character Phaedrus, who by Plato's account dialogued with Socrates about the symbiotic interplay between passion and reason creating the purest form of love. I was amazed at the relevance of a dialogue taking place nearly 2,500 years ago, as I charted my own course toward responsible adulthood.

The next day, in spite of nasty weather, I took Phaedrus for a test drive to the Oregon Coast. I enjoyed the one-hour drive over the Coast Range to Lincoln City, where I found an expansive windswept sandy beach. After a refreshing walk in a light rain, I drove south along scenic Highway 101 to Cape Perpetua where I got out to observe sea lions bathing on the rocky shoreline.

As I walked back to my car parked along the highway 101 roadside, I noticed a tagless, raggedy, pitch-black Dachshund with a typical hotdog body. When I got to my car, I pulled a couple of hotdogs out of the cooler and went back to see if the dog remained where I first spotted him. Sure enough, he was waiting for me. I fed my obviously abandoned new friend and we bonded. "Perpee" followed me back to Phaedrus, and without needing any more incentive, he hopped in as soon as I opened the door. Perpee's openness to building a new life matched my own—we became fast friends.

The second part of my plans for Phaedrus proved more difficult. I noticed that the car was leaking oil, so I decided to dive into car maintenance by changing the engine oil. I'll spare you the gory details. Suffice it to say that the leak worsened after my foray into car mechanics. I quickly realized that any attempt on my part to take the car apart and put it back together—an operation Phaedrus sorely needed—would require the expertise of a bona fide auto mechanic. Or I could immerse myself in grease and oil for the next couple of years instead of working on credentials to teach at a community college.

I found a reputable Volkswagen mechanic in the vicinity and asked for an assessment. He pointed out that engine leaks generally do not disappear after simply changing the oil. He would have to rebuild the engine, and he also recommended rebuilding or replacing the transmission and clutch. He took pity on me and said he could do the entire job for $1,500. There went my $250 bargain. When I acquired Phaedrus, the car was as prepared for the road as I was to teach at Colorado Mountain College. Phaedrus needed some work and so did I.

The Bumpy Road to Eugene

After repairing Phaedrus, I began earnestly scouting my next move. I discovered the Portland Scribe, an underground newspaper with a mission to expose the evils of the Vietnam War, promote gay rights, and organize community activists. I decided to pay a visit to this newspaper's downtown Portland office. I found no help-wanted sign in the window, but I inquired anyway. I offered my accounting expertise to further the organization's mission.

The person I talked with said, "We can't pay you, but we would gladly accept volunteer services." This underground newspaper impressed me as much as *The Walrus* captivated my imagination during my years at the University of Illinois. The Portland Scribe's mission was perfectly consistent with my ideals. However, I doubted that my talents matched their needs and developing them seemed like too much of a stretch. The encounter reminded me that while I knew my ideals, I was still figuring out the best way to act on them.

Next, I drove to Eugene to visit the University of Oregon, the school that had jumped to the top of my preference list. Oregon offered me probationary admission to their accounting doctoral program, with the stipulation that I take a doctoral seminar and some MBA classes during the upcoming Spring quarter. They also offered to immediately put me on the payroll as a teaching assistant for an MBA-level class in operations research, a subject I knew nothing about. Next, I drove to Berkeley, where I met with a pompous professor who didn't think I was graduate student material. This marked the second time that UC Berkeley—the school that most reflected my passion for making a difference in the world—had rejected my application for post-graduate education. Maybe they saw something that would hold me back or maybe they weren't listening. I wasn't giving up. Eventually, I would break through the sound barrier—because persistence, to me, has never meant refusing to change course, only refusing to let closed doors define my limits.

For now, I had pretty much decided to begin graduate school at the University of Oregon. I would decide between two paths. If I did well and liked the program and faculty, I could work toward a PhD. If that seemed too highfalutin, then I could finish the MBA in a year or two and leave qualified to teach at a community college—my original goal.

I didn't forget that before leaving Chicago I obtained a passport and had aspired to work my way around the world. I envisioned a job on a ship destined to points unknown. Not having completely abandoned that dream, I decided that—before finalizing plans to move to Eugene—I would drive to Mexico. I had been to Tijuana during the summer when I lived in Southern

California. Now, I decided I would drive more deeply into Mexico—beyond the tourists.

So, Perpee and I hopped into Phaedrus and began the long drive south. I remember stopping at a town about 100 miles south of the border. No one spoke English and my eighth grade Spanish didn't help. I quickly realized this was too much of a leap for my constitution. Rethinking my plan to rent a room and stay south of the border for a while, I turned around and drove back to the U.S. As I returned home—from a day that felt like a week in Mexico—I felt a stronger-than-ever connection to my homeland. On the way back to Oregon, Perpee and I visited friends living in Los Angeles. My friends were a married couple whose acquaintance I made at Illinois. I remember feeling deeply grateful for their warm hospitality.

My friends had tickets to see Carole King in concert and I decided to join them. Carole King burst on the scene as I was graduating from college in 1971, with songs like "Natural Woman," "Beautiful," and "Smackwater Jack" on her amazing second album, *Tapestry*—25th on Rolling Stone Magazine's list of the 500 greatest albums of all time. She performed these songs, along with new ones like "Only Love is Real." I practically floated above my chair listening to her mesmerizing music—one of the best concerts I've seen, and I've seen some great ones.

On my way back to Salem from Los Angeles, I stopped in San Francisco to visit my friend and fraternity brother, Barry Greenberg, who had moved there after college. Barry and I took a drive down the coast to Big Sur to visit Esalen, the self-proclaimed "birthplace of the human potential movement [62]." This was quite an experience, as we entered a world where nudity was encouraged and anxiety frowned upon. It seemed that a true Esalenian displayed equal parts of mellow and pretentious. I did my best to blend in but found myself lacking in both ingredients. We stayed in this picturesque pampering environment one night and the better part of two days, which was about my limit; I was too restless—or too driven—to fully surrender to Esalen's mellow.

Upon returning to Salem, I no longer had any doubt that I would move to Eugene and work as a teaching assistant, while taking spring quarter classes. The classes would count toward an MBA in case I decided against pursuing a Ph.D.

Chapter 19
Into the Current

Self-actualization

I began searching for a place to live in Eugene and found a cozy apartment in the walk-out basement of a house on an unimproved road not far from the main University of Oregon campus. The apartment contained a bedroom, living room, kitchen, and small windowless room off the kitchen that could serve as a spare bedroom.

Perpee and I settled into my new abode, and I passed the time by reading *Atlas Shrugged* by Ayn Rand. I had read *The Fountainhead* shortly before leaving Chicago. I was captivated by the vision of a society without government-imposed barriers to self-actualization, and with powerful incentives encouraging individual innovation, creativity, and freedom. These books make a strong case that only such unencumbered individuals can create a responsible, prosperous society.

While the ideas sounded good at the time, I soon realized that Rand's philosophy fails to encourage the type of self-actualization that builds compassionate community, as envisioned by Abraham Maslow [100]. Maslow's hierarchy of needs characterizes self-actualization as a holistic integration of self into the larger community. For Maslow, self-actualized individuals often find fulfillment through acts of service—helping to build healthy, connected communities. On the other hand, Rand envisions a society where each individual functions autonomously, with community seen as an obstacle to realizing one's full potential. In fact, I learned that Rand's Objectivism goes so far as to label altruism a moral evil. Eventually,

I realized that Rand's views conflict with the ideals I absorbed during the protest movement of the sixties, which advocated building community and caring for the earth.

Hard Left

While kicking back with Perpee, I prepared to feast on the beautiful outdoor environment surrounding me. I discovered a company specializing in production of rafts for professional guides and novices alike. Bill Parks, a business professor at the University of Idaho in Moscow, started the company in 1972 with the name Northwest River Supplies (NRS). I browsed the company's catalog and bought my first raft: a six-person inflatable boat suitable for all levels of river running. Since then, I have purchased rafts and accessories from the NRS catalogue on many occasions. This employee-owned company's values reflect sixties ideals by empowering "individuals to make the right decisions for the good of the customer and the company."

At first, my equipment consisted of the boat, a foot pump, and five paddles. One paddle was longer than the rest, as the captain used it to steer the boat from the back. The other four paddles were for the crew, with two people on each side of the boat. My trips with guides taught me to instruct the crew with commands like "hard left," "soft right," "backpaddle," and "power forward!" Knowing no one in Eugene, I tried out my new equipment by paddling solo on a lake. I quickly learned that simultaneously steering and paddling for power on water with no current was no fun—especially into the wind! It was exhausting, frustrating—and an early lesson in the value of a strong current.

I soon graduated to the Willamette River. I tackled a stretch running from downtown Springfield—

Eugene's twin city—to a take-out point near the University of Oregon Campus. This stretch has no serious rapids and enough current to use the long paddle for steering without needing to paddle for power. I parked at the put-in point and hitchhiked back to my car from the take-out point. My exhilarating first run on the Willamette set the stage for pleasurable and exciting rafting adventures that kept me harmonizing with nature for the next 35 years.

Pleasurable Commuting

To my repertoire, I soon added a bicycle that I could lock up at the take-out point and use for commuting back to my car. The bike also became an important vehicle for commuting to the Oregon campus once I started my work and studies. My bike had two important accessories: a backpack for books or hikes, and an attached milkcrate for carrying the backpack, small loads of groceries, and other items in need of transport. In Eugene, I began a tradition of commuting on my bicycle and, over the years, I have rarely owned a campus parking pass. The exercise on the way to work in the morning perked me up and the decompressing ride home after work readied me for family time. Furthermore, biking connected with values of sustainability, simplicity, and the joy of intentional physical engagement.

Chapter 20
Running

Not long after moving into my basement apartment, my friend Bruce from the tax department at Coopers & Lybrand called and said he would like to visit. Bruce and I had worked together, and we ran a 5-day stretch of rapids on the Colorado River with nightly campfires and—one of my favorite things in life—sleeping under the stars.

During Bruce's visit, he said that he, too, was thinking about moving from Coopers to something new. He held a degree in English from the University of Chicago, a law degree from Illinois, and a CPA license—credentials that supported his role as a Coopers & Lybrand Supervising Tax Specialist. He also dreamt of becoming a performing pianist, and my move inspired him to give that a try. By the end of the visit, he'd made up his mind to leave the firm and, to my surprise and delight, decided to claim the small room in my apartment. A few months later, he followed through. Our shared passion for communing with nature, building community, and finding our highest calling made us compatible roommates and close friends.

Pre's Trail
It wasn't long before I discovered one of Eugene's favorite pastimes: running. When Bruce arrived, he quickly joined in. Steve Prefontaine (Pre)—possibly the greatest runner ever to grace the streets of Eugene and the track at Hayward Field—tragically died in an automobile accident less than a year before I arrived in town. He made a profound impact on the community and has a lasting legacy. Shortly before I arrived, the

Oregon Track Club and the university completed construction of Pre's Trail, which Pre designed himself.

I hadn't run seriously since competing on the cross-country team in high school, and my first time on the woodchip trail, I could barely run a mile. It didn't take long before I was in good enough shape to run the entire 10,000 meter course. I caught the bug and—along with seemingly everyone else in Eugene—I was running everywhere. I ran on Pre's Trail, city streets, the road between Eugene and Springfield, and in the annual "Butte-to-Butte" 10-K run between Spencer's Butte and Skinner's Butte. Both Buttes are treasured Eugene landmarks covered with flowers and beautiful forest paths.

During the years I lived in Eugene (1976-1981), more people attended track meets at Hayward Field than the number attending football games at Autzen Stadium. The football team won 20 and lost 33 games at home, while the track and cross country teams were hosting the Olympic Trials, setting records, and producing Olympic athletes. During these years, the Oregon cross country team was touted as one of the best of all time, winning the NCAA championship in 1977 and finishing second in 1979.

I don't remember seeing Alberto Salazar on Pre's Trail, but I remember him as a student in my accounting class in 1978. I came to know Alberto as a fine young man and engaged student. Just a few years later, Salazar became the world's best distance runner, winning the New York City Marathon in 1980, 1981, and 1982, and simultaneously holding records at distances of 5,000 and 10,000 meters in 1982. Alberto pushed himself, and the women he later coached, beyond healthy limits. I was dismayed to learn that his extreme methods ultimately became unethical, attracted sanctions, and severely damaged his reputation. He was charged with doping, administering illegal drugs, and emotionally abusing the female athletes he coached. It pains me to think that the fine young man I knew was later driven to behavior that overshadowed his remarkable achievements.

Chapter 21
Starting Blocks

Perpee's Passion

Becoming familiar with our surroundings, Perpee and I enjoyed exploratory evening walks to the end of our rutted, lightly traveled road. Perpee was very protective of me and liked to run up behind dogs of any size and bark ferociously. Small dogs would quake in fear of him, and large dogs would *usually* ignore him. One evening, we walked past a house with two large dogs standing unattended in their front yard. Perpee made the mistake of threatening them with his bark and they didn't take kindly to the insult.

The two dogs leaped on Perpee and began tearing him apart. I screamed at the top of my lungs and kicked the dogs until they backed off enough for me to pick Perpee off the ground. He was barely breathing. I rushed home and then drove us to the animal hospital. I felt terrible thinking that Perpee would not survive. He surprised everyone.

I took him home, all bandaged up, and he could not move. The next morning, I watched him drag himself to his feet and move slowly toward the door, which I opened so he could drag himself outside. Then, I watched him walk ever so slowly around the perimeter of the small yard behind the apartment, marking his territory by—oh so gingerly—lifting his leg and peeing deliberately along his route. I have never been so impressed by the fortitude, loyalty, and dedication of another sentient being.

Perpee made a full recovery, only to be killed by a hit-and-run driver several months later. Sadly, I was not in town when it happened. I had flown back to Chicago for a short visit and had asked a friend to watch over Perpee while I was gone. Even now, decades later, I remember his determination and mourn the inspiring companion I lost too soon.

Steaming Stillness

Before spring classes, I began exploring the Cascade Mountains. I made three important discoveries, each one deepening my sense of awe for the wilderness east of Eugene. The first discovery was a great camping spot along the banks of the McKenzie River about an hour's drive upstream from Eugene. Along the way, I discovered Marten's Rapids only about 40 miles up the road from Eugene. I learned that one could include Class III Marten's Rapids in runs of 1 mile, 10 miles, or 15 miles, with corresponding put-in and take-out spots.

I knew I needed more practice on the Willamette and hoped to tackle my first run on the McKenzie once spring quarter ended. I followed through with my plan, gaining the confidence needed to invite classmates to join my crew during the following academic year. Not far from the car camping spot, I made my third major discovery. I found the road to Cougar Dam and a trailhead used by backpackers hiking into the Three Sisters Wilderness Area.

On the other side of the road from the trailhead, I noticed some hikers heading up a trail into the National Forest. I decided to check it out and much to my amazement I found several people soaking in a natural hot spring. I disrobed, carefully made my way over the rocks, and waded into the water. Wow, what a feeling— a deep primal calm descended as the warm mineral water enveloped me and steam rose to meet the cool mountain air.

Stumbling from the Starting Blocks

My first classes and teaching assistantship began at the end of March 1976. I had registered for three classes: a doctoral seminar taught by Paul Frishkoff and MBA-level classes in Management and Marketing. My teaching assistantship had me assigned to help one of the operations research professors with grading for a quarter-long project. With my never-all-that-great and now-rusty study skills, I managed to limp through my first quarter.

I understood little of the academic articles we read in the doctoral seminar. Somehow I earned a "B" in the course, while only partially understanding my own final paper. I managed to grade the project required of the students in the operations class while realizing that I could not have produced a passing paper myself. I earned an "A" in the Management course, the content of which I do not remember. Finally, I had a run-in with the Marketing Professor because I considered the 1,000 point system he used to motivate students dehumanizing and without substance.

I guess I had a chip on my shoulder, thinking that my experience in public accounting provided me with perspective lacking among ivory tower professors. To his credit, the marketing professor offered me the opportunity to write a paper to support my perspective, and my grade would depend on the quality of the paper rather than the accumulation of points for various activities that I considered inane. I ended up with a passing grade in the course, which I was taking on a pass-fail basis. I think we parted on good terms, or at least terms that would not get either one of us in trouble. I guess you could say that I stumbled out of the starting blocks.

A Gift of Sunshine

During that summer, I took plenty of time to enjoy Eugene and its surroundings. I graduated to the McKenzie River and Marten's Rapids with my raft-bicycle system. I built running endurance on Pre's Trail. I car-camped a few times at the spot I found on the McKenzie River, and I revisited the hot springs near Cougar Dam. I also discovered the Oregon Country Fair, which encouraged nudity and showcased ideas for living in deeper harmony with community and nature.

Shortly after Perpee died, I acquired a female puppy named Sunshine, an Australian Shepherd mix. To put this in context, that summer brought both a new dog and the end of a relationship. I met Ellie during the spring quarter when she was a graduating MBA student. Ellie found Sunshine at Eugene's Saturday Market and gave her to me as a going away gift. Then, during the summer of 1976, Ellie moved first to Portland and then to Seattle, leaving our relationship behind. Until much later, I didn't appreciate the benevolence behind Ellie's gift of Sunshine with whom I immediately bonded. Sunshine became an integral part of my life and lived to be 16. She rivaled Easy as the best dog I've ever known. When they met at Keith's wedding later that year, Easy and Sunshine became good buddies.

Chapter 22
"An Accounting Revolution"

You Graded this Wrong!

By the time fall quarter rolled around, I had decided to pursue the doctoral degree. In fall 1976, I taught two sections of a class in introductory accounting. While not entirely smooth sailing, teaching convinced me I was on the right career path. A few days after grading and returning first-exam papers, one student claimed that I incorrectly graded one of the problems. I suspected the student of changing his answer after the fact, but had no proof. The student had the audacity to do it again on the second exam. I was so sure that he cheated that—not realizing the importance of the student's father to campus life—I confidently changed his exam grade to zero.

A week or so later, I received a memo from the dean. It said that I needed to explain why I summarily accused the university vice president's son of cheating. I feared this might end my new career before it began. With some trepidation, I explained the situation to Dean Reinmuth, and he said to write a memo to him with that explanation. In the memo, I elucidated why I was so sure that the student had cheated and why I felt justified in changing his grade.

About a week later, Dean Reinmuth again summoned me. My heart was in my throat and my hands were clammy as I walked to his office. This time, he said, "I forwarded your memo to the vice president. His son confessed when confronted with your description of the events, and he agreed to retake the course. Good work!" We were on the best terms for the rest of my doctoral program.

Accounting Revolutionaries

During spring quarter, I took my second accounting doctoral seminar co-taught by two youngish assistant professors, Jerry Bowman and Larry Lookabill. Both men had recently graduated from Stanford and had studied under Bill Beaver and Joel Demski. Both Beaver and Demski graduated from the University of Chicago accounting doctoral program in the late 1960s.

Beaver and Demski were high-flying members of an elite group of late 60s and early 70s University of Chicago graduates who were changing the face of accounting as an academic discipline. Beaver and Demski landed at Stanford, where Jerry Bowman and Larry Lookabill were two well-regarded accounting doctoral students. The seminar with Jerry and Larry inspired me—and the handful of other accounting doctoral students taking the class—to love accounting research. Jerry and Larry were great at explaining the history of the seminal papers they assigned, as they knew the authors personally.

Three important 1960s events paved the way for scientific accounting research. First, the Standard & Poor's Company developed a machine-readable database containing corporate earnings and other detailed financial statement information, extending back to the 1920s. Second, the University of Chicago's Center for Research in Security Prices (CRSP) developed a machine-readable database with daily stock prices and returns on all securities traded on the New York and American Stock Exchanges, also extending back to the 1920s.

Third, four University of Chicago professors used CRSP data and Wall Street Journal articles to conduct a study of the efficiency with which stock prices react to a company's decision to split its stock [65]. The authors found that the market quickly impounds the implications of stock split decisions for future dividend increases. This led to the conclusion that the market responds *efficiently* to new publicly available information about the value of the firm. The evidence of market efficiency set the stage for thousands of future papers judging the relevance of accounting information by the stock price reaction to its release.

We learned that we were entering an academic profession with less than a decade of modern history. It started in 1968 when Ray Ball and Phillip Brown published their seminal paper demonstrating empirically the quality of the information contained in audited financial reports. The paper appeared in one of the two top accounting research journals, the *Journal of Accounting Research*, founded in 1963 at the University of Chicago [64]. The other top accounting research journal, *The Accounting Review*, had rejected the paper on the grounds that it was too disconnected from the style and conclusions of articles appearing over the last 50 years.

Ball and Brown introduced the scientific method to accounting research, while debunking current thinking about the efficacy of accounting information. They hypothesized that if reported earnings were simply meaningless combinations of abstract numbers—the conventional wisdom—then the study should find no systematic relation between reported earnings and changes in stock prices. The study's strong evidence of such a relation led these two University of Chicago doctoral students to reject their null hypothesis and conclude that accounting income reflects information relevant to investor judgments about the value of a firm.

Ball and Brown's 1968 paper revolutionized accounting research, bringing recognition of accounting as an academic discipline—a social science comparable to economics and finance. I appreciated the human interest story of the accounting revolution, but I struggled to understand the technical details of the revolutionary publications when I first read them. I have read the Ball and Brown paper many times, and—despite developing substantial expertise over the years—if I read it again today, I would still learn something new.

Michael Jensen was one of the authors of the seminal market efficiency paper that paved the way for Ball and Brown. Jensen—overlooked for a Nobel Prize—founded the *Journal of Financial Economics*, the top academic journal in finance, which he served as Editor in Chief for 22 years. With William Meckling, he coauthored another seminal article; this one cited more than any other paper in the history of economics. The paper heralded the study of agency conflicts between a company's owners and managers. It stimulated Jerry Zimmerman with his Berkeley Ph.D., and Ross Watts, one of Jensen's students at the University of Chicago, to found the *Journal of Accounting and Economics*, which quickly rose to the level of one of the top three accounting journals.

Watts and Zimmerman's seminal research focuses on the demand for accounting information to facilitate contracting between owners, managers, and lenders. The bookends to support accounting's scientific awakening are Beaver's *Financial Reporting: An Accounting Revolution* [70] and Watts and Zimmerman's *Positive Accounting Theory* [71].

To earn my Ph.D., I needed to pass three comprehensive exams based on four graduate-level seminars in each of three subjects: Accounting, Finance, and Econometrics (a blend of Economics and Statistics). This would prove a lot harder than earning an MBA, but the spring 1977 doctoral seminar with Jerry Bowman and Larry Lookabill hooked me. While taking that seminar, I began to develop friendships and intellectual relationships with Oregon's faculty and doctoral students.

It was an exciting atmosphere and close-knit community with frequent faculty parties to which doctoral students were invited. The accounting comprehensive exam didn't look anything like the CPA exam. A better name for it would have been a comprehensive exam in the science of information economics. Comparable in rigor to the exams faced by finance and economics Ph.D. students, it emphasized the usefulness of accounting information in resolving agency conflicts, promoting market efficiency, and facilitating economic exchange in financial markets. I was learning a lot!

Welcome, Bruce!

My housing situation changed dramatically during the summer of 1977. By then, Bruce had moved into my walk-out basement apartment. According to plan, he took the spare room off the kitchen, and this was fine until the mice showed up (not according to plan). We started laying mouse traps in the kitchen and we would typically catch two or three mice in each trap, no matter how many traps we set. We were inundated with mice and they eventually chased us out of the apartment. We looked for something a little more bourgeois, and we found a duplex unit about a twenty-minute bike ride from campus with easy access via a scenic bike path. The owners of the building, a sociable older couple, lived in the other unit.

I don't remember whether Bruce had a piano shipped from Chicago or whether he acquired one in Eugene, but I remember his practice sessions in our house, and I enjoyed seeing him perform for tips at a local pub. Bruce also became an avid running, rafting, camping, and hiking companion. Our exhilarating adventures included rafting through Marten's rapids, camping at the base of the trail to the top of one of the Three Sisters mountain peaks, and hiking to the summit the next day. With two cars, we could shuttle my raft from the take-out to the put-in a mile upstream multiple times in a day. We were getting good at navigating through the rapids with me paddling and steering from the rear, and Bruce paddling for power in the front right or left position.

Sunshine's Office Visits

Meanwhile, life on campus continued to evolve—enriched by Sunshine's office visits. I continued teaching during the summer of 1977, and graduated to an office in a building near the business school with a window at ground level—perfect for Sunshine's entrances and exits. She was navigating around campus better than I was—and probably had more friends. I can't recount her adventures—she always returned on her own, never having stirred up trouble.

My favorite fellow doctoral student, Roger Chope, occupied the office next door to me. We had a great time discussing teaching strategies and accounting research issues. I remember filling my office blackboard with our musings. While our advisors strongly suggested that we limit our teaching preparation to the bare minimum necessary to keep out of trouble, Roger and I enjoyed discussing strategy for our various teaching assignments. Throughout my doctoral program—even during summers—I taught two classes every quarter. The classes included introductory financial accounting, intermediate financial accounting, management accounting, and introductory statistics. I loved it as much as I loved developing the tools for accounting research.

Chapter 23

An Auspicious Encounter

Surprised by Joy

Between the end of the 1977 summer quarter and the beginning of the fall quarter, I put the relationship with Ellie behind me and made plans for a seven-day backpacking trip. My plan was for Sunshine and me to hike in the *Three Sisters Wilderness* for five days, meet Bruce on the fifth day, hike to the summit of the Middle Sister the next day, and hike out on the seventh day. Bruce planned a shorter one-day hike to our rendezvous spot.

The plan worked like a charm. My bond with Sunshine grew stronger as we hiked through the wilderness, marveling at beautiful wildflowers, ferns, meadows, streams, and wildlife. We camped each evening and left no trace. Back then, I drank directly from icy mountain streams and warmed myself by campfires at night. What a joy to meet Bruce on the fifth day! He even brought a bottle of wine, which we eagerly shared by the campfire to celebrate our reunion. According to plan, we climbed the Middle Sister the next day and camped for one more night. On our third day together—my seventh day backpacking— we hiked out of the wilderness and Bruce drove me back to my car parked near the hot springs by Cougar Dam. After soothing our muscles in the hot springs, we caravanned back to Eugene.

I don't think I have ever felt more confident or more at peace with my place in the world than I did after that seven-day backpacking adventure. I slept like a baby on the mattress on the floor of my bedroom that night. The next day I ventured back to campus and learned of a new secretary in the department chair's suite. I didn't waste time before I moseyed over to the office. The attractive young woman sitting behind the reception desk blew me away. I ambled over, perched myself on the front edge of the desk, and announced, "I came to meet the new secretary." I honestly believe it was love at first sight.

After several minutes of chatting, I suggested a picnic lunch by the Willamette River near campus. I was smitten. Her name was Sharon O'Neal. (To avoid confusion, I will henceforth refer to her as Neala, the name she adopted 30 years later.) Virtually all the women I dated to that point were non-Jews, so the name O'Neal didn't dissuade me.

As we got to know each other over lunch by the river, Neala shared that she moved from California's Bay Area to Eugene just a few weeks earlier and was attending church at the Faith Center. She said she had become a "new-born" Christian, and she was taking a break from dating for the foreseeable future. I said, "That's OK—let's be friends." That put us both at ease. We continued our idyllic lunch by the river and walked back to the office, chatting along the way.

This Is Not a Date

The next chain of events included an adventure and an invitation. First came the invitation. After a week or two interacting on campus, it was clear to me that we liked each other, so I decided to move our friendship along by inviting Neala to dinner at my house. I said, "This is not a date—just dinner and a chance to see where I live." She hesitated, then said, "OK." I excitedly drew a map to where I lived and as we parted, I said, "See you at 6pm."

This gave me just enough time to pick up some furniture on the way home. Bruce and I hadn't lived in our duplex apartment very long, and it still lacked a living room couch. I quickly combed the classifieds in the local newspaper and found an ad for a loveseat and chair combination—perfect! I made it home in time to prepare chili for dinner—my specialty. The evening was full of laughter and warmth. As we sat on my new couch facing the fire in the fireplace, a gentle first kiss turned our friendship into something more.

Our first adventure happened a short time later. At the end of a workday, I decided to introduce Neala to my raft. I offered a two-hour trip on the Willamette River. I thought we would have just enough time before an 8pm sunset. The trip began at a boat ramp near downtown Springfield and continued for about seven miles to a take-out point near the University of Oregon campus. Unfortunately, I miscalculated both the time and the weather. As we neared Eugene, darkness hid the small waterfall, known as Millrace Dam, that I knew was just ahead.

Neala and I have different recollections of what happened next. She remembers us going over the dam without capsizing, and I remember managing to get over to the right side of the river in time to float past the hazard. Either way, we made it into the current below— in the rain with very little light. These conditions prompted us to high-tail it for the shoreline, still upstream from the designated take-out spot.

As we pulled the boat from the water, we confronted a steep, slippery embankment. I remember pushing Neala from behind, as we struggled for footing on the slick terrain with the raft somehow hoisted over our heads. By the time we retrieved our car and loaded the boat, it was dark and still raining. Neala impressed me with her great attitude as we laughed and chalked up the trip as an exciting adventure.

Courting Neala

When I think of all the things that happened during my second academic year in the Ph.D. Program, it makes my head spin. Neala and I spent every minute we could together. She joined Bruce, Sunshine, and me jogging on Pre's Trail. We went camping in the mountains and at the coast. And we enjoyed the hot springs I had discovered near the McKenzie River and Cougar Dam.

We took up cross-country skiing in the winter, and Neala outpaced me. We enjoyed the rhododendrons at Hendricks Park in the spring, and hiking to the tops of Skinner's and Spencer's Buttes in various seasons and weather conditions. One night we even good-naturedly endured miserable conditions with just our sleeping bags—in the rain from dusk to dawn at the top of Spencer's Butte. The next morning, Neala pointed out that I huddled against her downwind side throughout the night—so much for my masculine image!

After binging on spaghetti the night before—in accord with the conventional wisdom of the day—we enjoyed competing with a thousand or so runners early in the life of the annual "Butte to Butte." The first Butte to Butte was in 1974, and the race didn't require a police escort until 1977. Today, nearly 5,000 participants compete. Neala still has her Butte-to-Butte T-shirt, and I remain proud to have maintained a seven-minute-mile pace over the 10,000-meter course.

Early in our relationship, Sunshine and I introduced Neala to Hobbit Beach, which I had discovered during my first academic year. At this stage in its history, Hobbit Beach was an unmarked well-kept secret that only the most tuned-in locals knew about. To find it, you had to know to look for the camouflaged trailhead near highway 101 milepost 177 just north of Heceta Head. From there, the trail winds through a dense fern-filled canopied forest. The canopies are so low that hikers have to duck to get under them. It's as if hobbits built the trail. After a half-mile of walking, a beautiful view of the ocean and beach opened up. On our first trip to Hobbit Beach, we camped on a forested cliff overlooking the beach, and we played in the ocean waves the next day.

The one-hour drive from Eugene to the coast passes a quaint restaurant where we always stopped for warm gingerbread and ice cream. Today, the restaurant goes by the name, Old World Gingerbread Village, but it was established in 1966 as The Gingerbread House, which is the name by which we knew it. It's part of the magic of the Hobbit Beach experience.

We also enjoyed the charming town of Yachats and its quaint "Pie and Kite" shop, only 12 miles north of Hobbit Beach. I remember one of our many visits to Yachats when we stayed in a peaceful beachfront cabin. There were several cabins, and the proprietor sat in a small office receiving guests and managing the property. The proprietor grew fond of us and entrusted me with tending the office whenever she had to run an errand. We briefly considered moving to Yachats. When choosing a path, I didn't *always* take the road less traveled.

With her roommate Diane, Neala rented a big house on West 31st Avenue, which served as a gathering place for the many friends we made in the university and religious communities. Diane and Neala were the perfect hostesses. Diane introduced us to the Oregon Shakespeare Festival, which we attended for the first time in spring 1978 in the enchanting town of Ashland.

Before seeing them, we read the plays out loud with each of us assuming different roles. I remember seeing the *Taming of the Shrew* at the festival's Elizabethan Theater. For accommodations that year, we chose campsites and set up a small tent city, where Neala and I had heart-to-heart connections with Bruce and Tam, Diane, Diane's friends, Rich and Judy, and Diane's brother and sister-in-law, Dave and Marci. I thrived in this rich cornucopia of community—academic, Jewish, Christian, Diane circle, and Bruce's circle.

Part IV: Launchpads

Chapter 24

Existential Leaps

Becoming an Accounting Professor

During my years in Eugene, I made two existential leaps—one that launched my academic career and another that launched my family life. While Neala and I enjoyed an active social life, I was hitting my stride in the doctoral program. My classes now consisted entirely of graduate seminars. During the 1977-78 academic year—my second in the program—I passed comprehensive exams in econometrics and finance. Then, I focused my attention on my dissertation, as well as research with one of my professors.

I wanted my research to mean something besides fulfilling the degree requirements. I decided to explore whether corporate social responsibility, especially environmental stewardship, held value in the eyes of investors. When I attended classes as an undergraduate student at the University of Illinois, I thought my accounting professors were the biggest nerds on the planet. Now I signed up to become one of them. To motivate this leap, it helped to embrace the notion of joining an accounting revolution—one that promised to transform a once stodgy discipline with preachy professors into a vibrant empirical social science—a legitimate branch of economics.

Do Investors Act Like They Care?

I was lucky that the only scientific study related to corporate social responsibility appearing in a major accounting journal was authored by Barry Spicer, and he joined the Oregon faculty as an untenured assistant professor shortly after I arrived. Barry earned his Ph.D. at the University of Washington in 1976 and was on the University of Arizona faculty for a year before coming to Oregon. I took his spring 1978 cost accounting doctoral seminar and earned an A+. I guess we were hitting it off.

I told Barry about an idea I had for a paper. I suggested posing the question: Do investors care about whether a company is socially responsible? This event study would be scientific, as it would test the null hypothesis that investors do not care. Evidence that stock prices increase with news of good pollution control performance and decrease with news of poor pollution control performance would lead us to reject the null hypothesis in favor of the alternative hypothesis that investors do care.

Barry listened and then pointed to five boxes sitting on the top shelf of his office bookcase. He threw them up there when he arrived from Arizona. He told me that the boxes contained notes and documents related to a similar study he had proposed at Arizona. Due to preoccupation with his move to Oregon, as well as his research interests shifting toward management accounting issues, he hadn't gotten around to designing or conducting the environmental performance study. We moved the boxes into my office.

I took it upon myself to comb through Barry's notes, develop a research design, and report the results of tests of our null hypothesis that investors do not care. By this time in the program, I had acquired the computer programming skills, as well as the understanding of the theory of finance and statistics, needed to conduct this study.

The results of our empirical tests showed that firms' stock prices move in the direction of news from the Council on Economic Priorities of the firms' good and bad performance in protecting the environment. On average, the market reacted positively to good news and negatively to bad news, and we found economically and statistically significant differences between the reactions. Thus, information about a firm's environmental performance affects the value of the firm as perceived by investors, suggesting that investors *do care* about a firm's social responsibility.

Barry took the lead in writing the paper, and we published it in *The Accounting Review* in 1983. I didn't realize the magnitude of this accomplishment until much later, when I learned about the rarity with which accounting doctoral students publish in top journals over the course of their careers. I'm gratified and humbled to know that our study—now cited by more than 900 subsequent papers—has helped open doors for further empirical research investigating the role of accounting information in promoting corporate social responsibility.

A Sacred Bridge

As my academic identity solidified, I faced challenges to my cultural and spiritual identities. My second existential leap involved the realization that the long-term potential for my relationship with Neala depended on confronting my feelings about Christianity. I grew up with the notion that Jesus, the symbol of Christianity, was the enemy, and I dared not set foot in a church— just seeing a church from the outside gave me the creeps. Until I met Neala, if I wanted to walk to or from campus on the block where the Faith Center was located, I avoided the perpetual stream of Bible-carrying devotees by walking on the other side of the street.

The Faith Center Community was becoming increasingly important to Neala, so I mustered the courage to attend some services. What better way to start than the day Neala chose to be baptized in front of the congregation. I decided to surprise her. As the service began, I sat in a pew near an outside door at the back of the church. I had a good view of the baptismal tank at the opposite end of a long runway.

While waiting for the baptism ceremony, I became quite uncomfortable as everyone around me joined the chorus in heartfelt worship with hands extended skyward to embrace the Holy Spirit and connect with God through Jesus. Intellectually, I understood the liturgy but experiencing it firsthand was too much at this stage of my spiritual development. I remembered my experience with psychedelic drugs in college, and thought to myself, "Either I am tripping or everyone else is."

Finally, the baptism ceremony began, and I saw Neala disappear into the water before emerging to join the singing with a most joyful look on her face. We had not yet spoken of marriage. After all, we were barely dating. However, as she joyously walked down the aisle in my direction, unaware of my presence, I had the strongest sensation that this woman in a dripping white gown was my bride. I thought, "How can that be?" as I made a quick dash for the exit. Unaware of its impact while growing up there, the atmosphere in Skokie left me with a complicated approach-avoidance attitude towards Judaism and deep discomfort with all things Christian.

I decided that if destiny were leading me to explore the Christian faith, I would at the same time reconnect with Judaism by engaging in local synagogue activities. I became a regular participant in Friday night and

Saturday morning Shabbat services, and I got to know the rabbi and his family. At one point, Neala and I received the honor of an invitation from the rabbi to join his family for a holiday dinner. I had confided in him that I was also attending services at Faith Center with Neala, and I was considering adopting the Christian faith. He was cool about this and did his best to expose me to a spiritual side of Judaism that I might have missed growing up.

The Forces Pulling Us Together

Falling in love with Neala has been and continues to be the greatest adventure of my life, with powerful forces pulling us apart and more powerful forces pulling us together. Our backgrounds and ancestry suggest that we have nothing in common. Neala was born in Dallas and raised mostly in Dumas, Texas, a small town in the Texas Panhandle.

As places to grow up, Dumas and Skokie have about as much in common as day and night. With about 65,000 people, Skokie has about five times the population of Dumas. Skokie is a suburb of Chicago, and Dumas is a rural Texas town. In the 2024 election, 28% of the people in the county where Skokie sits (Cook County) voted for Donald Trump, as compared to 83% of the people in the county where Dumas sits (Moore County). To see a fish out of water, move a Dumas native to Skokie or vice versa.

Neala traces her heritage to 17th century pioneers in twelve of the thirteen original American colonies. My ancestors arrived more than 200 years later. Neala is a product of the American melting pot with a strong dose of Scandinavian and Scottish origins, whereas I am the product of a much smaller insulated Jewish gene pool with Middle Eastern and East European origins. While

Neala's ancestors were busy colonizing America, my ancestors were living cloistered, persecuted lives in Europe. We have the same skin color, but I imagine her bloodline's skin color has darkened over the centuries, while my bloodline's skin has lightened, and we met in the middle as white Americans.

Neala had her introduction to religion in the Southern Baptist tradition, whereas my introduction had a Jewish fence. The only intersection in our heritage is that we each have some German ancestry, representing about 5% of Neala's bloodline and about 38% of my bloodline.

Neala's ancestors fought in the Revolutionary War creating the United States of America, as well as the Civil War that nearly destroyed the South in the process of saving the union. They fought on the side that won the Revolutionary War but on the side that lost the Civil War. My ancestors migrated to Illinois, a northern state, two generations following the civil war.

Faith Center pastors, one of them Jewish, advised Neala and me to carefully consider the challenges of "unequally yoked" partners in a relationship. The forces pulling us together were too powerful to heed this advice. We thoroughly enjoyed one another's company, and we shared a love of the vibrant environment and culture that drew each of us to Eugene from disparate places of origin. We had similarly free and pioneering spirits that created a powerful attraction. We were on paths toward self-discovery that came together with perfect timing. I was ripe with passion for starting a family. Furthermore, the magnetism that drew us together attracted friendships and community that we both enjoyed.

The academic and spiritual communities began to merge. Jerry Bowman, my strongest role model in the academic community, was also an integral part of the Faith Center community. Jerry is about 10 years older than Neala and me, and he had experienced much more of life. His journey to Eugene took him through tours of duty as a captain in the Navy, a manager in a CPA firm, and a Stanford University student in one of the world's most demanding and pioneering accounting doctoral programs. While a doctoral student, Jerry became increasingly counterculture in inclination and appearance.

When I first met him, Jerry had a beautiful head of long red hair hanging down to the shoulder blades of his athletic six-foot-two-inch frame. Jerry's boundless intellect and passion for truth inspired my enthusiasm for opening my mind to economics-based accounting research and opening my heart to an unbounded spiritual journey beyond the fence around Judaism.

Hosting An Accounting Revolutionary

It wasn't long before my ambitions adjusted to incorporate my twin passions for a new career connecting social responsibility with the revolution in accounting research and a loving marriage promoting tightly knit and deeply committed family life. However romantic, teaching at a community college—with its low salaries and no connection to academic accounting research—no longer held my interest. Instead, I threw my heart and soul into developing a meaningful dissertation idea and conscious spiritual life, while nurturing my relationship with Neala and connections in the academic community.

I began to realize that the accounting revolution was forging a close-knit community of young accounting scholars with greater loyalty to the scientific community than to the individual universities where they happened to teach. The accounting revolution was spreading from the University of Chicago, Stanford, and the University of Rochester to include research-oriented universities throughout the United States and ultimately throughout the world. We were like free agents—accounting revolutionaries—eager to learn about opportunities unfolding at a host of universities determined to develop the personnel and resources needed to participate in the accounting revolution. George Foster was one such accounting revolutionary.

With Bill Beaver as his mentor, Foster's first academic position was as an assistant professor at the University of Chicago. After earning tenure at Chicago, Beaver invited Foster to return to Stanford, and shortly thereafter George Foster came to Oregon to present a paper at our burgeoning accounting workshop series. Jerry Bowman and Larry Lookabill became good friends with George during their doctoral studies at Stanford, and the three of them shared Bill Beaver as their dissertation chair. Jerry and Larry wanted George to have a memorable experience connecting with Oregon's natural environment. They enlisted my services.

I played the role of raft guide, leading the way to the McKenzie River and the site of Marten's Rapids. Three Oregon faculty members, two doctoral students, and George Foster piled in with paddles and life jackets. I sat in the back with the long paddle. I put three paddlers on each side straddling the heavy-duty Hypalon chambers that formed and floated the raft. The four chambers, one on each side, one in the front, and one in the back had thin but strong rubber walls between them, so the raft would not sink if one chamber burst.

The chambers did their job. However, the trip provided almost too much excitement. When the boat dipped from its high point in the middle of one of the large waves comprising Marten's Rapids, George slipped from his perch into the water. When he was deep in the water, I reached out, grabbed his arm and, as his body began to rise with the next wave, I pulled as hard as I could and he flopped back into the boat. This deft move saved me years of embarrassment and spared the University of Oregon Accounting Doctoral Program unwanted notoriety. We breathed a collective sigh of relief. The near catastrophe reminded us of the responsibility we carried as accounting scholars and as stewards of each other's journeys in scholarship and life.

Visitors

During spring 1978, we welcomed visitors. First, Neala's mom, Trella, came to visit, and we immediately hit it off. She was so enthusiastic about our relationship that I worried it might drive Neala away. The last thing Neala wanted was to have an interest in a suitor her mom heartily supported.

Our next visitors were two of my closest friends from my fraternity: Bob and Morry. They came at a time when I was on the fence between pursuing spiritual growth on a Christian or Jewish path. Would I leap off the fence on the side of Christianity and a life with Neala, or would I go my own way in search of a Jewish partner? During Bob and Morry's visit, I thought hard about the ramifications of a Christian lifestyle for my relationships with Jewish friends and family. We had a great visit and, after they left, I made my decision.

Then, my mom and dad showed up. I thought we had a great time with them, but Neala felt a strong dose of what I can best describe as "shiksa phobia" coming from my mother—an anxious resistance to me marrying a gentile. Dad was relaxed and supportive. His only concern, which he expressed in just a few words, was whether I was taking on too much with a new home, new religion, new relationship, and new career. He still didn't understand why I left the Chicagoland community that had encouraged and supported him all his life.

I assured him that I was on a path right for me, and we never again spoke of such matters. We simply enjoyed the time we had together. Neala and I showed Mom and Dad the sights in Eugene, including a hike that ran out of gas at about the halfway point on the trail ascending to the top of Spencer's Butte.

Rogue River Revelation

Neala and I had many camping, hiking, Nordic skiing, and rafting adventures in the Cascade mountains and along the Oregon Coast. On one such occasion, we backpacked on a National Recreation Trail along a 40-mile stretch of the Rogue River, one of the eight rivers in a system of waterways designated for protection by Nixon's Wild and Scenic Rivers Act of 1968. As of today, Oregon has 59 rivers designated for protection, twice as many as Alaska, the next closest state.

In the Rogue River Canyon, we were with my roommate Bruce and his girlfriend Tamara. We thoroughly enjoyed hiking through some of Oregon's most pristine and wild countryside. Bruce kindly included a couple of bottles of fine wine in his 60-pound backpack, which we enjoyed drinking by the campfire after dinner each evening.

Sometime after I asked Neala to marry me, she told me that she had a premonition that surprised her while hiking ahead of me on the Rogue River Trail. The premonition—that we would someday be married—surprised her because she previously thought she would learn about Judaism from me, I would learn about Christianity from her, and we would move on with our individual lives. So much for my control over the situation!

Neala's premonition came to fruition on a fine spring day on May 10, 1978. I asked Neala to marry me while we were jogging stride for stride on Pre's Trail. While jogging, I said, "What would you say if I asked you to marry me?" To which she responded, "You'll have to ask to find out." I then managed, "Will you marry me?" Of course, she said "yes," and we kissed without breaking stride but almost breaking teeth. Without further ado, we celebrated with friends and began planning our wedding.

Christianity Is Jewish

Once committed, I devoted myself to participating with Neala in the full force of spiritual energy pouring from the Faith Center congregation. We prayed with pastors and fellow congregants, sang with the congregation at services, attended Bible studies, and nurtured spiritual relationships. I internalized the message that Jesus was a Jewish revolutionary who came to challenge hypocrisy among Jewish leaders, and to encourage all Jews to enjoy personal, heartfelt relationships with God.

I was so sure of the path I had chosen that I sent my closest friends and relatives, including my parents and siblings, the book *Christianity Is Jewish*. The author, Edith Shaeffer, makes a strong case for Jews to embrace Christian teachings just as Christians have embraced Jewish teachings. These Jewish friends and relatives graced us with their presence at our wedding, but none of them mentioned the book I sent, nor did they ever broach the subject of my choice to follow a Christian path with a Jewish foundation. They gave me love without judgment, but also without understanding why anyone would choose to dilute their Jewish lineage.

Under the Chuppah

We created our own wedding and enlisted Ken Klein, the Faith Center's Jewish pastor, to marry us. The ceremony on August 31, 1978 took place under a traditional Jewish chuppah, a canopy with four poles symbolizing our home together. Rather than resting them on the floor, four men held the poles and raised the canopy above our heads. The men who so honored us included my cousin, Steve, and my friends, Bob, Morry, and Keith. My brother Rick was best man, my sister Linda sang a song, as did Neala's sister PJ. My brother David ushered guests to their seats.

Our wedding went off without a hitch, with the vows we made to one another as the centerpiece. Neala promised to be a lovingly supportive, encouraging, and trusting wife, and I promised to be a protective and loving husband. I promised to walk with Neala on a spiritual path with Jesus as the bridge on which the purest of Christian and Jewish teachings come together and on which we were already experiencing God's sustaining love and mercy. Neala promised to support me through all the seasons of our lives. The music during the ceremony included *Morning has Broken* by Cat Stevens, and *Amazing Grace*, sung by PJ. After the wedding, a good time was had by all at the reception, an ice cream social in the church basement. After the celebration, Neala and I departed for a honeymoon that began in the Cascades and culminated at the coast three weeks later.

Chapter 25

Honeymoon Diaries

Paul or Paula?

Our honeymoon began with a stop for the night at a small lodge with a few cabins on the McKenzie River—near the unincorporated town of Blue River in the Willamette National Forest. When we checked in at the lodge, the proprietor wanted to socialize before we retreated to our cabin. He told us about his career in high-level administration of a large food chain headquartered in Southern California, and he told us that he and his partner had recently retired to Oregon.

Neala immediately picked up on his sexual orientation and his interest in me. I was oblivious. The three of us sat down at a table in the lobby and, after picking up on an antisemitic remark, Neala revealed my Jewish heritage. Our host then gave Neala's hand a hard slap. Later, Neala explained that this was our host reprimanding her for embarrassing him in front of me.

I missed another cue when "Monkey," the muscular sidekick-caretaker showed up with refreshments. Neala later explained that "Monkey" was the host's partner, and they had a romantic relationship. I said, "How do you know that?" Neala responded, "Didn't you hear him refer to his romantic partner as Paul? Monkey's real name is Paul." I said, "Oh… I thought the partner was someone else entirely—named Paula." Neala assured me that I had subconsciously changed the name to Paula in order to avoid my discomfort with a gay man's attraction to me. I learned something new that evening and, when talking to Neala, I have had many such revelations over the years.

Near Death Experiences

The next stop on our honeymoon was a camping trip into the Three Sisters Wilderness with the goal of ascending to the peak of the Middle Sister, 10,000 feet above sea level. This would not be easy, as it involved 4,500 feet in elevation gain from the base camp. We had perfect weather conditions when we started the ascent.

As we approached the Hayden Glacier, about halfway to the mountaintop, we encountered a snowstorm and "white-out" that shrank our field of vision to less than three feet ahead. We hunkered down behind some boulders and huddled against each other, while worrying that we might freeze to death before conceiving children. Eventually, the storm passed, the snow lifted, and we made it safely back to camp.

Next stop on our honeymoon was to cash in on a wedding present—a three-night stay at the Sunriver Resort southwest of Bend in the Deschutes National Forest. After a relaxing few days, we headed for Hells Canyon on the Snake River along the border of Oregon and Idaho. We drove to a spot on the river downstream from the canyon, and we hired a speedboat to take us upstream to a secluded section of the river deep in the canyon.

We found ourselves in an idyllic setting with canyon walls on either side of the river, and a lovely small beach just above a narrowing where waves crashed around boulders piled up in the middle of the river. At this point, the speedboat turned around, and the captain said he would return to pick us up at the end of the day.

We had two near-death experiences at this low point in the deepest canyon in North America. First, I decided to try shimmying up a slit in the canyon's rock wall overlooking the river. I thought I might be able to climb to the top of the canyon, which Neala later informed me was ridiculous. Hells Canyon is much deeper than the Grand Canyon, and it would take at least four hours to climb the nearly 8,000 feet from the riverbank to the canyon rim. As it was, while shimmying up the crevice in the rock wall, I dislodged a rock that nearly killed Neala. The rock bounced down the canyon wall and came within an inch of Neala's head about 100 feet below.

The second near-death experience in Hells Canyon occurred when I decided to cool off with a refreshing swim in the river. I had no life jacket and swam away from shore until a current caught me. The current prevented me from swimming back to shore no matter how hard I tried. Instead, it was pulling me into the river's main channel which was powerfully rushing toward rapids flowing over the large pile of boulders.

My only chance to avoid crashing into the rocks was to let the current take me past the beach and—before reaching the rapids—swim as hard as I could toward another rock wall that plunged directly into the river. When I reached the wall, I managed to grab one of the protruding rocks and pull myself out of the water. I had to climb high and out of sight before angling back to the beach where Neala was waiting. I'm not sure whether witnessing these events increased Neala's confidence in me—or made her question my survival instincts—but they bonded us just the same.

Roosters

After our honeymoon, we moved into our first home together. Neala decided that she had gained too much weight on the honeymoon, so we fasted. We had nothing but water for the first two or three days, and then added all the juice we could drink for the remainder of the nine-day fast. Quite the relationship-building experience for the start of a marriage! The home we rented gave us the opportunity to try out country living. It was a trailer in Marcola, Oregon, about 17 miles from the University of Oregon campus. The trailer sat on two acres of property, covered with tall weeds that I mowed with a push mower. The trailer was small. It had a bedroom with just enough room for a bed and two nightstands, and a tiny bathroom, kitchen, and living room. The grounds came with a pen housing about six hens. The hens pecked at me when I tried collecting the eggs from their nest, and eventually I said, "have it your way; let's see what happens when they hatch."

The chicks were cute at first, but this experiment didn't end well. Before long, six of the chickens became roosters who created a lot of ruckus. Luckily, we had gotten to know Pastor Minski at the local Pentecostal Church, and he saved the day. He came over and wrung the roosters' necks. Then, he took them home and made chicken soup. Pastor Minski bounced around his pulpit like Jiminy Cricket, fully inhabited by the Holy Spirit. He was a sight to behold!

Portland Marathon

While living in Marcola during the fall of 1978, Bruce and I decided to train for the Portland Marathon, scheduled for November 25. Once we hit our stride, we were running 50 miles per week, including at least one long run. On a couple of occasions, we ran the 17 miles from the University of Oregon campus to the trailer where Neala and I lived. Exhilarating!

Finally, the day of the marathon arrived, and we drove to Portland. With Neala and Tamara cheering us on, Bruce and I began the race in a sea of about 1,200 runners. I remember feeling great until the halfway point when my knee started throbbing. I gutted out the next seven miles thinking mostly about the pain in my knee.

I was thrilled when Neala snuck under the ropes and joined me at the 20th mile. We ran together for a couple of miles, and just like that, I forgot all about my knee. Neala gave me a second wind. I pulled away and finished strong with a time of four hours over the 26.2-mile course, which breaks down to nine-minute, ten-second miles, close to my goal of running a nine-minute pace—a personally satisfying performance in my one and only marathon.

Chapter 26
Creative Energy

During the fall quarter of 1978, I passed the accounting comprehensive exam, and Neala helped me celebrate with a 24-can case of black olives, one of my favorite foods. After passing the exam, I began developing my dissertation idea [72].

Dissertation Research

Building on the philosophy of John Rawls, I developed the notion that firms have implied contracts holding them accountable for the internalization of costs that their operations impose upon society. Results of my empirical tests were consistent with the inferences that: (1) investors recognize firms' obligations to mitigate externalities; and (2) investor perceptions of the value of the firm depend on the firm's performance in fulfilling such obligations.

I submitted my dissertation paper to *The Accounting Review* and received excellent reviews from three referees. In perhaps the worst case of "dropping the ball" in my career, I obsessed about the reviews. By the time I submitted my response, the journal's editorship had changed, and the new editor rejected the paper on the grounds that it didn't have enough to do with accounting. Eventually, I published the paper in a strong second-tier journal—the *Journal of Accounting, Auditing, and Finance*—but not until 1995. The paper has not received nearly the attention received by the Shane and Spicer paper.

Brother David

David turned 13 on December 26, 1978. Soon afterwards we traveled to Chicago to attend his bar mitzvah. The gala affair gathered the Shane and Herr families and friends. During the celebration, I made a toast, and Neala and I lit a candle, showing our support and best wishes for David, as he embraced his path toward adulthood.

David was quarterback of his high school football team, and he also had a passion for hockey. He married his middle-school sweetheart, Stacy. He enjoyed four fun years of college at Indiana University, where he majored in finance. At Indiana, David also excelled in the *Little 500*, a 200-lap bicycle race around a quarter-mile track at the school's soccer field. One of my all-time favorite sports movies, *Breaking Away*, tells the story of this iconic race.

After college, David initially worked in financial services and then pursued a career in public accounting. He rose to the level of managing audit partner for the Great Lakes Region of one of the world's five largest CPA firms, McGladrey. He then moved back to financial services, facilitating mergers, acquisitions, and initial public offerings (IPOs) within the industry.

David and Stacy have three lovely daughters. An active family and work life has not detracted from David's athletic pursuits. For many years after college, he played organized hockey, and at age 59, he still competes in triathlons and marathons. He has run in the Boston and Chicago Marathons multiple times, and he recently completed a bike race in Italy. To put this in perspective, my Portland Marathon time at age 30 was four hours, whereas David completed the Boston Marathon in three hours and fourteen minutes at age 44. Ironman triathlons require athletes to run a 26.2-

mile marathon, bike 112 miles, and swim 2.4 miles. At 56 years old, David completed the Arizona Ironman in just under twelve hours. Amazing! I consider myself a good athlete, but I'm not in a class with my brothers, Rick and David, who are great athletes.

Grandmother-in-law Máma

Neala and I conceived our first child on or about November 17, 1978. I was going to be a father! Of course, we didn't learn of this event until the new year when we realized that Neala had missed her December period. At that point, we began preparing for the new arrival. Neala's grandmother Máma came to help. I immediately liked Máma. She was fun to have around and overlooked my shortcomings.

One rainy night, as Neala, Máma, and I drove to the Coburg Inn for dinner, I intermittently stuck my arm out Phaedrus' side window with a squeegee. I explained that the windshield wipers didn't work, and Máma just laughed. When she noticed that I was not in the habit of shining my shoes, she discreetly mentioned to Neala that she'd gladly shine them for me. I heard from Neala that Máma was secretly horrified by the hair that I was sure I had extracted from the tub after giving Sunshine a bath. Our fondness for one another grew over the years, and I genuinely enjoyed the times Máma lived with us.

Jake Joins the Family

We knew we couldn't raise our first child in a tiny trailer, so we made plans to move from Marcola back to Eugene. The Marcola trailer had been home to some interesting activity. Between raising chickens, gathering eggs, mowing two acres of weeds with a push mower, attending Pastor Minski's Pentecostal Church, and running the 17 miles home from campus, we also dealt with frozen pipes in winter—and could entertain no more than two guests at a time in better weather.

Jerry Bowman was our final guest before the exodus. In early April, he joined Neala and me for a blended Easter-Passover celebration. This would be the first of many times over the years that we celebrated both holidays by marrying the rich tradition of Passover (known in Hebrew as Pesach) with the spirit of Easter. After all, Jesus' "Last Supper" was a Passover celebration.

From Marcola, we moved into student housing near campus, and we prepared our new home for the arrival of our first child. Neala was sure it would be a boy. In a dream even before she knew she was pregnant, Neala heard the name, Jacob, a name she wrestled with—much like the biblical Jacob wrestling the angel. We had no idea what—or whom—our Jacob might "supplant," but we trusted his best efforts would meet with success and that God would watch over him.

Once Jacob was born—at 7am on August 17, 1979—we both knew the name suited him perfectly. During Neala's pregnancy, we also enhanced our already-healthy lifestyle by emphasizing vegetables, avoiding alcohol, and swimming. I could not compete with Neala's swimming buoyancy. I boiled soybeans and separated the curd from the whey to make our own tofu, while Neala visited the nearby McDonalds to satisfy her craving for animal protein. Life felt full and joyful—we were hopeful, healthy, and ready for whatever lay ahead.

Chapter 27
Life, Loss, and Legacy

During the fall 1978 and winter 1979 quarters, I developed my dissertation idea for presentation to recruiters—in Hawaii at the Annual Meetings of the American Accounting Association (AAA) to begin on August 22—assuming our first child didn't arrive too many days beyond the August 10 due date. The prospects of spending several days at a convention in the vicinity of Waikiki Beach never seemed so uninviting. Nothing would stop me from supporting Neala and witnessing the birth of our first child.

We functioned as a team every step and every breath of the way. We attended Lamaze classes and enjoyed the camaraderie with other pregnant couples. I did not, however, enjoy one brutal exercise. The father had to pinch an especially vulnerable part of his partner's anatomy—just below the ear at the top of the shoulder—while both the father and expectant mother focused on in-and-out breaths. Neala got to the point where she could do this without feeling the pinch, but she needed to be looking me in the eye as we breathed—a brutal bonding experience!

Gut Punch

We were enjoying the beginning of Neala's second trimester—beyond months of morning sickness—when we received a phone call with terrible news. At the other end of the phone, a voice—probably my mom's— told me that my father had undergone tests that came back positive for pancreatic cancer. I felt a *gut punch* like nothing before, as I contemplated how to simultaneously hold space for the joy of the pending arrival of my first child and the sadness of saying goodbye to my father.

Dad had just celebrated his 52nd birthday and was the pillar of strength in the family. Linda tells the story of a cold Chicago winter day with snow blowing everywhere when her car got stuck. When she tried to move the car, the back wheels spun deeper and deeper ruts in the snow. She called Dad, and he was there in minutes. He told her to get in and with super strength he lifted the back end of the car while pushing it out of the rut. I remember times when everyone in the family was sick except Dad, and he would say "I never get sick." He was invincible!

Still fighting her depression, my mother was dazed and unable to support my father in his time of need. In fact, she made things worse with demands for Dad's attention to *her* needs. With Neala's encouragement, I offered to come in for the month of June. Mom might calm down with me there, and I knew I could help Dad with his client load. He accepted my offer to help. By the time I got to town, he had lost a lot of weight and was obviously suffering. I accompanied him on visits to clients' offices, helping wherever I could but mostly providing moral support. He was not good at expressing feelings, but I felt close to him during this time, and I believe the feelings were mutual.

I was sick with grief when I returned to Eugene. I received pressure from some Christian acquaintances to talk with my dad about Jesus. I know they meant well, but their insistence pushed me over the edge, and I just sobbed (privately). I felt that they cared more about proselytizing than they cared about my father—or my relationship with him—and I stewed with resentment.

Before his cancer diagnosis, I had sent Dad a letter explaining my spiritual journey and Christian experience—a letter he never acknowledged and I regretted sending. My father was the best person I've known. He most generously took care of everyone— his wife, parents, children, partners, and clients. If he didn't receive a royal welcome to the kingdom of heaven, I don't know who would.

With the joy of a child on the way and needing to support my wife, I could not wallow in grief. Dad didn't want that. He had the attitude of a fighter—determined to beat the disease. None of us—including my dad— knew how to talk about the prognosis. We were all in denial.

Jake Arrives!

To help prepare for the new arrival, Trella joined us in early August. Lamaze birthing classes were in full swing and Neala and I eagerly anticipated greeting our first child. Would it be a girl or a boy? We were on the edge of our seats to find out. Our son Jacob Brian Shane arrived late. After more than 12 hours of labor, with the help of a midwife, a pediatrician, and our breathing prowess, he was born naturally at 6:43am on August 17. As my father's life was slipping away, a grandson arrived to carry on the Shane family name.

Dr. Jacobs cut the umbilical cord and examined little Jacob. We all breathed a sigh of relief when his skin turned from blue to a healthier color. Then, Dr. Jacobs handed my son to me, and I in turn delivered him to his mother's yearning embrace. At thirty years of age, I was a father!

Just a few days after we settled in at home, I boarded a plane and headed for job interviews in Hawaii, Trella departed for her home in San Francisco, and my mother came from Chicago to "help" Neala. This created a lot of stress, as Lois was more interested in getting Neala out shopping than she was in providing much help with the baby or the house. I remember nothing about my job interviews and nothing about being in Hawaii, as my mind was elsewhere. I was anxious to return home.

While carrying the weight of my father's sickness, I was at the same time the happiest I had ever been, thoroughly enjoying the family that Neala and I had created. The University of Oregon campus grounds were a short walk from our house, and while we were still having nice fall weather, Neala would put Jacob in the stroller, and they would meet me for picnic lunches. How moving it was to see my family walking toward me in these idyllic surroundings.

Saying Goodbye

We traveled to Chicago as a family in September of 1979 for Rick's wedding. Rick, the class president and star athlete, married his high school sweetheart, Karen Rice, a popular cheerleader. They planned to move to Albuquerque, where Rick ultimately would launch a career as a budding district attorney. Rick became the second member of the family to marry a woman demeaningly referred to in the Jewish community as a "shiksa."

Having dated Rick since they were youngsters, Karen felt the full force of my mother's dismay. I'm sure this provided much of the impetus for Rick and Karen's decision to leave Chicago, and it didn't hurt that Rick and especially Karen worshipped the sun. Albuquerque was the right distance from Chicago and their new home came with plenty of sunshine. After he graduated from high school, Rick and I became quite close, and the challenges faced in bringing gentile women into the family only brought us closer. Neala and Karen connected well, too, as they commiserated about my mother's condescending attitude.

In December, it became clear that my father's health was rapidly deteriorating. Neala and I made a momentous decision. With my dad at death's door, we decided we would move to Chicago temporarily to help my mother. We planned the move for immediately after Christmas, and our friends, led by Jerry Bowman, offered to pack up our belongings and transfer them to storage.

I told Jerry and the rest of the faculty that I would continue working on my dissertation in Chicago and I would send them a complete proposal soon. They could then advise me about whether to stay in the program for an extra year or accept invitations to interview for faculty positions at other universities.

When we arrived in Chicago, I found my dad mostly incoherent and still visiting his clients' offices. I went with him, as he managed to go through the motions for a few more days. Dad loved his work. During his final week on this earth, I heard him tell my mother, "Don't worry, Lo, there must be an important job waiting for me upstairs." He spent his final few days with his adoring family around him. He loved watching his four-month-old grandson, Jacob, bounce up and down in the Johnny Jumper that we hung from the doorframe leading from the den to the utility room.

Dad died on January 4, 1980. Thankfully, Rick was with him in the hospital room when he breathed his last. I was in the hallway taking care of our mother. I regret that only Rick was in the room. Dad should have been surrounded by his wife and all of his loving children. I should have been with him. His untimely death attracted throngs of mourners, who crammed the synagogue and the funeral procession to Shalom

Memorial Cemetery. There, we laid him to rest next to the plots reserved for his mother and father. A child is not supposed to die before their parents. Grandpa Mort and Grandma Selma were devastated, as were Aunt Sermata and Aunt Ila.

For a week, we sat shiva at the Skokie home on Kilbourn Avenue where I lived during my teenage years, where Mom, David, and Linda still lived, and where Neala and I were living temporarily. Rick and Karen were living on their own in Chicago, where Rick had recently finished law school. Rick was studying for the bar exam, and I was writing a dissertation proposal. We put it all on hold, while Rick took care of legal matters associated with Dad's death and while I took care of loose ends at Dad's office. Rick and Karen delayed plans to move to Albuquerque until May.

Together, Rick and I made sure that bills were paid and that Mom got everything left over, which wasn't a lot. Dad had set up a trust to ensure David would have enough money to get through college when the time came. Dad knew Mom would spend any money not tied up in a trust designated for David as the beneficiary. I always felt it unfair that my parents didn't encourage Linda to go to college, and I remember telling them so, without effect. This was a serious oversight on their part, one that my siblings and I didn't repeat. My daughter and five of my nieces have college degrees. My sixth niece is working on her degree at the University of Illinois as I write this.

Dad's death was hard on David, who was only 14 at the time. I felt horrible for abandoning him and Linda. The insufferable abuse associated with Mom's relentless struggles drove Linda to realize that she had become the parent of both Mom and David. The longer she stayed the worse it got for David witnessing the craziness of Mom berating Linda for not catering to her obsessions. Mom became more removed from David and more dependent on Linda. Finally, Linda did the only thing she could. She moved out hoping the environment would become less toxic. She hoped Mom would become the responsible parent that David needed. She had done all she could and was beyond her capacity to help Mom or stabilize life for David.

I doubt that we'll ever know the impact of Mom's struggles on David once we all departed. He lost the most important person in his life, his mother was out of control, and it would have been reasonable from his perspective to feel abandoned by his three siblings. While abandoning David was never our intention, we were busy living our own lives without the capacity for the intervention that David surely needed.

Rick and Karen needed to get away in order to have a chance at happiness. I had already departed and could not return with a five-month-old child and nursing mother. My marriage to Neala would not have survived close proximity to Lois. None of this made it any easier to leave Linda and David with the burden of a mother in poor mental and emotional health. Of course, Rick and I provided support from a distance, but it wasn't the same as being there. David takes after our dad, rarely expressing feelings, and I have not been able to talk with him about the repercussions of Dad's premature death. One of my biggest regrets in life is the awkwardness in my relationship with David stemming— I believe—from the impact of my father's early demise on our family dynamics.

Dad's death deeply affected us all. I had recurring dreams about watching Dad's profile turn into mine on an operating table. Then, I'd see my skull explode from the pressure of too much responsibility and stress. If my dad—the invincible savior—couldn't live past 52, how could I? In the back of my mind sat the fear that I would meet the same fate—dying in my fifties before experiencing the fullness of a life well-lived. On the flip side, I lived with a strong sense of Dad's presence—inspiring a legacy of integrity, loyalty, generosity, joy, and unconditional love of family.

Chapter 28
Family Road Show

Seeking Employment

Once Dad's affairs were settled, Rick and I turned our attention toward launching our respective careers. Rick continued studying for the bar exam, and I worked on my dissertation proposal. Universities so eagerly wanted to hire accounting faculty trained in modern scientific research methods—accounting revolutionaries—that I needed only a defended proposal to apply. Moreover, universities commonly hired accounting professors with incomplete dissertations, with the stipulation that they earn their Ph.Ds. and demonstrate strong research and teaching before the six-year tenure review.

I didn't have the time or money to fly back to Eugene before applying for jobs, so I completed the proposal in Skokie and sent it to the members of my committee, chaired by Barry Spicer. I then asked if I could defend the proposal by way of a conference call. This request had no precedent, and I have always appreciated the flexibility and support of the Oregon accounting faculty who granted my request.

We didn't have cell phones or video conferencing in 1980. Instead, Barry, Jerry, Larry, and other members of the committee sat around a conference table in Eugene with a landline conference phone sitting between them. My proposal defense succeeded in gaining the necessary permission, and I applied for assistant professor jobs at about ten universities.

I received invitations to interview at The University of Colorado, Penn State University, the University of North Carolina, the University of New Mexico, the

University of Arizona, and the University of Kansas. I didn't get invitations from Berkeley, Cornell, and one or two other universities. Now, Berkeley had rejected my applications three times—once for law school, once for accounting doctoral studies, and once for an accounting faculty position. This was getting old, but I knew it was a long shot, and I was grateful for the opportunities other schools presented. Years later—after developing a respectable research record—I broke the sound barrier, as the Berkeley accounting faculty invited me to present a paper at their weekly workshop series.

At this preliminary stage in my career, I needed a "road show"—a paper based on my dissertation proposal, adapted for presentation to faculty and doctoral students at university workshops. These workshops would be the centerpieces of my six campus interviews. Neala and Jacob, six months old and still nursing, accompanied me on the interview trail. The interview season was nearly over. To complete the interviews under the wire, we decided that we would do them in a single trip. I managed to schedule the interviews over a three-week period. Each interview took place over two or three days.

Upon arrival, a couple of faculty members would pick us up at the airport, get us settled at the designated hotel, and take us to a fancy restaurant for dinner. On the second day, I would make a 1½ hour presentation of my dissertation proposal, meet privately with every accounting faculty member, have a group meeting with the doctoral students, and meet with the dean. This day included another fancy evening dinner and a campus tour.

The third day generally involved a tour of the city with a realtor and departure. It was a grueling and exciting experience. When it was over, I received offers to join the faculty at five of the six schools. Only Arizona rejected me—despite faculty support—because I had, in their words, "rubbed the dean the wrong way." I never learned exactly how, but it served as a lesson that "fit" mattered as much as credentials.

Choosing between schools was not easy. My committee preferred North Carolina, which had the best resources for supporting the type of accounting research they had trained me to conduct. But North Carolina was not head and shoulders above Kansas and Penn State. I thought long and hard about university resources and family life in the community.

I believed Kansas offered a supportive work environment in a wholesome community. I was not ready to move to the South, and Penn State seemed too remote. Kansas felt more like home, albeit in a setting without mountains and wild rivers. Furthermore, while faculty at all three schools wined and dined us, we felt the most affinity for Kansas' Professor Larry Friedman and his wife Janet. We saw the potential for the four of us to become close friends and this sealed the deal for Kansas.

Leaving Oregon

Dean John Tollefson brought me on board as an assistant professor and promised a raise in an already sweet salary once I completed my degree. The initial $26,000 salary purchased as much then as $100,000 purchases today. I know this sounds like a lot, but it's nothing compared to the $250,000 starting salaries of assistant accounting professors at top tier public universities.

Salaries rose as accounting established itself as an academic discipline, and accounting firms increased their financial support of the nation's top accounting programs. While the job at Kansas was advertised to begin with the fall 1980 semester, Dean Tollefson granted me an extension—to January 1981—so I could make progress on my dissertation before facing the responsibilities of a new faculty member.

We returned to Eugene in April 1980, and moved into another student housing property at 1311 W. 8th Street. Neala, Sunshine, and I enjoyed introducing Jacob to all of our favorite Oregon attractions. We continued picnic lunches on campus, camped in the mountains, hiked on the trail to Hobbit Beach, and shopped at Eugene's iconic Saturday Market. During the month of April, we met cousins Steve, Pettra, Jeff, Joel, and Amy for fun at the Oregon Coast, and during the summer of 1980, we ventured beyond U.S. borders.

We visited friends in Vancouver, B.C. and then camped in Victoria on nearby Vancouver Island. Of course, Jacob also accompanied us to the many gatherings with our communities of friends from Faith Center and the university. Everyone loved Jacob, and life was good. Around this time, reflecting the love in our hearts, Neala experienced another "knowing:" we would soon have another son. And sure enough, about nine months later, Adam was born.

During fall 1980, Máma came to visit again, this time with plans to move with us to Kansas. My dissertation research was moving slowly, and my committee cautioned me that I would have a hard time convincing accounting journals that my research addressed an accounting issue. Nonetheless, the committee applauded my ambition for developing scientific evidence that might inspire regulation requiring greater transparency in reporting the environmental impact of corporate activity. While still in Eugene, I spent a lot of time thinking and reading about social contracts and corporate social responsibility (CSR). I also developed my computer programming skills and a solid understanding of econometrics.

We had no laptops or internet in those days. Running computer programs involved a laborious process of writing the program, transferring each step onto a separate punch card, delivering the deck to a computer technician in another campus building, waiting for the results, finding errors, and repeating the process until the program ran correctly. Only then could I analyze the results, which involved testing the study's null hypotheses in hopes of disproving them in favor of insightful alternative hypotheses. Failing to reject the null hypotheses meant repeating the whole process with new null and alternative hypotheses that might bring evidence to bear on the research question. I don't remember producing meaningful results at this stage, but I learned a lot about conducting empirical research.

Eventually, we needed to leave Eugene with my dissertation unfinished. On our way to Kansas, we stopped in the Bay Area where Trella lived with her partner, Rod. We pulled Phaedrus behind the U-Haul, Sunshine lay on a couch in the cargo area with our other furniture and belongings securely tied to the truck's walls, Máma sat in the passenger seat with Jacob strapped into a child seat on the floor at Máma's feet, and Neala at almost eight months pregnant sat between Máma and me while straddling the manual gear stick.

I couldn't believe my good fortune—less than five years earlier I had arrived in Oregon alone, carrying only a backpack and a dream of finding my way in the world. So much richer now, I was departing with a family, a job offer, and a strong sense of purpose. When we arrived at Trella and Rod's place in San Francisco, we received a royal welcome and Jacob received a little red wagon, which I pulled to his—and my—heart's delight. It felt as though I was pulling us into two journeys at once—one with me as a young father and the other with me as a newly minted faculty member—each promising adventures I could barely imagine.

Chapter 29
Acclimating

The Mohel at First Christian Church

Upon arriving in Lawrence, Kansas, we rented a townhouse on a month-to-month lease. I set up shop at the university in an office not much bigger than a closet and without windows. After about six months of renting, we found a house we could afford to buy—record-high mortgage interest rates of 17% limited our purchasing power.

We found a single-family home at 1603 W. 2nd Street, a not-too-busy street a couple of blocks from the bottom of the hill leading to campus. The three-bedroom home had an attached garage converted into a den with a drop-down ceiling. We used a small space heater to heat the den, and for light we used a couple of kerosene lamps. It was a start. If I had stayed with my job at Coopers & Lybrand, I might have been approaching promotion to partner with a big office in a fancy downtown Chicago building, and a salary that would have doubled my KU salary—but I had no regrets and never looked back.

Shortly after arriving in Lawrence, Máma encouraged Neala and me to take some time to enjoy ourselves. So, she watched Jacob while we headed out to get the lay of the land and have dinner at a local restaurant. When we sat down, we overheard a couple in the booth next to us talking about their campus ministry. We thought maybe they wouldn't mind getting acquainted, so we said hello and they invited us to join them. We hit it off immediately with Alan and Charlotte Rosenak. He was the campus minister, she was a psychology doctoral student, and we delighted in learning that he was Jewish.

One thing led to another and Alan agreed to fulfill the role of Mohel upon the birth of our second child, assuming a boy arrived two months hence. In those days, ultrasound technology was not prevalent, and doctors typically didn't give parents the option of learning the baby's sex before birth. The Mohel performs or presides over the traditional Jewish circumcision ceremony, offering prayers over the eight-day-old baby boy. This was a big deal to us. Two months later when our son, Adam, was eight days old, it was a big deal to him, too! Adam thrilled us with his arrival at 1:58pm on March 8, 1981. I liked having brothers, so I delighted in now having two sons who I hoped would bond as brothers.

Alan and Charlotte told us that they attended the First Christian Church, and that sounded good to us. Alan invited us to a talk he was giving at another local church. His talk encouraged congregants to participate in a program providing housing for international students while they waited for dorms to open. Alan pointed out that this program provided the opportunity to connect with foreign cultures without needing to travel. We liked this idea and signed up to participate. A Pakistani student stayed with us temporarily and became like a member of the family, visiting us from time to time over the years we lived in Kansas. We continued this practice with several more students from different universities over the years.

Elijah's Car and the Holy Spirit

We quickly became connected with the people and goings-on at the First Christian Church. Neala was a favorite of Pastor Ron Goodman, and I played racquetball with Ron's wife, Barb. I also enjoyed playing softball on the church team.

Every year, Neala and I conducted a Passover Seder that blended Jewish and Christian experience and theology. In Lawrence, it grew into a community event. One year we sat at a long table with about fifteen people, including our four-year-old son Jacob. We got to the point in the Seder of preparing the way for Elijah, who Malachi prophesied would come to announce the coming of the Messiah. To prepare the way, we readied our hearts, set the table with a glass of wine for Elijah, and sent Jacob to the front door, located in sight of the table where we sat in the living room. When Jacob returned to the table, we asked, "Did you see Elijah?" To which, he replied, "No, but his car is there!"

Around this time, Neala came to believe that the fullness of Christian experience required a deep personal relationship with the Holy Spirit. This made me a little nervous, so I audaciously decided to lead a Bible study on the topic. The ensuing rich blend of intellectual inquiry and spiritual exploration attracted a community of a dozen or so dedicated participants. About six months of weekly meetings brought Neala and me into deeper spiritual alignment—with the Holy Spirit opening our hearts and minds to a fuller embrace of God's love and creative energy.

Chapter 30
Polar Bear Shock

Adam emerged from the womb as an activist. He powered out with an extended arm and a tiny, fisted hand at the end of it. Neala wanted to name our new son, Micah. When she learned it would be a great blessing to Grandma Selma to name him after my dad, she graciously complied. We narrowed the names to Aaron or Adam, and when he appeared with a reddish tint to his skin, we knew he was Adam—meaning "man of the red earth [75]." The name connotes creative energy, and Adam has impressed us with creative intelligence throughout his life.

We wanted a rabbi's stamp of approval on Adam's Hebrew name, Avram, the same as both Grandpa Orv's and Orv's uncle—the former rabbi turned jeweler. I thought this would be a "big ask" considering our unconventional spiritual orientation. So, I decided to connect with Rabbi Neil Brief, the presiding rabbi at the Niles Township Jewish Congregation—where the Shane family had been members for the past 25 years and where my siblings and I had our Bar/Bat Mitzvahs. My letter to Rabbi Brief on June 27, 1981, laid out our spiritual journey and our desire for Jacob and Adam to have proper Hebrew names—Ya'acov for Jacob and Avram for Adam. Much to our delight, he agreed, and on our next trip to Chicago, we brought six-month-old Adam and two-year-old Jacob to meet him. Rabbi Brief graciously blessed both boys with their Hebrew names complete with certificates to commemorate the occasion. Thank you, Rabbi Brief!

Adam was born with strawberry birthmarks on his chest and forehead—where an angel kissed him—and a large hematoma on top of his head, which the delivery doctor diagnosed as a harmless hematoma that would either go away on its own or become part of his skull. The doctor said that either way, after about five years, it would not remain visible. Way ahead of schedule, the birthmarks and hematoma disappeared after about one month.

Adam learned early to withstand discomfort. Our pediatrician implored us to make him wear a brace designed to straighten both of his bowed legs. This was so tortuous to Adam and to us that, against doctor's orders, we discontinued the therapy. Adam's legs straightened anyway. He also battled night terrors—episodes so intense that we felt as frightened as he did. We disobeyed orders again—this time they were, "Lock him in his bedroom and let him cry it out." Instead, we held him—helplessly trying to console him—as he wailed at the top of his lungs night after night. Only Máma could calm him. Thank God for Máma!

I smile when I think about my relationship with Máma, who lived with us from time to time. We had lots of fun. Every night, once the kids were settled, Neala, Máma, and I would sit down at the kitchen table to play Scrabble. We kidded one another, laughed playfully, and when I won, Neala and Máma joined together in raucous disapproval. Neala says I always won. The kids loved Máma, as did we, and we were a happy family—supporting one another through challenges, while sharing daily episodes of hearty laughter and pure joy in the midst of loving and supportive community.

When Adam was about two-and-a-half years old, I decided to take him on a trip to Chicago—just the two of us. The trauma of night terrors and a leg brace were behind us, but I worried that post-traumatic stress hampered his development in other ways. Specifically, I wondered whether he should be saying more than just a few words by now. I thought some dedicated time together might help, so off we went, with me driving and Adam strapped in his car seat.

I remember three highlights from that trip. First, a simple ride in the front seat of the front car of the Chicago El gave us quite a thrill. I don't remember our destination, but I'll never forget the excitement on Adam's face as we rumbled above the streets of Chicago, mesmerized by sights from the giant window directly in front of us.

The second highlight involved a visit to Lincoln Park. We drove there from Skokie along Lake Shore Drive, parked the car, strolled through the park, found the zoo, and began exploring the exhibits. We walked down a ramp toward the polar bear exhibit. No one else was around. We approached the rail just three feet away from the thick Plexiglas wall separating us from the bear habitat. Suddenly, an agitated bear came charging toward us from the center of the enclosure. We instinctively backed away. The bear crashed into the Plexiglas, which bulged on impact. Hearing a crack, we jumped and hastened the pace of our backward shuffle. Well, the glass didn't *actually* crack—but our hearts were in our throats, nonetheless.

The third highlight was all the fun we had with Nana Lois, Aunt Linda, Uncle David, and the rest of the family, all eager to interact with Adam. I smile to think about how deeply bonded I felt with Adam on the drive home to Kansas. Playful chatter replaced worries about his vocabulary.

Chapter 31
Crash Course

In hindsight, I was on a crash course in establishing myself at work, at home, and in the community during the Kansas years.

Lauren Friedman

We became close friends with several members of the First Christian Church community, and at least one of the families associated with KU's Accounting Department, Dave and Lynne Smith and their two children, Rebecca and Ballard. We thought we'd be close friends with another university family—the Friedmans—but fate intervened in unexpected ways.

Larry Friedman led the recruiting effort that brought us to KU, and he helped unload our truck when we arrived in town. We played bridge with Larry and his wife Janet a few times, but then the relationship withered and we wondered why. Not much later, along with the rest of the business school faculty, we received a shocking memo—no email in those days—from Dean Tollefson announcing that Larry was leaving. The reasons he could not presently disclose, but he said, "You will later understand."

Months later we discovered that Larry had transitioned to Lauren, moved to San Francisco to work for a bank, and started a new life. Her rare distinction of publishing in *The Accounting Review* under both first names reflected not only academic excellence but personal courage—no small feat!

I'll Teach That!

Dave Smith and I hit it off as soon as I came on board. During my first semester (spring 1981), I was assigned to teach the first half of Intermediate Financial Accounting. It didn't go well, as I aimed too high by designing two major projects to elucidate the economics of financial reporting. Students and parents petitioned the dean to rein in the course requirements and shift the focus more practically toward CPA exam preparation. The dean had a talk with me but did not require any changes to the course requirements or my approach to engaging students. Nonetheless, end-of-semester teaching evaluations reflected substantial student frustration that I resolved to assuage without compromising my principles.

Once spring semester ended, the dean's curriculum committee assigned faculty to courses scheduled for the fall. Dave was assigned the introductory accounting course in a large lecture hall. He didn't want to teach that class, as he was more comfortable teaching smaller groups. I received the assignment to again teach intermediate accounting.

I came up with the brilliant idea for Dave and me to switch teaching assignments. Without informing the administration, we made the switch. The fall semester had barely started when the associate dean summoned Dave and me to his office. He admitted that the switch was a good idea, while imploring us to, "Never do such a thing again!" We never did.

Connecting with Students

I had a fantastic experience teaching the introduction to financial reporting course. One day, Neala surprised me by leaving Jacob with Máma and crashing my class with our infant son, Adam, in tow. They walked toward the front of the lecture hall, and I introduced my awestruck students to my newest son.

The course inspired many students to become accounting majors, and the students nominated me for a H.O.P.E. Award (Honor for Outstanding Progressive Educator). The award process involved a vote across the entire university student body narrowing the field of dozens of nominees to a manageable set of finalists. Then, a panel of alumni interviewed each finalist to determine the winner. In spring 1982, I didn't win, but I was one of the thirteen finalists interviewed.

I hired some of my best students as teaching assistants to help with the next iteration of the course (spring 1982). When these outstanding students reached the second half of intermediate accounting in spring 1984, they once again drew me as their instructor. The reunion was magical. I had perhaps my best teaching semester ever.

For the third year in a row, I attended the spring banquet for the Beta Gamma Sigma fraternity of the university's top business school students. This year, Neala accompanied me and we sat at a table with some of my former students. When the evening climaxed with the announcement of the Beta Gamma Sigma teacher of the year, everyone in the room including me expected Maurice Joy—a popular and highly regarded finance professor with an international reputation—to win.

Much to my amazement, the student presenting the award called *me* to the podium. In a dazed state of disbelief, I accepted the award. I had the capacity only to say, "Thank you." To make sure she attended, the students let Neala know the winner in advance, and she surprised me by keeping the secret. She was very proud of her husband—perhaps our proudest moment aside from welcoming our kids into the world.

Connecting with Colleagues

I worked as hard on research as I did on teaching. Mike Ettredge joined Dave Smith and me on a project eventually published in *Auditing: A Journal of Practice & Theory*. The paper demonstrates that a company's stock trades at a premium when the company's auditor is one of the Big-8—potentially due to higher quality audits. An alternative explanation, which we didn't explore, is that auditing firms have the deepest pockets for settling shareholder suits in the event of a failed audit. Larger firms' deeper pockets offer client shareholders greater security in the event of fraudulent financial reporting. That explanation suggests that accounting firms provide a form of insurance against shareholder damages.

I also started a project with John Robinson, ultimately published in a 1990 issue of *The Accounting Review*. Our paper demonstrates that managers of acquiring firms paid premiums for the stock of target companies willing to cooperate in structuring acquisitions to take advantage of an accounting method with cosmetically favorable profitability boosts. This effectively required acquiring firm shareholders to sacrifice wealth for purposes of making managers look good. Our paper foreshadowed elimination of said accounting method by accounting regulators, and the paper found its way onto the syllabi of faculty teaching accounting doctoral seminars at various major universities.

Working on research with colleagues at KU wasn't the only thing that kept me busy during my first year. I also worked on my dissertation, as well as the paper with Barry Spicer, started at Oregon. I needed to learn a new computer system and, for the first time, I was teaching intermediate financial accounting. I also developed and taught a doctoral seminar for previously neglected students starving for an introduction to modern accounting research.

As in my own doctoral program, KU's tenured faculty lacked training in applying the scientific method to accounting research, so the burden fell on untenured assistant professors: Smith (Illinois), Ettredge (Texas), Robinson (Michigan), and me (Oregon). Just two generations removed from the genesis of the accounting revolution, we were trained by Chicago school disciples who had landed at major public universities. As faculty in our generation grew to obtain tenure, the time for assistant professors to develop their own research programs became more protected, as was typical in more mature academic disciplines.

A Fateful Ride

I developed the habit of riding my bicycle up the hill to work every day. Coming down in the evening could be a harrowing experience, especially in the rain. One day it was raining hard, as I headed downhill toward a bend in the road. The next thing I remember is opening the sliding glass door on our patio—rain-soaked and disoriented—saying to Neala, "I think you better take me to the hospital."

Several stitches later, we returned home to a worried Máma watching our two boys. Apparently, the wheels on my bike had slipped from under me as I made that turn on the hill, and I came crashing down with my bare head hitting the pavement so hard that I blacked out. Not to be dissuaded, I somehow got back on my bike, rode the rest of the way down the hill, crossed a busy street at the bottom, and arrived home before regaining consciousness. To this day, the memory gap remains. The incident inspired me to wear a helmet on all subsequent bike rides.

Congratulations

On or about February 17 of 1982, less than 14 months after arriving in Kansas, and less than a year after Adam's birth, Neala and I took a break from all the stress and conceived another child. I was thrilled because I was hoping to have a daughter. However, the stress of raising kids while establishing a foothold in my new profession created a dulled response when Neala told me she had missed a period and tested positive on a home pregnancy test. I'm not sure she has ever forgiven me for—somewhat weakly—responding, "congratulations," when she relayed the news.

There has never been any doubt about the deep and intense love between us, as we have fallen in love innumerable times over the years. However, experiencing life largely through emotions, as we both do, can create periods of volatility in even the most loving relationships. Looking back, Kansas was my crash course not only in launching an academic career, but also in navigating the rich chaos of marriage, fatherhood, and carving out my place in the world. The crash taught me to wear a helmet. In life, I was still learning—sometimes the hard way—how to keep pedaling through it all…with protection!

Chapter 32
Barn Burning

On a harrowing day not long after the news of a third child on the way, I received a chilling anonymous phone call at work: "You don't know me, but you better come home quick, because your house is burning!" After a few stunned seconds, I bolted from the office, drove home in record time, and skidded to a stop at the roadblock. I jumped out of the car and came face-to-face with an officer telling me I could not proceed. I said, "That's my house!" and I broke through to see an inferno where our house once stood.

I ran down the block, desperately looking for my family, and I experienced more relief than any other day of my life when I spotted Neala, Jacob, and Adam incredulously watching the scene, still in their pajamas and sitting on the doorstep of the house across the street. When the relief finally penetrated, I realized Sunshine was missing. A moment later she appeared, and the pile of ashes where our house once stood no longer concerned me. My family was intact. Fortunately, weeks before, Máma left to visit Neala's aunt and cousins in Maryland.

So, how did this fire start? You may recall the attached garage without integrated heat or light, and the space heater and kerosene lamps we used to make it livable. On the morning of the fire, Neala turned on the space heater and inadvertently left it too close to the couch. She was talking on the phone in the bedroom while nursing Adam when she heard 2½-year-old Jacob running down the hallway yelling, "Moke! Moke! Moke!" Neala got the message, came out of the bedroom, and ran for the fire extinguisher, which wouldn't operate.

She gathered Jacob and Adam, opened the front door and yelled, "Help! Help!" A man in a car stopped in front of the house, rolled down the window, and yelled, "Get out of there, now!" Alarmed by the urgency in the man's voice, Neala heeded the admonition and moved as fast as she could with Adam and Jacob in tow. Seconds later, as the man was driving away and as Neala was crossing to the other side of the street, the fire exploded through the den's front windows. I came terrifyingly close to losing Neala, our two sons, and our unborn child. The gravity of it all shook Neala and me to our core—while Jacob, Adam, Sunshine, and our unborn baby seemed remarkably unscathed.

The response of our friends in Lawrence overwhelmed us. Pastor Ron and his wife insisted that we move in with them until suitable housing became available. The insurance company quickly provided money to rent a house on the other side of campus. The process of finding a contractor and rebuilding the house took about six months.

At the beginning of the process, we visited the site to see what possessions we might retrieve. It was still winter and the waterbed in the bedroom where we slept had literally turned into a giant ice cube. Any clothes that remained had so much smoke damage that no amount of cleaning could save them. Nothing was salvageable.

The insurance company came through for us with enough money to build a brand-new house and buy all the appliances, furniture, and clothing we needed. We moved into the new house later in the summer of 1982, in time to prepare for the arrival of our third child—

due on November 17. Out of the ashes, we rose—
scarred but whole, grateful beyond words, and ready to
welcome new life.

Chapter 33
Flirting with Fame and a New Arrival

Flirting with Fame

The year 1982 brought good news for my research regarding environmental performance. I submitted the final draft of my dissertation, which my committee approved with minor changes, and the accounting faculty invited me back to Oregon for a formal dissertation defense and graduation ceremony. Then, the editor of *The Accounting Review* notified Barry Spicer and me that our paper would appear in a 1983 issue of the journal. To this day, the paper with Barry remains one of my most cited works. Quality research output, combined with teaching excellence and a positive presence among accounting faculty and doctoral students—including chairing a dissertation committee—established me as an up-and-coming accounting scholar.

I also served as a member of our friend Charlotte's psychology dissertation committee. Charlotte's research introduced Neala and me to Jungian psychology and Myers-Briggs personality type indicators. We loved getting together with friends and discussing the fit of the descriptions of each other's personality types, derived from responses to a diagnostic questionnaire in a popular book called *Please Understand Me* by David Kiersey. The book elucidates sixteen personality types identified by Isabel Myers and Katharine Briggs through the lens of Carl Jung's archetype-oriented philosophy. In addition to Alan and Charlotte, our closest circle grew to include Rodge and Linda Moore. Rodge ran the Christian Counseling Center, which enjoyed an affiliation with First Christian

Church, and Linda was a vivacious flight attendant with a deeply spiritual Christian faith.

In October of 1982, when Neala was eight months pregnant, we decided to take a trip to Chicago to visit family. The Chicago visit was a stressful one, and we got a late start coming home. We hoped the boys would sleep through most of the nine-hour drive if we traveled at night. The stress of the visit killed our conversation on the way home. We had a Dodge van with enough room in the back to lay down a mattress on which one of us could rest while the other drove.

At about 10pm, after turning onto highway 35 heading south toward Kansas City, I needed to pee, so I pulled over under a viaduct. When I got back in the driver's seat, I didn't see Neala and assumed she crawled into the back of the van where she could rest her eight months pregnant body. Instead, unbeknownst to me, Neala got out to pee, too. Pulling away, I noticed that the passenger door was open. I thought it strange that Neala had not closed it when she repositioned herself to the mattress in the back. I covered for her by reaching over, grabbing the door handle, and pulling the door shut. I continued on my way, while Neala watched from the side of the road with her jaw dropped open.

An hour and a half later, I pulled into our driveway. Both boys were cranky. I grabbed Adam out of his car seat, set him down in the house and went back to the van to retrieve Jacob. I was surprised not to see Neala. "She must have gone to bed," I thought out loud. I grabbed Jacob out of his car seat, re-entered the house, and checked the bedroom. No Neala. This was becoming alarming. I went back to the van, looked more carefully in the back, and then looked more carefully in the house. By this time, I had put 1½-year-old Adam in the bathtub to calm him down, and I was carrying 3-

year-old Jacob. When I became pretty sure I had lost Neala, I started repeating, "Oh my God …. Oh my God …" Then Jacob started echoing me, and I knew we were in trouble.

By this time, I deduced that I must have left Neala under that viaduct. I knew it was approximately an hour and a half back to the spot, but I had no further information on the spot's location … and why would Neala still be there? Eventually, I got the bright idea to start calling police stations along highway 35 an hour or so from Lawrence. I explained the whole story to the officer who answered the phone at the first station. At the end of my explanation, he said, "Nope, she's not here." When I called the next station on my list, I simply said, "Is Neala Shane there?" The voice on the other end laughed and said, "Do you want to talk to her?" I said, "I'm not sure, does she want to talk to me?" I don't remember the answer to that question.

The next thing I remember is dragging the next-door neighbor out of bed to come to our house and watch over the boys while I high-tailed it to that police station. I drove as fast as I could without getting arrested, not knowing if I would still have a marriage when I arrived. Luckily, Neala was glad to see me, and we forgot all about whatever it was that made us not want to talk to one another. On the way home, I said, "Now, we don't need to tell anyone about this, do we?" I don't remember her response, but I felt assured that we were going to keep this between ourselves. Well, she must have had her fingers crossed, because it seemed that everywhere I turned during the next week or two, friends and colleagues were inquiring about this misadventure. One day, I came home from work and somewhat playfully said, "why don't you just put an ad in the newspaper and get it over with already?!"

Once we could look at the episode in the rear-view mirror, we found ourselves entertaining friends, colleagues, and family, alike, with the telling of the story. I would tell the story to the point of driving away, and Neala would then describe her situation while I was figuring things out. She would start by saying, "Well, I left the door open as a pretty strong signal that I was not in the car." Then she would describe her state of disbelief as she watched me pull away. Then Neala would say that she waddled about a half-mile down the road to a gas station, where the attendant made her wait until he closed for the night. Neala would mimic the attendant acting very nervous about the chance he'd have to deliver a baby, as he drove her to the nearest police station. At this point, our audience would be howling with laughter, as they accusingly pointed their fingers at me. I would then try to gain some sympathy for myself by describing my consternation in Lawrence, but this would only intensify the accusatory amusement.

Eventually, the story found its way into the accounting departments of major public universities in the U.S. and elsewhere. I remember one occasion many years later, long after I had moved on from the University of Kansas, when I invited Abbie Smith, a University of Chicago professor to present a paper at an accounting workshop I had organized. My colleagues and I took Abbie to dinner and, at one point, a look of realization came across her face, and she said, "You're the guy who left his wife on the side of the road! Please tell me the story." One year, I had a position as a visiting professor at the University of Auckland in New Zealand, and one of the faculty members wanted to know if the rumors he heard about me having left my pregnant wife on the side of the road were true. I was famous—or at least I had achieved a degree of international notoriety.

Bethan Arrives!

Soon after we settled back into life in our new home in Lawrence, excitement returned as we prepared for a new baby. We set up the crib in our bedroom, the boys shared the second bedroom, and Máma slept in the third bedroom. We loved our new house, but we were running out of space. On November 17, exactly on schedule, Neala's contractions quickened and she nonchalantly announced, "It's time." Then she said, "Let's walk to the hospital." And so, we walked the half-mile from our house to the hospital. Neala thought the walk might help move things along, and by now I think you know that we enjoyed living dangerously.

Neala was now so good at this that we barely had time to get to the birthing room, with me situated as the breathing coach, when Bethan Kay Shane popped out on this fine Wednesday afternoon. Tears of joy ran down my face when we saw that we had a daughter. We knew this would be our last child, and we both hoped for a girl. Thankfully, our hopes were fulfilled, as we didn't have a boy's name picked out. We were ready with the name Bethan for a girl. Our friends, Clive and Jill Emanuel, had a daughter named Bethan, apparently a popular name in Wales. Clive came to KU from Wales as a visiting professor during my second year on the faculty, and we got to know him and his family. The root meaning of the name Bethan is "house of God [75]." It is a form of Elizabeth, thus derived from the Bible in the same spirit as the names we chose for Bethan's brothers.

In December 1982, with 3-year-old Jacob, 1½-year-old Adam, and 1-month-old Bethan, we flew to Oregon for my graduation and to see friends. It was a triumphant and most enjoyable trip. The year 1983 was a good one for us. We loved our family life, I enjoyed the glow of success at work, and we thrived on fellowship at First Christian Church. We also enjoyed many visits from family and friends during our Kansas years. The years 1982-83 brought me publication prestige and international notoriety—for leaving my pregnant wife on the side of the road. But the true headline was Bethan's arrival. Kansas taught me that unexpected interruptions of best laid plans can create some of life's most cherished memories.

Chapter 34
The Mountains Beckon

Big Sky Opportunity

To alleviate financial stress, Neala—already caring for our three children—decided to operate a day care center out of our home. For about three months, she cared for two infants in exchange for $16 per day. It was so hard to keep all five kids calm at once that she resorted to nursing the two infant clients, while still nursing Bethan. It was more exhausting than anything I was dealing with at work—even amid escalating tensions in my department.

Larry/Lauren's departure shook up the dynamics and fed dissension between assistant professors and tenured faculty, as she had been the *de facto* department leader. The stress at home and work— along with a longing to return to the mountains—made me start thinking about a move. We tried a trip with our raft on the Kaw River near Lawrence. This disappointing float, with virtually no current and not much in the way of scenery, reinforced my growing ambition to raise my young family in the mountains of the west.

I came out of my doctoral program into a community of scholars organized by the American Accounting Association. The AAA transcended the individual universities where its members worked. The AAA published *The Accounting Review*, organized annual meetings, facilitated recruiting and cross-university research, and organized discipline-specific and region-specific sections within the broader association. During the summer of 1983, I saw a posting by the University of Montana, inviting letters of interest from candidates wanting to interview at the August AAA Meetings in Chicago. With Neala's blessing, I sent my letter of interest to Bruce Budge, the Chairman of Montana's Accounting Department. I received a warm response and scheduled a time to meet.

In spite of my enthusiasm when I met with Bruce and other Montana faculty members, the interviewing team expressed concern about the seriousness of my interest. Essentially, they said, "With your training and accomplishments, you could get a job on the accounting faculty of some of the most research-focused public universities. Why are you interested in us?" I must have had a convincing response, because later that fall, I received a call from Bruce Budge inviting me to campus for a spring 1984 interview. They invited Neala, too, so they could assess our family's commitment to the fullness of community life in the remote mountain town of Missoula, Montana.

Hitting it Off

I think we won over the faculty from the moment we stepped off the jetway at the Missoula airport and gave one of the flight attendants hearty goodbye hugs. Later we explained this gesture by telling our hosts that the flight attendant Linda Moore went to our church, and we were close friends with her and her husband Rodge. In any case, it looked good when we hugged Linda just before spotting the two accounting faculty members acting as our Montana reception committee.

We had a fantastic time on this trip. The faculty seemed stimulated by my one-hour workshop presentation. I connected well in half-hour office visits with the dean and each of the school's accounting professors. Finally, a faculty potluck reception, campus tour, real estate tour, and meals with faculty members and spouses drove our enthusiasm through the roof.

By the time we left Missoula, we were sold and so were they. Shortly after returning to Lawrence, I received a call from Bruce Budge with an offer to begin work as an assistant professor with a salary that matched what I was earning at Kansas. I negotiated a January 1985 start date. I intended to complete all the empirical research I had in progress, because I would not have the resources to do so once I moved to Montana. A seductive but faulty voice in my head told me that giving up accounting research would be a small price to pay for the chance to raise my children in the mountains. I convinced myself that if I missed it and wanted to continue doing accounting research, I could successfully do so with resource-rich coauthors at other universities.

When I told Dean Tollefson about my decision, he gave me all the same reasons that everyone else gave me for not moving. The bottom line was that I would be throwing a promising academic career away, because no university in Montana had the resources to support an active program of modern accounting research. The University of Montana housed the state's only graduate program in accounting and that was at the master's level. The business school had no doctoral programs, so I was giving up the opportunity to train doctoral students. Dean Tollefson eventually gave up trying to convince me to stay, and began telling me of his own love for the mountains and the northwestern United States. We had a warm connection, and shortly after getting settled into my new office, I received a call from him inviting me to return to Kansas with a hefty raise in pay. I politely turned down the invitation.

In fall 1984, without finishing even one of my research projects in progress, we nonetheless excitedly prepared for our move to Montana. We put our house on the market to sell but found no buyers. Eventually, we convinced our realtor to buy the house from us for a price equal to what we owed on the mortgage. Thus, in spite of completely rebuilding the house, we had to sell it for a substantial loss in a horrendous housing market.

Linda Ties the Knot

Also in 1984, my lovely sister Linda married her high school sweetheart Jimmy. A few days before the September wedding, my family arrived from Kansas and Rick's family arrived from Albuquerque. Rick and I escorted Linda down the aisle. Normally, this would have been our dad's job, and we all missed him terribly. Linda became the third Shane child to marry outside the Jewish faith. Jimmy's devoutly Catholic family welcomed Linda with open arms. Mom was not so welcoming. Nonetheless, it was a beautiful ceremony, Linda was a beautiful bride, and her three brothers looked on with love and pride.

A Rocky Beginning

Around Christmas time, our friends helped us load a U-Haul truck and sent us on our way to Montana. What awaited us on that road, however, nearly turned the leap of faith into disaster. I drove the truck with Adam strapped into a car seat next to me. Neala drove our car with Jacob and Bethan strapped into car seats and with Sunshine riding in the car's hatch area behind the back seats. We left in the dead of winter and the roads were slick.

As we set out, I noticed the truck pulling to the right, but eager to get on the road, I ignored it. About halfway across Kansas, the truck veered to the right, slipping onto a steeply inclined shoulder. With my brake foot slowing the van, I desperately tried to turn the wheels back toward the right lane of the highway. I couldn't do it, and to my horror, the truck teetered on its right-side wheels before crashing to the pavement and rolling onto its roof. I managed to extract Adam from his seat and crawl with him through the passenger side window. I was afraid the truck would explode, so I scurried with Adam across two highway lanes to the center median strip.

Neala saw what happened in the rear-view mirror of our hatchback, turned around, and drove back to us on the median dividing the highway. When she arrived, I opened the hatch and climbed in holding Adam, who had blood dripping from his head. Neala drove back toward Lawrence. We got off the highway at the first exit with a hospital sign, drove to the emergency room, and waited only momentarily before seeing a doctor. Thankfully, Adam was okay—with minor cuts not requiring stitches—but the whole incident scared Neala and me half to death.

The policeman who appeared at the hospital was an angel. He waited with us while we arranged with U-Haul to have the truck towed to the nearest transport station, and he helped us get settled in a hotel for the night. No tickets were issued. Once settled, I bought us a bottle of wine so we could celebrate the fact that no one was seriously hurt. We lost nearly all our belongings, but we were together and safe. Once again, insurance softened the blow—affording us the chance to start anew. The next day, U-Haul agents transferred all of our belongings—damaged or not—to a new truck and without judgment sent us on our way.

I'd like to say that we had an uneventful remainder of the dead-of-winter trip from Kansas to Montana, but that wouldn't be entirely true. We made it to the border between Wyoming and Montana without incident. However, we encountered black ice as we entered Butte on the way to Missoula. Neala's car began spinning on the ice in city traffic, and she almost lost control. I wasn't doing much better in the truck, but at least the truck had some weight. Somehow, we skated through this harrowing ordeal and made it to a hotel without hitting anything or anyone. With our first step into Montana—bruised, lighter in possessions, but bound by faith and purpose—we looked forward to forging our way in the mountains of the west.

·· · ·

This completes Volume One. It tells the story of eight immigrant families—with roots in the shtetls of nineteenth-century Central and Eastern Europe—coming together in Chicago's West and South Side Jewish neighborhoods where they embraced American culture. They celebrated during the Roaring Twenties, fought or cheered for America in the first and second world wars, and scraped through The Great Depression on the streets of Chicago. I came along during the Cold War and came of age in a culture of possibilities—for living harmoniously in community, in nature, and in the world. These possibilities embrace the ideals of three great social movements—Civil Rights, Antiwar, and Environmental—which converged with profound consequences during my most impressionable years.

Volume Two describes how I carried those ideals with me while raising a family, building a career, and engaging in community. Themes of faith, identity, assimilation, resilience, communion with nature, and responsible citizenship bridge from the first to second volume. Like Volume One, Volume Two explores the political and economic currents shaping our journey. The journey crisscrosses America, and extends to the far corners of the world. Along the way, we encounter rich community, adventure, and adversity testing our core beliefs, the strength of our family ties, and the very fabric of our existence. Volume Two ends with my grandchildren—fulfilling the hopes and dreams of my great-grandparents—carrying the mantle of a family sustained by love and the promise of freedom, democracy, and prosperity in America.

Acknowledgments
Both Volumes

I am grateful to the many people who encouraged me in the process of writing this two-volume memoir. Most of all, I appreciate my wife Neala who graciously supported me through two years of immersion in this project. I am also especially grateful to Neala, as well as my sister, Linda Wehrheim, my former student, Professor Dov Fischer, and my friend, Charlotte Rosenak, for investing many hours reading the manuscript and providing astute comments throughout the process. My friends, Keith Boxerman, Alan Morris, and Bob Goodman, and my son, Adam Shane, read parts of the manuscript and provided much-appreciated encouragement and thoughtful comments. The insightful comments of all these supporters contributed greatly to the best of what the memoir has to offer. Any remaining errors or gaps in clarity are my responsibility alone.

Appendix A
Neala's Heritage
A 75th Birthday Gift

I (Phil) have enjoyed working on your genealogy in anticipation of your 75th birthday. Now it's time to tell you (Neala) what I have learned. As a preamble, let me tell you that your heritage is deeply steeped in Colonial America. Your ancestors helped discover, settle, and expand this country over the course of the 400+ years since the establishment of the Jamestown Settlement in 1607. That's approximately 10 generations of your family in America. This means that any one of your pioneer relations carries only about 1/10 of a percent of your DNA and traces of your heritage into where they started their journey to America are even more tenuous. However, I can see that they arrived from England, Scotland, Ireland, and Germany. Once arriving in America, I see evidence of your ancestors having lived in all but one of the original 13 British Colonies, including the colonies in Virginia, Maryland, Connecticut, Pennsylvania, Georgia, Massachusetts, Rhode Island, New York, New Hampshire, New Jersey, North Carolina, and South Carolina. The only original colony that I didn't see mentioned anywhere in your lineage is Delaware. Now let's continue with a point-by-point detailed description of what I have learned.

1. You were born in Dallas, Texas on September 24, 1948 to William Coyt O'Neal (spelled Coyet on birth records) and Trella Fern (spelled "Ferne" on her birth records) Davis, who were, respectively, 26 and 18 years old at the time.

2. Your heritage on both your father and mother's side comes almost exclusively from the British Isles, with most coming from England, second most from Scotland, and third from Ireland. And the documentation indicates that your Irish ancestors most likely got to Ireland by way of Scotland. The only place of origin other than the British Isles is Germany. Of course, the lineages of virtually all of these ancestors extend back to places prior to arriving in Germany and the British Isles. Those places are only accessible with your DNA test.

3. Your German heritage is on your mother's side and comes through your great-great-great-great grandmother Leah Sappenfield Davis, who carries about two percent of your DNA, and through your great-great-great grandmother, Phoebe Catherine Bower, who migrated from Germany to Texas in the mid-19th century and who carries another three percent of your DNA. As far as I can tell, Leah was 100% German with three of her grandparents and two of her great-grandparents immigrating from Germany to the Colonies in Virginia and North Carolina. Leah and her husband, Brinkley Davis, moved the family to Texas in the early part of the 19th century. As far as I can tell, Phoebe also was 100% German with both of her parents born and raised in Germany. Thus, 5% of your ancestors arrived in America from Germany.

4. Let's get the bad news out of the way. Twenty-five percent of your DNA rests with your ne'er-do-well grandfather on your mom's side named Randall Morgan Davis. The only record we have of him is on your mom's birth certificate which says he was

22 years old in 1930, born in Texas, and had no occupation. Your mom's memory book says "Never knew him as I was little when Mother left him. He didn't want children." Máma was only 16 when your mom was born in Borger, Texas. The rest of the bad news is that another 25% of your DNA rests with James W. O'Neal who was born in Texas in 1900 and died in Georgia in 1973. We have no record of this grandfather's heritage. All we know is that he married your grandmother, Lula Mae Davis, in Texas in the early 1900s and had four children with her between the years 1919-1930. By the time of the 1940 census, James W. O'Neal was gone and Lula Mae was listed as the head of the household. So, 50% of your DNA rests in Texas with your grandfathers whose lineages are unknown to us.

5. The good news is that we have substantial documentation of the lineage associated with the 50% of your DNA that extends back from your two grandmothers, Lula Mae Davis on your dad's side and Stacy Azile Rasco (Máma) on your mom's side.

6. Let's start with Máma's lineage. Her parents, Leonard Lee Rasco and Dora Katherine Medders (Mama Dode), married in 1912 in Limestone, Texas. Leonard Lee Rasco's Texas roots go back three generations on his mother's side and three generations on his father's side. His mother and father met and married in Texas, but their family trees extend back in very different directions. Leonard's parents (your great-great-grandparents), Captain Maloy Rasco and Martha Evelyn Lindley lived in Texas their whole lives.

7. The lineage of Captain Rasco's father, John Bunyan (Jack) Rasco, extends back to ancestors who came from England and Ireland and made their homes in North Carolina and Tennessee. The Tennessee branch included some of the first Quakers to arrive in America in the early part of the 18th century. The North Carolina branch extends back to 17th-century Jamestown, Virginia.

8. The lineage of Captain Rasco's mother, Susan Davis, extends back to Germany on her mother's side. We have no documentation of the lineage of her father, Brinkley Davis, who came from Maryland to Texas in the early 19th century. His wife, Leah Sappenfield (Susan Davis's mother) has a strong German heritage. Your German branches arrived in North Carolina in the early 18th century and migrated to Texas in the early 19th century. The surnames of your German-rooted ancestors include Bower, Myers, Albert/Albrecht, Grimes, Reighert, and Sappenfield.

9. The ancestors of Captain Rasco's wife, Martha Evelyn Lindley, came to Colonial America in the first half of the 18th century from England, Scotland, and Ireland, and the family spent time in Pennsylvania, Virginia, and Tennessee, before settling in Texas in the mid-19th century. Martha's father, Elijah Lindley, fought in the Texas Calvary on the side of the Confederacy. During the Civil War, your father's ancestors lived in Arkansas, and your mother's ancestors lived in Texas. Thus, on both sides of the family, any soldiers would have fought for the Confederacy. On Martha's mother's side, the documentation dates back to 1715 when William McGill was born in Ireland. This branch of the family migrated from Ireland to Tennessee.

10. William McGill's wife, Jean Fowler, has a lineage extending back to John Rice Burton, who came from England to Massachusetts in the mid-17th century and was prosecuted as a Quaker in Salem. He married Elizabeth Handcorne Bowers who came from England to Rhode Island. Martha Lindley's branch of the family settled in Tennessee until the Reverend Walter Marshall McGill moved them to Texas before the Civil War.

11. The remaining branches of your tree on your mom's side pass through Máma's mother, Dora Katherine Medders (Mama Dode), whose parents were born in the mid-19th century and lived into the 20th century.

12. Mama Dode's father, William Sebastian Medders, has a lineage arriving in Colonial America primarily from England and Scotland. Thomas Medders was born in Bristol, England in 1612 and migrated to Virginia to join the early settlers of the Jamestown Colony. The Medders branch of the family spent time in the Carolinas, Georgia, and Arkansas before settling in Texas shortly after the Civil War. At one point on this branch in the mid-18th century (before the American Revolution), Jason Medders married Mary Elizabeth Harrison Stone. Mary Elizabeth's family came to Virginia from England as far back as the Reverend Robert Hunt, who was the first Chaplain of the Jamestown Colony, and Robert Harrison who came to Jamestown from England in the early years of the Colony.

13. You have some Scotch heritage on the branches leading to William Sebastian Medders. In particular, William's great-grandmother Mary Heath either joined her Scottish family in America in the early part of the 18th century or she was born to this

family after they arrived in Colonial America. Either way, her heritage is Scottish and in 1743 she married Captain William Miller who had arrived in Virginia from Scotland. Captain Miller may be Mary Heath's distant cousin, as he most likely bore some relation to Lady Margaret (Fanny) Miller Heath who arrived in Virginia during the early years of the Jamestown Colony. Mary Heath most likely bears some relation to Lady Margaret's husband, Sir Robert Silcock Heath, who was Chancellor of England and instrumental in the colonization of America. In 1621, Sir Robert was Knighted. He served as Chief Justice of the Court of Commons from 1631-1634. The Millers picked up some more Scottish heritage when Jesse Miller married Martha Elizabeth McNair in Georgia in 1783. The Millers moved from Georgia to Arkansas where they met up with the Medders when James Benjamin Medders married Elvira Dora Miller Medders in Arkansas in 1847. The family lived in Arkansas until moving to Texas after the Civil War. The surnames on the branches associated with Mama Dode's father include Medders, Miller, McNair, McFate, Bailey, Hughey, Mobley, Stone, Harrison, White, Hunt, Heath, Lee, Owen, and Felton.

14. I can trace the Medders branch of your tree to Colonial Virginia by way of England. John M. Medders and Elizabeth White were married in 1677 and lived in Colonial Virginia, and their respective lineages trace back to England. Their son, Jason Medders married Mary Elizabeth Harrison Stone, and they moved from Virginia to North Carolina in the mid-18th century.

15. Mary Harrison Stone descended from George Stone, "a wealthy banker and a stockholder in the Virginia Land Company of London." He was married to Mary Nelson and they immigrated together to join the Jamestown Colony in its very early years. On her mother's side, Mary Stone descended from Robert Harrison and Mary Sutton who were married in England around the turn of the 17th century and migrated to Colonial Virginia. Their son, Robert Harrison, married Elizabeth Cummins whose parents, Nicholas Cummins and Eleanor Elison, married in 1618 in England and migrated to Colonial Virginia.

16. Robert and Elizabeth's son, Samuel Harrison, married Sarah Ann Hunt whose lineage extends back to the Reverand Robert Hunt, the first Chaplain of the Jamestown Settlement. He married Marjorie Cummins in 1570 in England before migrating to Virginia. This reverend's son Captain William Hunt and his wife Anna Tyler Hunt also lived in Colonial Virginia. The Hunts were an important colonial family.

17. Mama Dode's mother, Catherine Eudora (Dora) Hall Medders, was born in 1871 and lived to be 95 years old. Dora's mother, Phoebe Catherine Bower Hall was born in Germany in 1843, married Isham Belcher Hall in 1859 in Texas, and died in Texas sometime between 1870 and 1880.

18. On Dora's father's side, the Hall family extends back to the early English settlers of the Maryland Colony in the mid-17th century. This branch includes John Hall who married Katherine Primrose in the second half of the 17th century. Katherine's parents lived in Scotland, but she was born in England in 1650.

19. In 1700, John Aaron Hall, Dora's great-great-great-great-grandfather, married Jane Rawlins in Maryland. The Rawlings branch extends back to Anthony John Rawlings, whose father, Anthony John Rawlings Sr., was a "Cornish Royalist," born in 1619 and died in 1652. This Cornish Royalist likely had Celtic roots. His son married Catherine Elizabeth Beckwith whose parents immigrated from England to Connecticut in the early days of the colony which started there in 1636.

20. Other maternal lines extending from the Hall branch of the family have deep roots in the Maryland Colony and these maternal lines arrived in Maryland from England and Scotland. John Aaron Hall's grandson, Thomas Hall, married Ann Wheeler in 1778 and moved the family from Maryland to Kentucky. Ann's family arrived in Maryland from England and Scotland in the latter half of the 17th century. Thomas Hall's son married Mary Ann (Polly) McDonald in Kentucky in 1809. Polly's family came from Northern Ireland to Kentucky in the 17th century (well before the potato famine). Thomas Hall's grandson married Sarah (Sally) Belcher and moved the family from Kentucky to Texas in the mid-19th century. Sally's family most likely came to Kentucky from Scotland, perhaps by way of one of the original 13 colonies.

21. On your father's side, your grandfather, James W. O'Neal, was 20 years old at the time of the 1920 census, so he was born in 1899-1900. The 1920 census record shows that this grandfather was born in Texas, and he and his wife, May O'Neal, had an infant daughter, Rubie Lee, living with them. May O'Neal is listed as Lula Mae Davis on James

W.'s social security application, which also lists William Coyet O'Neal as their child. The 1920 and 1930 census records identify your grandfather's occupation as farming. The 1930 census shows that the family increased in size due to the births of your father in 1922, your uncle JW in 1925-1926, and your Aunt Bette in 1929-1930. There is some confusion as to where James W.'s parents (your great-grandparents) were born. The 1920 census says Oklahoma, while the 1930 census says Georgia and Arkansas, and that's as far back as the documentation goes for your paternal grandfather's branch of the family. It's not clear when or where James W. died. In any case, this branch of the family tree contains 25% of your DNA and it appears that the documentation goes back only as far as the birth of James W. O'Neal in Texas in 1900.

22. James W. O'Neal married your paternal grandmother, Lula Mae Davis, and they had five children, including your father, who was born on December 17, 1922 in Sherman, Texas, Ruby, James (who died fighting in WW2), Betty Louise, and Wanda Polly. The documentation for the 25% of your DNA that comes from Lula Mae runs deep into Colonial America. You have relatives who fought in the Revolutionary War, the Civil War, and both world wars. The most recent immigrants in Lula Mae's lineage arrived in America from England in the mid-19th century (before the Civil War). As your great-great-great grandparents, these immigrants carry 1/32 (or about 3%) of your DNA. We don't know their names, but we know they came from England and gave birth to your great-great-grandmother, Juda Marshall. Juda was

born in 1843, possibly in England, but more likely in North Carolina from where she migrated first to Arkansas and later to Texas. She married your great-great-grandfather, Aron A. Davis, in Arkansas in 1867, and she died in Texas in 1920.

23. Aron and Juda Davis were the parents of Joseph Washington Davis, who was born in Arkansas in 1869 and died in Texas in 1940. Joseph married Sarah Ellen Caldwell in 1890 and these great-grandparents were the parents of your grandmother, Lula Mae. Aron's lineage on his father's side includes the Quaker colonist, Thomas Mitchell, who immigrated from England to Philadelphia at the beginning of the 18th century. He married Sarah Densey whose Quaker parents had immigrated from England to Philadelphia in the latter part of the 17th century. This branch also includes Abraham Thomas Mitchell III who was born in 1761 and became a documented Revolutionary War soldier. He married Lucinda Williams whose parents, Nathaniel Williams and Ann Hawkings, arrived in America from Scotland in the mid-18th century.

24. Aron Davis's lineage on his father's side also includes his mother, Kate Standlee, whose great-grandmother on her father's side was a full-blooded Cherokee Indian named Red Bird Moytoy. That's right, your great-great-great-great-great-great grandfather, John Nolichucky Standlee, moved from England to North Carolina and married a full-blooded *Cherokee* princess named Red Bird Moytoy. It's possible that Red Bird Moytoy is the woman your mom had in mind when she wrote "my father's grandmother was a full-blooded Comanche princess." Red Bird Moytoy

actually accounts for about four-tenths of one-percent of your DNA. Red Bird Moytoy's father and grandfather were Cherokee Indian chiefs. Their names were Chief Willenawah The Great Eagle of Tellico Corntassel (1703-1788) and Chief Amahetai "Pigeon of Tellico" Moytoy (1650-1741). John Nolichucky Standlee and Red Bird Moytoy had a daughter-in-law, Polly Stratton, and the documentation says she was an end-of-line Cherokee Indian, but the documentation also indicates that her father, Colonel John Bryant, and her mother, Mary Ann Hille, were both white. I suppose it's possible that she was Cherokee but lived her life among white people who took care of her as if she were their child. This is a mystery. If it's true that Polly was Cherokee, then she accounts for seven-tenths of one percent of your DNA, as she was your five-times great-grandmother on your father's side. The white person lineage attached to Polly Stratton extends back to colonists coming from England to Virginia.

25. I followed the rest of the branches of your family tree on your father's side through parents, grandparents, and all levels of great-grandparents. I didn't include aunts, uncles, siblings, or cousins in the analysis; although in one case I discovered that a husband and wife had the same grandparents (i.e., they were cousins). Yes, Kate Standlee's great-great-grandparents, William Charles Boren and Sarah Elizabeth Larkin had a grandson, William Boren, and a granddaughter, Mary McIntosh, who married each other in 1780 in North Carolina. In 1803, William and Mary had a daughter, Sukey Boren, who married John Standlee, thus connecting with the family's Cherokee heritage, as

John was ¼ Cherokee. John and Sukey parented Kate Standlee, who was introduced in the previous paragraph. Mary McIntosh's father, John Mohr McIntosh, came to America from Scotland in the mid-18th century.

26. Sarah Elizabeth Larkin's grandfather on her father's side, John Coloner Larkin married Katherine (Lucy) Holland in England and came to America in the middle of the 17th century. Lucy Holland's roots extend back to her grandfather, Sir John Philemon Holland, the Duke of Exeter (England), and his wife, Mary Fletcher Mollenax, whose father, Sir John Castellan, lived in England during the second half of the 16th century. They settled in Maryland and bore a son, Francis Gabriel, who settled in Jamestown during the colony's early years. Francis Gabriel Holland married Mary Jane Elizabeth Pinke in Jamestown. Mary Pinke's roots extend back to England, and she arrived in Jamestown by way of Massachusetts. Sarah Elizabeth Larkin's father, Captain Thomas Larkin, married Margaret Jane Elizabeth Gassaway, whose parents, Colonel Nicholas Gassaway and Anne Hester Besson Sutton, migrated to Maryland from England.

27. From William Boren's mother, Mary Brashears Boren, your tree branches to her great-grandfather Major Peter Jones who was born in England in 1634, moved to Virginia with his parents at the age of one, and became part of the Virginia militia. He was known as a fur trader and an Indian trader, and his parents, Sir Reverend Captain Richard Peter Jones and Lady Ann (Mary Ann) Jeffries Heiress of Manor Ley, migrated to Virginia from England in 1635. Major Peter Jones married Margaret

Lewellen Cruse Wood in the Virginia Colony. Margaret's parents, Captain Burgess (Sheriff and Gentleman of Chelmsford) Daniel Lewellen and Mary Ann (the immigrant) Matthews, migrated from Essex, England to Virginia during the early days of the Colony. From Mary Brashears Boren the tree also branches to "the carpenter," Samuel Barton Brashears whose grandfather on his mother's side, Thomas Spriggs, immigrated from England to Maryland in the mid-17th century., Thomas Spriggs married Katherine Graves in Maryland. Her parents, Captain Thomas Graves II and Katherine Crosher, immigrated from Jamestown in the Colony's early days. In fact, Captain Thomas Graves II was a "justice for the court" and was known as Captain Esquire of Berkshire and one of the "adventurers/stockholders of the Virginia Company of London." Samuel Barton Brashears' grandfather on his father's side, Benjamin Brashears, came to America from France, and Benjamin's wife, Mary Ann Richford, came to America from England. They met and married at Jamestown and the family eventually migrated to Maryland. Samuel Barton Brashears' mother-in-law, Dorothy Cager lived in Maryland and her grandparents, Robert Thomas Cager Sr. and Elizabeth Yates Powell, came to Maryland from Ireland and England in the early part of the 17th century. Their son, Robert Cager Jr. married Dorothy James in Maryland. Dorothy's parents, Sir Owen James II (a Baron) and his wife Joanne Maddock migrated to Maryland from Northern Ireland, also in the early part of the 17th century. Dorothy's grandparents, John "Madog" Maddox

(Lord of Morgan) and Lady Elizabeth Aubrey, had lived in Wales in the latter part of the 16th century. Thus, you have tiny bits of French and Welsh heritage.

28. The Boren lineage in your family tree extends from Sukey Boren back through time to John Boren (also spelled Bourn) who married Anne Sawyer. Anne's parents, Thomas Sawyer and Mary Prescott, moved from England to Jamestown, Virginia, in the early 17th century, perhaps as original colonists. They married in Maryland in 1650 but lived in Virginia, and their descendants lived in Virginia throughout most of the 17th century. After leaving Virginia, the family spent time in several states, including Massachusetts, Maryland, North Carolina, Kentucky, Tennessee, and Missouri before Sukey Boren married John Standlee and settled in Arkansas. John and Sukey's descendants stayed in Arkansas for two full generations before Joseph Washington Davis and Sarah Ellen Caldwell moved the family from Arkansas to Texas in the latter part of the 19th century.

29. John Bourn's son, Richard Bourn, married Mary Martin in 1675. Mary's branch of the tree extends back to Captain John Martin who married Maud Marshall and moved to Jamestown in the early days of the colony. Their son, John Martin, married Christian Pettus, whose father, Colonel Theodore Pettus moved from England to Jamestown in the early days of the colony, and he married a Powhatan Indian named Jane Kaokee Patawomeck. Jane Kaokee's parents were both Powhatan Indians, and her grandfather was a chief named Chief Japasaw Paowomeck Nemattanson who

lived in the Jamestown area from 1520-1597. This Indian Chief's daughter, Jane Kaokee, was your 11 times great-grandmother, meaning that she carried about one one-hundredth of one-percent of your DNA.

30. Another branch extends from Sarah Ellen Caldwell to her great-great-grandfather, John Mitchell, who immigrated from Scotland to Virginia in the middle of the 18th century. John Mitchell married Rachel Anna Chrisman whose grandparents, Daniel Donald McDonald and Elizabeth Grant, moved from Scotland to join the South Carolina Colony and eventually migrated to Virginia in the mid-18th century.

31. The rest of the branches of the tree on your father's side are rooted in England, Scotland, and Ireland. The Davis branch extends from your grandmother, Lula Mae Davis, back to 16th century England. Captain James Davis was born in England in 1583. He captained one of the two ships that landed in Maine and established the first New England colony in America in 1607. According to the *Carolina Journal*: "Born around 1580 in Gloucester, England, Davis was the son of Sir Thomas Davis, an original member of the Virginia Company of Plymouth. Already an experienced sailor by the age of 27, James Davis joined the Company's 1607 expedition to New England to plant a colony." The Popham Colony began just a few months after the establishment of the colony at Jamestown by the same Virginia Company. Captain John Davis briefly served as its Governor before the dissolution of the Popham Colony in 1608 due to harsh winters. To sail back to England, the Popham colonists constructed the first ship

built in America. Captain Davis subsequently participated in the development of the Jamestown Colony. The article goes on to describe the role Captain Davis, a storied Indian fighter, played in the establishment of the colony at Jamestown, Virginia, and in the subsequent development of the Massachusetts Colony.

32. Captain Davis married Cicely (Sissila) Thayer in England. She was the daughter of John Edward Thayer and Joane Lawrence, the Baron and Baroness of Thornbury. Included in this lineage is the life of the "legendary bear hunter" Zacharias Mason Davis who lived in Virginia between 1765 and 1830. Zacharias' grandparents on his mother's side came to America in the late 17th century from Scotland and Northern Ireland and settled in Philadelphia. On his father's side, Zacharias' grandmother, Mary Knight, came from England to New York in about 1700, and his great-great-grandparents, Ralph Blaisdell and Elizabeth Ann Parker, migrated from England to the Massachusetts Colony in the mid-17th century.

33. The Caldwell branch of your family tree extends from your great-grandmother, Sarah Ellen Caldwell (mother of Lula Mae), to John Caldwell and Isabel Wasson who were born in Northern Ireland and migrated to New Hampshire before marrying in 1734. John and Isabel were both buried in New Hampshire. The family eventually migrated from New England to South Carolina, spent some time in Illinois, and settled in Arkansas for at least two generations including the Civil War years. Sarah Caldwell and her husband, Joseph Washington Davis, moved from Arkansas to Texas in 1899 when Lula Mae was one-year-old. Sarah Caldwell's

roots also extend back through her great-great-grandmother, Ruth Maybin, who lived in South Carolina and Connecticut between 1780 and 1844. During the mid-18th century, Ruth's parents, William Maybin and Mary Jane Duncan migrated from Scotland to Northern Ireland to America, eventually settling in South Carolina.

Appendix B
Eulogy of Orville Shane, by his Children, January 1980

Our father was the most unselfish man we have ever known. He was a man who never put himself first but rather was devoted to serving and loving people—especially his family—but also his friends, clients, and the Jewish community in which he lived. He was not a religious man, but was a man who believed in God—a man of deep faith and integrity. He fought, even against the greatest of odds, with real hope right up the moment of his death to live life the way he knew in his heart that he should. So, let's not have pity or feel sorry for him because Dad would not want us to do that. He would want us to carry on our lives and do the very best that we can, just like he did right up to his life's final moment.

We are very proud of him and are immeasurably thankful for all he has given us. We are even more thankful for the tremendous impact he had and continues to have on our lives by simply being the wonderful human being that he was.

We love our Dad very much as we know you all do. He has always been ready to make us smile—to stop our fears—to help anyone in need. His heart has never stopped giving. He touched everyone who knew him in a beautiful and unique way. You couldn't really know him without loving and respecting him.

We believe from the bottom of our hearts that Dad is in a better place now. He is at peace and deeply and richly fulfilled. He's working as hard as ever and has his same personality that we all know and love. His body is now free of any disease.

We will miss him terribly and know that life will never be the same without his physical presence. But we are thankful for the one special gift that we all have, and that is being loved by someone as wonderful as Dad. We only hope that our own wives, husbands, and children will love and respect us as much as we and our mother love and respect our father.

References

1. Romey, Kristen. 2017. "Living Descendants of Biblical Canaanites Identified Via DNA." *National Geographic*: https://www.nationalgeographic.com/history/article/canaanite-bible-ancient-dna-lebanon-genetics-archaeology.

2. Gassel, Rafi. 2022. "Israelis and Palestinians are Both Indigenous and Why that Matters." *The Times of Israel*: https://blogs.timesofisrael.com/israelis-and-palestinians-are-both-indigenous-and-why-that-matters/

3. Feldman, Noah. March 11, 2024. "The New Antisemitism." *Time Magazine* 203(7/8): 34-41. https://time.com/magazine/us/6836631/march-11th-2024-vol-203-no-7-u-s/

4. University of Chicago Library website. 2024. "New Jews" vs. "Old Jews": Emancipation, Assimilation, and the Ostjuden as Other:" https://www.lib.uchicago.edu/collex/exhibits/exeej/new-jews-vs-old-jews-emancipation-assimilation-and-ostjuden-other/

5. Deutsch, Gotthard and Mannheimer, S. "Bismarck, Prince Otto Eduard Leopold." *Jewish Encyclopedia*: https://www.jewishencyclopedia.com/articles/3337-bismarck-prince-otto-eduard-leopold

6. Elon, Amos. *The Pity of It All: A Portrait of the German-Jewish Epoch, 1743-1933* (p. 206). Henry Holt and Co. Kindle Edition.

7. Rosenberg, Hans. 1943. "Political and Social Consequences of the Great Depression of 1873-1896 in Central Europe." *The Economic History Review* 13(1/2): 58-73.

8. *Time Magazine*, December 31, 1999, Volume 154, Issue # 27.

9. Okrent, Daniel. 2020. *The Guarded Gate: Bigotry, Eugenics, and the Law that Kept Two Generations of Jews, Italians, and Other European Groups Out of America.* Published by Scribner.

10. Sarna, Jonathan; and Zollman, Joellyn. "Jewish Immigration to America." *My Jewish Learning*: https://www.myjewishlearning.com/article/jewish-immigration-to-america-three-waves/

11. *Jewish Virtual Library.* "Hungary:" https://www.jewishvirtuallibrary.org/hungary.

12. Levitats, Isaac (1943). *The Jewish Community in Russia, 1772-1844.* New York: Columbia University Press. pp. 20–21.

13. Trepanier, Lee. 2017. "The Russian Empire (1721-1917)." Voegellin View: https://voegelinview.com/russian-empire-1721-1917/

14. "A New World: The Soviet Remaking of the Pale Jews" appears in *The Nation's* September 18/25, 2023 issue.

15. Avrutin, Eugene. 2021. "Pogroms in Russia's Borderlands, 1881-1884." 2021. In *Pogroms: A Documentary History*: Avrutin, Eugene and Elissa Bemporad, eds.

16. *Columbia University Club of Chicago History of Chicago Series.* 2021. "Chicago: City of Horses. A Journey Through an Urban World of Horses and the Origins of Mass Public Transit, 1859-1910:" https://chicago.alumni.columbia.edu/history_of_ch icago_series_chicago_city_of_horses

17. Lyle. 2013. "Horses Go Out of Business: Technology That Changed Chicago." Chicago Public Library:

https://www.chipublib.org/blogs/post/technology-that-changed-chicago-horses-go-out-of-business/#:~:text=By%201940%20there%20were%20fewer,changes%20happened%20in%20the%201920s.&text=In%201950%20only%20329%20horse,for%20rags%20and%20scrap%20metal.

18. Jewish Treats. 2021. "Courland Jews, An Interesting History." *National Jewish Outreach Program*: https://njop.org/courland-jews-an-interesting-history/

19. The YIVO Encyclopedia of Jews in Eastern Europe, Courland, by Sarunas Liekis.

20. The JewishGen Latvia & Estonia Research Division. https://latvia.jewishgen.org/history-and-geography/history-of-latvia-and-courland

21. Polansky, Antony. 2010. "The Position of the Jews in the Tsarist Empire, 1881-1905." Chapter One in *The Jews of Poland and Russia*: https://www.brandeis.edu/tauber/events/Polonsky_vol2%20_%20ch1.pdf

22. Barrett, James. "Canaryville." *Encyclopedia of Chicago*. http://www.encyclopedia.chicagohistory.org/pages/2476.html

23. Museum of Jewish Heritage. "German Patriots: Jewish Germans During World War I." 2022. https://mjhnyc.org/blog/german-patriots-jewish-germans-during-wwi/

24. Markazi, Arash. 2015. "Meet the 73-year-old Lady Fighting for Shoeless Joe Jackson." https://www.espn.com/mlb/story/_/id/13560985/arlene-marcley-73-leads-fight-clear-shoeless-joe-jackson-name-get-baseball-ineligible-list

25. DCASE. "History of the Maxwell Street Market." https://www.chicago.gov/city/en/depts/dca/supp_info/maxwellstreetmarket0.html

26. Jewish United Fund. "Chicago's Jewish West Side." https://www.juf.org/news/arts.aspx?id=52474

27. Betsy. 2018. "100 Years Ago: Chicago Celebrated the End of WWI." Chicago Public Library Archives: https://www.chipublib.org/blogs/post/100-years-ago-chicago-celebrated-the-end-of-wwi/

28. Roos, Dave. 2019. "How Prohibition Put the Organized in Organized Crime." *History*: https://www.history.com/news/prohibition-organized-crime-al-capone

29. Teasdle, Holly. 2002. "Jewish Farming in Michigan." In *Michigan Jewish History* (Vol. 42), ed Aimee Ergas https://www.jhsmichigan.org/assets/docs/Journals/Michigan_Jewish_History_2002_09.pdf

30. Cook County Democratic Party. History: https://www.cookcountydems.com/history/

31. Green, Paul. "Kelly-Nash Machine." *Encyclopedia of Chicago*: http://www.encyclopedia.chicagohistory.org/pages/686.html

32. *The Conversation*. 2021. "How Did Uncle Sam Become a Symbol for the United States." https://theconversation.com/how-did-uncle-sam-become-a-symbol-for-the-united-states-171283

33. Deutsch, Tracey. "Great Depression." *Encyclopedia of Chicago*: http://www.encyclopedia.chicagohistory.org/pages/542.html#:~:text=Like%20much%20of%20the%2

0nation,%2Dwattage%2C%20independent%20radi
o%20stations.

34. Medoff, Rafael. 2020. "Joe Biden, FDR, and the
    Nazis," Roosevelt's Prewar Attitude Toward
    Hitler. Published by the *Jewish Virtual Library* with
    permission of the *Algemeiner*.

35. Photograph in United States Holocaust Museum
    (Chicago). 1933. Caption: "Jews march in Chicago
    to protest against the Nazi persecution of
    German Jews." Appeared in Chicago Herald and
    Examiner:
    https://collections.ushmm.org/search/catalog/pa83
    26

36. Gross, David. 2015. *The Smithsonian Magazine.*
    The U.S. Government Turned Away Thousands of
    Jewish Refugees, Fearing That They Were Nazi
    Spies | Smithsonian

37. New York Times. 1939. "22,000 Nazis Hold Rally
    in Garden." February 1, 1939 (p. 1, 5).

38. Mottlow, Martin. 2002. *Fast Break to Glory:
    Marshall High School's 98-Game Basketball Winning
    Streak.*
    https://basketballmuseumofillinois.com/weintraub-
    lou-1985/

39. Atomic Heritage Foundation. 2014. "Debate over
    the Bomb."
    https://ahf.nuclearmuseum.org/ahf/history/debate-
    over-
    bomb/#:~:text=In%20the%20initial%20days%20fol
    lowing,5%20percent%20had%20no%20opinion.
    June 6, 2014.

40. History Extra. 2022. "Was the U.S. Justified in
    Dropping Atomic Bombs on Hiroshima and
    Nagasaki During the Second World War?"
    https://www.historyextra.com/period/second-

world-war/atomic-bomb-hiroshima-nagasaki-justified-us-debate-bombs-death-toll-japan-how-many-died-nuclear/*. April 6, 2022.

41. Freeman, Hadley. 2021. "The Rosenbergs were executed for spying in 1953. Can their sons reveal the truth?" *The Guardian* (June 19, 2021): *https://www.theguardian.com/world/2021/jun/19/rosenbergs-executed-for-spying-1953-can-sons-reveal-truth*

42. Reich, Howard. 2010. "The Life and Times of Skokie." *Moment: May-June 2010. https://momentmag.com/the-life-and-times-of-skokie/*

43. Sutherland, J.J. 2010. "L. Frank Baum Advocated Extermination Of Native Americans." *NPR Must Reads*: October 27,2010.

44. Blake, John. 2023. "'I Have a Dream' is MLK's Most Radical Speech — Not Because of What He Said Then, But Because of How America Has Changed Since." *CNN* (January 16, 2023): *https://www.cnn.com/2023/01/15/us/mlk-i-have-a-dream-speech-blake-cec/index.html#:~:text='I%20Have%20a%20Dream'%20is%20MLK's%20most,century.%E2%80%9D%20As%20the%20nation%20celebrates%20the%20Rev*

45. Engler, Mark, & Engler, Paul. 2021. Why Martin Luther King Jr. Didn't Not Run for President." *Rolling Stone* (January 18, 2021): *https://www.rollingstone.com/politics/politics-news/martin-luther-king-run-for-president-55331/*

46. King, Donna. 2023. "How a NC professor almost built a King/Spock presidential ticket." The Carolina Journal (January 18, 2023): *https://www.carolinajournal.com/how-a-nc-professor-almost-built-a-king-spock-presidential-ticket/*

47. *American Rhetoric.* "Top 100 Speeches." *https://www.americanrhetoric.com/speeches/rfkonml kdeath.html*

48. Jackman, Tom. 2018. "Who killed Bobby Kennedy? His son RFK Jr. doesn't believe it was Sirhan Sirhan." *Washington Post* (May 26, 2018): *https://www.washingtonpost.com/news/retropolis/wp/ 2018/05/26/who-killed-bobby-kennedy-his-son-rfk-jr- doesnt-believe-it-was-sirhan-sirhan/*

49. Stone, Oliver. *JFK Revisited: Through the Looking Glass. https://www.imdb.com/title/tt11173544/*

50. Patrick Nolan. 2015. *CIA Rogues and the Killing of the Kennedys: How and Why US Agents Conspired to Assassinate JFK and RFK. Skyhorse Publishing.*

51. Goldstein, Richard. 2018. "Ernest Medina, 81, Army Captain Acquitted in My Lai Massacre, Dies." New York Times (May 13, 2018): *https://www.nytimes.com/2018/05/13/obituaries/ern est-medina-dies-my-lai-massacre.html*

52. Nick Turse. 2013. *Kill Anything that Moves: The Real American War in Vietnam. McMillan Publishers: https://us.macmillan.com/books/9781250045065/kil lanythingthatmoves/*

53. *University of Illinois Library.* "The University of Illinois in the Cold War Era 1945-1975: March Riots (1970):" *https://guides.library.illinois.edu/c.php?g=348250&p= 2350901*

54. *New York Times* (March 19, 1970): https://www.nytimes.com/1970/03/19/archives/ba n-on-kunstler-revoked.html#

55. Evensen, Dave. "Illinois at the Crossroads: A Time to Protest." *A Gift for the Ages: The Lincoln Hall Project:*

http://www.lincolnhall.illinois.edu/history/crossroads/protest/

56. *Metz, Michael. 2019.* "Flash Point: Unfolding the Events that Led to the Climax of the Student Protest Movement at Illinois." *Radicals in the Heartland.* University of Illinois Press: https://uiaa.org/2020/03/25/flash-point/

57. *Lewis, Jerry, & Hensley, Thomas.* "The May 4 Shootings At Kent State University: The Search For Historical Accuracy." Published In Revised Form By *The Ohio Council For The Social Studies Review,* Vol 34, Number 1 (Summer, 1998) Pp. 9-21: *https://www.kent.edu/may-4-historical-accuracy*

58. Heim, Eric. 2011. "The 1970 Student Strike in Protest of Kent State Killings." *The Public* (May 19, 2011): *https://publici.ucimc.org/2011/05/1970-student-strike-in-protest-of-kent-state-killings/*

59. Williams, Albert. 1989. "Siegel-Schwall Band." *Chicago Reader* (March 16, 1989): *https://chicagoreader.com/arts-culture/siegel-schwall-band/*

60. Reid J. 2020. Hitchhiking and kinship practices in the Navajo Nation. University of North Carolina Press: *https://uncpressblog.com/2020/06/16/jack-reid-hitchhiking-and-kinship-practices-in-the-navajo-nation/*

61. Chicago Tribune. May 25, 1994. Ex-Oak Brook official dies in tri-state crash. https://www.chicagotribune.com/1994/05/25/ex-oak-brook-official-dies-in-tri-state-crash/

62. https://www.esalen.org/about

63. https://www.nrs.com/about/

64. Ball R, and Brown P. 1968. An empirical evaluation of accounting income numbers. *Journal of Accounting Research* 6(2): 159-178.

65. Fama E, Fisher L, Jensen M, and Roll R. 1969. The adjustment of stock prices to new information. *International Economic Review* 10(1): 1-21.

66. Watts R, and Zimmerman J. 1990. Positive accounting theory: A ten-year perspective. *The Accounting Review* 65(1): 131-156.

67. Spicer B. 1978. Investors, corporate social performance and information disclosure: An empirical study. *The Accounting Review* 53(1): 94-111.

68. Shane P, and Spicer B. 1983. Market response to environmental information produced outside the firm. *The Accounting Review* 58(3): 521-538.

69. Hasselback J, Reinstein A, and Abdolmohammadi, M. 2012. Benchmarking the productivity of accounting doctorates. *Issues in Accounting Education* 27(4): 943-978.

70. Beaver W. 1981. *Financial Reporting: An Accounting Revolution*. Prentice Hall.

71. Watts R, and Zimmerman G. 1985. *Positive Accounting Theory*. Prentice Hall.

72. Shane P. 1982. *Internalization of Social Costs and the Value of the Firm: A Descriptive Empirical Study*. Ph.D. Dissertation, University of Oregon (December 1982).

73. Guenther S. 2024. Six Good Things Richard Nixon Did for the Environment. *Treehugger: Sustainability for All*. https://www.treehugger.com/six-good-things-richard-nixon-did-for-the-environment-4869322

74. Wallis J. Eyes Wide Open: Discussing Israel and Palestine with Wesley Granberg-Michaelson.

Sojourners: https://sojo.net/media/eyes-wide-open-discussing-israel-and-palestine-wesley-granberg-michaelson

75. Shane, N. 2015. *Inspired Baby Names from Around the World*. New World Library: Novato California.

76. Montana International Choral Festival webpages: https://www.choralfestival.org/about/#:~:text=The%20Montana%20International%20Choral%20Festival%20was%20founded%20in%201987%20by,every%20other%20year%20in%20Missoula.

77. ICT, Benjamin Harrison: Busted Up Sioux Nation, No Remorse for Wounded Knee: https://ictnews.org/archive/benjamin-harrison-busted-up-sioux-nation-no-remorse-for-wounded-knee

78. Beaglehole A. Immigration regulation. Te Ara.govt.nz. https://teara.govt.nz/en/immigration-regulation/print

79. Clarity, J. 1999. Latoon Journal; If You Believe in Fairies, Don't Bulldoze Their Lair. *The New York Times*: June 15.

80. Drum K. February 1, 2011. America's love affair with Ronald Reagan. *Mother Jones*: https://www.motherjones.com/kevin-drum/2011/02/americas-love-affair-ronald-reagan/

81. Kunz K. 2017. Political engagement grows among students. *The Daily Wildcat*: https://wildcat.arizona.edu/127223/arts/political-engagement-grows-among-students/

82. Strom D. How to Get to Oventic, Rebel Headquarters of the Zapatista Army of National Liberation ★ Mexico Photos by Dane Strom

83. Leeds School of Business. Building bridges in the accounting world: https://www.youtube.com/watch?v=yx3fNuf95Xk

84. Gupta S, Laux R, and Lynch D. 2016. Do firms use tax reserves to meet analyst' forecasts? Evidence from the Pre- and Post-FIN 48 periods. *Contemporary Accounting Research* 33(3): 1044-1074.

85. Blouin J, and Robinson L. 2014. Insights from academic participation in the FAF's initial PIR: the PIR of FIN 48. *Accounting Horizons* 28(3): 479-500.

86. Rees L, and Shane P. 2012. Academic research and standard setting: The case of other comprehensive income. *Accounting Horizons* 26(4): 789-815.

87. Shane P. 2023. Mitigating probate costs. SSRN: https://papers.ssrn.com/sol3/papers.cfm?abstract_id=4453270

88. Whitaker I. December 12, 2022. Street mural takes shape with community effort. *Merced County Times*: https://mercedcountytimes.com/street-mural-takes-shape-with-community-effort/

89. Kamenetz R. 1994. *The Jew in the Lotus: A Poet's Rediscovery of Jewish Identity in Buddhist India.*

90. The Mob Museum (National Museum of Organized Crime and Law Enforcement): https://themobmuseum.org/notable_names/arnold-rothstein/

91. CNBC: https://www.cnbc.com/2009/12/29/Top-10-Best-(and-Worst)-Mergers-of-All-Time.html

92. Holy Land Trust webpages: https://holylandtrust.org/about/

93. Bacon D. 5 February 2025. Trumps executive orders—the return of Cold War repression.

Peoples World:
https://www.peoplesworld.org/article/trumps-executive-orders-the-return-of-cold-war-repression/

94. U.S.-El Salvador Sister Cities. Popular education: https://www.elsalvadorsolidarity.org/advocacy/popular-education-school/#:~:text=Popular%20education%20has%20been%20an,and%20sisters%20in%20El%20Salvador.

95. Leah Greens Compassionate Listening Project webpages: https://www.compassionatelistening.org/staff

96. *The Exhibit.* The era of mass migration from the dual monarchy to the U.S.: https://www.austriainusa.org/panel-4

97. Searching for Identity Support Groups Webpages: https://www.searchingforidentity.org/support-groups

98. Heschel S. October 3, 2010. The Aryan Jesus. https://press.princeton.edu/books/paperback/9780691148052/the-aryan-jesus?srsltid=AfmBOorABu0EBY6q5gpy1ScVkvnobQmEt9YHC-JnYYi01h_jCmHCU6wb

99. Top40 Weekly. https://top40weekly.com/1964-all-charts/#US_Top_40_Singles_for_the_Week_Ending_4th_April_1964

100. Whitson E. 2024. Self-actualization. EBSCO: https://www.ebsco.com/research-starters/psychology/self-actualization

101. Zohar, Shantam. *Mideast Tango: A Story of War and Awakening.* The Peace Press: August 1, 2010.\

102. Duerk, Judith. 1989. *Circle of Stones: A Woman's Journey to Herself.* Most recent edition published by New World Library in 2004.

103. Oxford Dictionary of World History

104. GMA: Gospel Music Association. https://gospelmusichalloffame.org/hall-of-fame-inductees-and-honorees/mahalia-jackson

105. This Day in History. https://www.history.com/this-day-in-history/august-26/democratic-convention-besieged-by-protesters

106. Genius. https://genius.com/Barry-mcguire-eve-of-destruction-lyrics

107. Library of Congress. https://www.loc.gov/resource/rbpe.24404500/?st=text

108. Trump D. 2025. Restoring Law and Order in the District of Columbia. *The White House.* https://www.whitehouse.gov/presidential-actions/2025/08/restoring-law-and-order-in-the-district-of-columbia/

109. Rubin J. 1976. *Growing Up at Thirty-Seven.* M. Evans & Company. Kindle Edition. ISBN 978-1-59077-291-1.

Figure 1
Israel and Palestinian Territories

The Ancient Levant included virtually the entire area of this map, including modern day Syria, Lebanon, Jordan and the Sinai Peninsula region of Egypt.

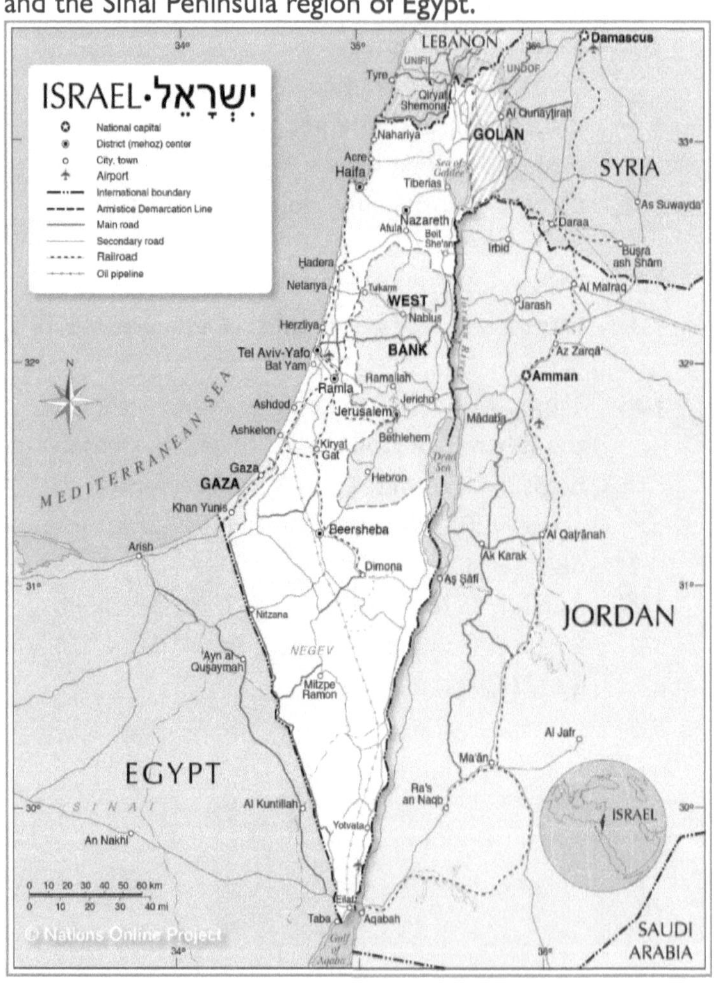

Figure 2
Family Tree

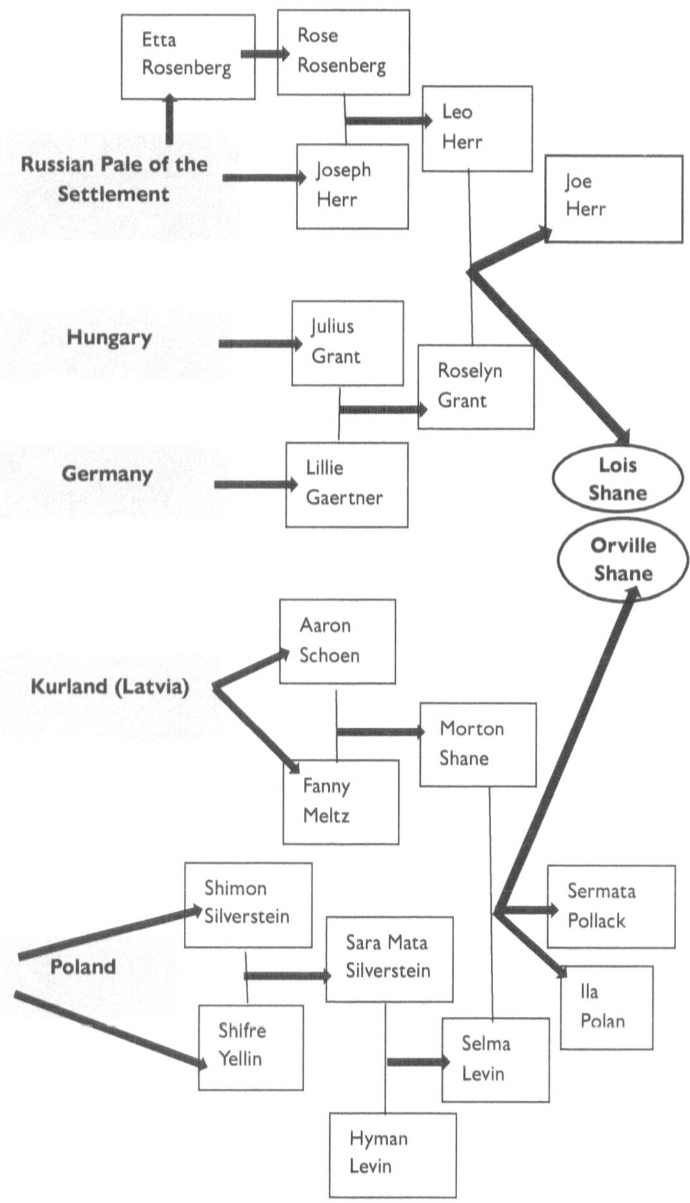

Figure 3
Pale of the Settlement